HISTORIC ANTIGONISH: TOWN AND COUNTY

LAURIE C. C. STANLEY-BLACKWELL
R. A. MACLEAN

NIMBUS
PUBLISHING

To my daughter, Ruth Lillie Hong Qiu Stanley-Blackwell (LCCS-B)

To my family (RAM)

May they find illumination for the path of life in both the future and the past

---

Nimbus Publishing Limited
PO Box 9166, Halifax, NS B3K 5M8
(902) 455-4286

Printed and bound in Canada

Design: Peggy Issenman, MGDC

Library and Archives Canada Cataloguing in Publication

Stanley, Laurie C. C. (Laurie Catherine Christina), 1956-
Historic Antigonish : town & county / Laurie Stanley-Blackwell
& Ray MacLean.

Includes bibliographical references.
ISBN 1-55109-480-0

1. Antigonish (N.S. : County)—History. 2. Antigonish (N.S. : County)—Biography. I. MacLean, Raymond A., 1927- II. Title.

FC2345.A53S72 2004   971.6'14   C2004-903567-3

Canadä

The Canada Council | Le Conseil des Arts
for the Arts | du Canada

We acknowledge the financial support of the Government of Canada through the Book Publishing Industry Development Program (BPIDP) and the Canada Council for our publishing activities.

Acknowledgements

In the writing of this book, we have incurred many debts of gratitude. First and foremost, this book could not have come to fruition without the tireless assistance of Jocelyn Gillis, curator of the Antigonish Heritage museum. Right from the outset, she threw herself wholeheartedly into the project and played a pivotal role in gathering photographs and historical information, and providing us with working space at the Museum. Jocelyn retrieved files, photocopied documents, scanned images, made countless phone calls, and chased down leads with a ready smile. At tea time, she played host, fortifying us with cups of tea and brownies. We are profoundly grateful for her professionalism, generous hospitality, and invaluable help over the past year.

We are also indebted to the expert advice and guidance of Scott Robson (Nova Scotia Museum), Alison McNair (Waldren Photograph Collection, Dalhousie University Archives), John MacLeod and Peter Hartling (Nova Scotia Archives and Records Management), Karen Smith (Special Collections, Killam Library, Dalhousie University), Kathleen M. MacKenzie (St. Francis Xavier University Archives), Photographic Division (National Archives of Canada), Maureen Williams (Special Collections, MacDonald Library, St. Francis Xavier University Library), Sister Marie Raymond (Bethany Archives), Keith Gallant (Sherbrooke Village Commission), Betty Webber (North Shore Heritage Schoolhouse Museum), Alfred Benoit (Pomquet Historical Society), and Margie MacIsaac (Royal Canadian Legion—Arras Branch 59). We also wish to record our thanks to Professor Tony MacKenzie and Dr. J. B. Stewart, who demonstrated great generosity of spirit in sharing their knowledge about Antigonish County's history. Another contributor who deserves special mention is Hattie Farrell, whose efforts to rescue from oblivion John Hattie's photographs of Antigonish and Guysborough Counties are truly commendable. The contribution of Mary Jane Paulette should also be highlighted. She brought great enthusiasm to our project and this book has been greatly enriched by the images of the Mi'kmaw way of life that she located. We are especially grateful to Francis Johnson, William Paulette, Robert Pictou, Kelly Prosper, and Annie Prosper of Paq'tnkek First Nation for sharing their photographs with us. We also want to acknowledge the assistance of Eileen Adams, Allan Armsworthy, Margie Bailey, Peter and Angela DeGruchy, Francis DeWolfe, Claire Dickson, Rick Grace, Jean Graham, Ronnie Gunn, Gilbert Landry, Joyce MacEachern, Terry Murphy, Joan Phee, Gordon and John Randall, Paul Randall, Roy Smith, Edgar Whidden, Isabel Whidden, Hugh Webb, and Mary Rose Wong. We applaud their dedication to preserving aspects of Antigonish County's photographic legacy and their willingness to make their rich collections available to us. Our work on this project was also expedited by the involvement of Isabel den Heyer, Yvonne

Maas, Agnes MacDonald, Gerard MacDonald, Sheldon MacDonald and Merle Taylor who enabled us to cast our net more widely when gathering photographs and information. CJFX also helped in this capacity with their public service announcements. Others who gave generously of their time and memories were Hattie Ash, Margaret Bowie, Leo Chisholm, Christina Connors, Fraser Dunn, Florence Helm, Archie Mills, Mag Lowe, Robbie and Connie MacDonald, and Pat Skinner.

We have also profited from the creativity and talents of others in the completion of our manuscript. Special thanks goes out to Heather Rankin who magically improved the quality of many of the photographs with her digital expertise. Jim Hubley also gave the photographs the benefit of his skill and painstaking labours, and Colleen Gillis's technological know-how in scanning and wordprocessing was a great boon to us. As well, Anne Marie MacPherson, Frances Baker, Marleen Hubley, Mary Beth Carty, and Lily Carty helped along the way in the production of this book. We are grateful for their cheerful efficiency. Thank you to Marleen as well for sharing her wisdom about making the perfect cup of tea. Other assets to the project were Patrick Wallis and Daniel Paintsil, both participants in Canada World Youth, who checked newspaper references in the *Casket* files. Furthermore, the manuscript benefited from the careful editing of my good friend, Marie T. Gillis, whose patience is rivalled by her precision. Dr. Ron Johnson helped the project along by providing much-appreciated office space. Thanks are also due and given here to the many other people who made our work both productive and enjoyable, namely: Michael Anderson, Paul Appleby, Arthur Arbuckle, Phil and Mary Margaret Arsenault, John Blackwell, Lloyd Boucher, Jim Boyd, Bernadette Brow, Mary Brown, Anne Haley Cameron, Sara Carty, *Casket* Printing and Publishing, Dolan Simpson Chaddock, Don Chapman, Jolene Chisholm, Katherine "D. A." Chisholm, Katherine Ann Chisholm, Kit Chisholm, Marie Chisholm, Murph Chisholm, Sandy Chisholm, Val Perry Chisholm, David Crerar, Evelyn DeCoste, Joanne DeCoste, Veronica and Joe Delorey, Joan Dunn, Margaret Enright, Kenny Farrell, Kevin Fehr, Brian Fougere, Robert Francis, Kenny Gallant, Gerry and Bernadette Gillis, Mary Gillis, Richard and Betty Glencross, Angus Grant, John A. Grant, Bill Hardie, Havre Boucher Kinsmen, Zoe Hayes, Debbie Helm, Al and Margaret Jennings, Stephen Jewkes, Dolorosa Kelly, Marian Kerr, Thomas Kinney, Alfred Landry, Bill Landry, John Landry, Arthur LeBrun, Betty MacDonald, Dadie MacDonald, Ducky MacDonald, Mary MacDonald, Lawrence MacDonald, Mary Anna MacDonald, Mona MacDonald, Paul MacDonald, Ronald MacDonald, Allan Francis MacDonnell, John P. MacEachern, Annie MacGillivray, Janice MacGillivray, John Allan MacGillivray, Mary MacGillivray, Rev. Gerard MacInnes, Anthony MacInnis, Mabel MacInnis, Tisty MacInnis, Collie MacIntosh, Neil MacIsaac, Anita MacKay, Grace MacKay, Anne MacKenzie, Catherine MacKenzie, Rev. Greg MacKinnon, Nancy MacLean, Agnes MacLellan, Cella MacLellan, John

MacLellan, Donnie MacMillan, Barbara MacNeil, Catherine MacNeil, Pat MacNeil, Mike MacPherson, Angus MacQuarrie, John MacQuarrie, Sadie MacQuarrie, Elizabeth May, Dr. David McCurdy, Marlene McLarty, Beryl Phee, Nancy Pitts, Ella McVicar, Rev. James Elliot O'Neal, Sandra Perro, Wilfred Prosper, Anne Sears, Roseanne Septon, Evelyn Smith, Ruth Stanley, Catherine Steele, Jean Swansburg, Charlie and Alice Taylor, Henry Van de Weil, and Edith Williams. At Nimbus Publishing, the dynamic team of Penelope Jackson, Heather Bryan, and Sandra McIntyre contributed significantly to the realization of this book.

The final word of thanks goes to our families, who have served as our touchstone of sanity and provided us with support and encouragement.

LCCS-B and RAM

Unfortunately, these acknowledgements must end on a sad note. Ray MacLean, co-author of this book, died before the manuscript went to press. When I first approached him with the idea for this project he did not hesitate to assist. A true exemplar of the scholar and gentleman, his career embodied the adage: "We make a living by what we get; we make a life by what we give." Ray gave his time and talents generously to academe, community and church. As a teacher, writer and colleague he was respected for his integrity, work ethic, and rigorous standards. His goals were neither acclaim nor self-aggrandizement. Ray's inspiration flowed from purer places than that: a love of family; a pride of place; and a reverence for history. Therein lay his honour and reward. His legacy to Nova Scotians is a richer sense of themselves and their storied past.

LCCS-B

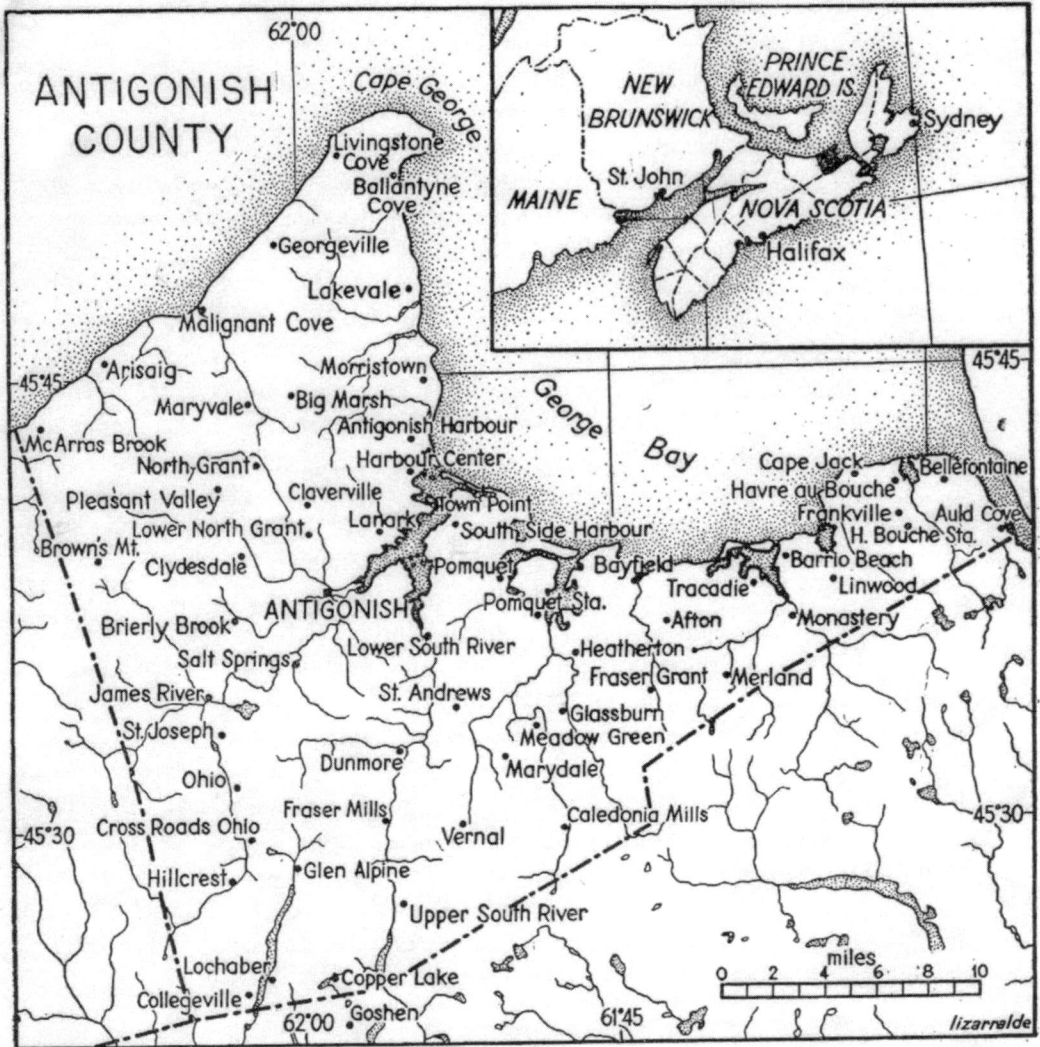

MAP OF
ANTIGONISH
COUNTY

MAIN STREET, ANTIGONISH, C.1910

Contents

Introduction

The name of Antigonish calls up thoughts of the Antigonish Movement, St. Francis Xavier University, and the Highland Games. These historic references, however noteworthy, belie the diversity of Antigonish's past and present. This book is a story about people, and how they lived, worked, and played—a story told in photographs as well as words. Readers are invited on a visual journey into the late nineteenth and early twentieth century worlds of Antigonish town and county. In frozen frames of black and white, the camera has recorded the maturing of a remarkable community, chronicling both its everyday life and events of historic importance. Photography was once described as a "mirror with a memory." We hope that readers will see reflected in this photo album the tapestry of human experiences, both public and private, in Antigonish.

Antigonish County is located in northeastern Nova Scotia. Originally it was known as the Upper District of Sydney County, which was created in 1784. In 1863, twenty-seven years after Guysborough County became a separate entity, Sydney County was redesignated Antigonish County. The county of Antigonish bears a rough resemblance to a triangle, its outline defined by the Gulf of St. Lawrence, St. George's Bay and several ranges of hills. The geography is marked by contrasts ranging from the rugged stone-bound coastline of Arisaig to the gentle rolling intervales of Lochaber, from the scraggy land of Merland to the lush, fertile stretches of St. Andrews.

This landscape of variations is a metaphor for the history of its people, enriched by a diversity of languages, cultures, and traditions. The placenames—Meadow Green, Cross Roads Ohio, Malignant Cove, McArras Brook, Cape Jack, Brown's Mountain, Mattie Settlement and Upper Village—capture in tones both poetic and poignant the unique quality of this county. Colour, character, and originality abound, mirrored in the expressive practice of nicknaming to identify people with identical names. Here is a place once populated by the likes of Holy Kate, Bernie Buttermilk, Bowtie Angus, Hockey Beau, Anthony à Ben à la mouche, Maggie in the Sky, and Monkey Joe. (Where appropriate in this book, nicknames are indicated parenthetically after an individual's given name and surname.) There is nothing bland or sepia-toned about the topography, people, or history of this region.

Archaeological evidence confirms that the history of Antigonish dates back to prehistoric times, when it served as a seasonal base for aboriginal peoples. In fact, the placename Antigonish is of Mi'kmaw origin. One early variant of the name was "Articougnesche," which appeared in Nicolas Denys's *The Description and Natural History of the Coasts of North America*, published in 1672. Originally Antigonish was alleged to mean "where branches are torn off by bears trying to gather beechnuts." A more plausible theory is that of "forked river," for there are three small rivers flowing through the town into the harbour: the West River, Wright's River and Brierly Brook.

VIEW FROM GREGORY'S HILL, C.1907

In addition, the South and North Rivers, outside the town limits, also empty into the harbour. Thus, "forked river" (or "place where the waters meet") offers a more logical, if less romantic, explanation.

During the summer months, Antigonish Harbour was the favourite camping site for the Mi'kmaq drawn to its natural abundance of gaspereaux, water fowl, seals, and shore birds. The migratory way of life for these aboriginal people depended on a "rotation of regions" rather than a "rotation of crops." The area was so closely identified with its native residents that later European settlers designated the area Indian Gardens. Tracadie and Pomquet were also well-established centres for Mi'kmaw activity on St. George's Bay. Other seasonal bases existed at such inland locations as Gaspereaux Lake and Lochaber Lake.

In the 1770s, newcomers arrived in the form of the Acadian French, as scattered remnants of the Deportation converged at such locales as Tracadie, Pomquet, and Havre Boucher. The region was soon populated by families with the surnames Benoit, Delorey, Doiron, LeBlanc, and Decoste. They drew their livelihoods from both the sea and the land, a people truly merged with place.

The year 1784 is regarded as a pivotal date in the history of Antigonish. In that year, Col. Timothy Hierlihy and a party of disbanded soldiers recently serving with the Royal Nova Scotia Volunteers settled on land grants on both sides of Antigonish Harbour. Town Point, a peninsula close to the harbour's entrance, emerged as the main locus of settlement. Renamed Dorchester in 1786, this embryonic village was part of a string of Loyalist communities that dotted the north shore of the Northumberland Strait. It is doubtful that these refugees from the American Revolution deserved Benjamin Marsden's harsh epithet of "riotous vagabonds." Still, many of those who vied for land, rations, and stature were better suited to shouldering muskets than clearing land and quickly succumbed to the temptation to sell their land grants and leave. Others abandoned the original landing district of Town Point to move inland to what is now the eastern end of Antigonish. The fertile intervale land at the head of the harbour drew them like a magnet. During the winter of 1810, Maj. John Cunningham set out from the harbour with several men and two yokes of oxen to forge a path to Antigonish. The arduous trek, which lasted from morning to late afternoon, was considered a progressive step. A ball was organized to mark the event. The settlement of Town Point, or Dorchester, was gradually abandoned. A dream that far exceeded realistic expectation, it never came to fruition, as the early residents tried to build a village before cultivating the soil in any systematic fashion.

Farther down the coast, the Black Loyalist settlement at Little Tracadie, led by Thomas Brownspriggs, also struggled into existence. In 1787, the government allocated a three-thousand-acre (1214-hectare) land grant to seventy-four black families. The Brownspriggs Black Loyalist grantees were a tenacious lot; a strong sense of community ensured their survival, carrying their descendants such as the Reddicks, Ashes, Geros, and Desmonds into the present day.

Notwithstanding the departure of the faint-hearted, there were those early white settlers who demonstrated a firm allegiance to their new home, such as the Hierlihys, Dunns, Kells, Mahoneys, and Cunninghams. By the late 1780s, several soldier-immigrants from the Montague Regiment, most notably Nathan Pushie and Zephaniah Williams, were prominent landowners in Antigonish County. This nucleus of New England-born settlers was further augmented by the arrival of the Hulberts and Wrights, followed by another significant infusion represented by the Symonds family in 1804. Nathaniel Symonds epitomized Yankee entrepreneurial spirit, earning the distinction of being one of Antigonish's earliest merchants. As time progressed, the strands of settlement grew more tangled. Here evolved a complex mosaic, where First Nations, Acadians, Planters, Loyalists and English, Irish, and Scottish émigrés intersected.

The influx of Scottish Highlanders, which started as a trickle in the 1790s and steadily increased in the early 1800s, also confronted the grim realities of "making land." They came predominantly from the Western Highlands and Islands, more specifically from Inverness-shire and the Isles of Barra and Eigg, regions that contained sizeable pockets of Roman Catholics. They came bearing proudly such surnames as MacDonald, Chisholm, Cameron, MacMillan, Gillis, MacNeill, Livingstone, and Ballantyne. Driven more by necessity than choice, these exiled Scots carved out and reshaped their communities from trackless wilderness. Motivated by a compound of homesickness and native pride, they took a nostalgic look backward and borrowed the familiar toponymy of their past. The new landscape soon resonated with such names as Arisaig, Moidart, Lochaber, Keppoch, and Strathglass. Long after the initial impact of the Hierlihy regiment, Irish immigrants also continued to contribute to Antigonish County's complex weave of ethnicity and became a formative force in the development of Antigonish, Lochaber, Donnybrook, Hallowell Grant, and Afton. Hardships tested the fortitude and faith of these early pioneers. They endured the 1815 plague of mice, the devastating 1844 potato blight, and "the year of the yellow meal," which brought virtual starvation to

ANTIGONISH HARBOUR, C.1930S

the inhabitants of St. Andrews in 1851. The Mi'kmaq endured trials as well, for white settlement often meant encroachment on their traditional hunting and fishing areas. This assault on their resource-based lifestyle spelled uncertain subsistence and raised the ugly prospect of extinction.

Although it was a hard-scrabble existence for first-generation immigrants, they built a resilient, self-reliant society. Permanence came in the structured form of churches and schools. By the early nineteenth century, the Catholics, Presbyterians, and Baptists were established institutions in Antigonish County. The religious zeal of these people is epitomized by the pioneer Catholic Scots of Arisaig who built their first log chapel in a single day in 1791. More than any other force, the firm hand of religion and its stern ethic shaped the contours of early Antigonish. It prevailed in every home and school, moulding the minds of the children of both the Catholic and Protestant churches, and providing formidable momentum for educational advances. There is no better example of this historical fact than the grammar school at St. Andrews, established by Rev. Colin MacKinnon in 1838, which trained some of the best intellects in the county. It is also mirrored in the pioneer contributions of the Rev. Thomas Trotter, Presbyterian minister *cum* schoolmaster, who devoted his energies to educational reform in early nineteenth century Antigonish. A further example can be found in the vast legacy of the Congregation of Notre Dame, which opened the doors of Mount St. Bernard to female students in 1883. Today, St. Francis Xavier University, founded in 1853, stands as a monument to this early seriousness of intellectual purpose. The paramountcy of Catholicism spilled into other avenues of life. For example, the *Casket*, established in 1852, became the voice of religious orthodoxy and moral regulation, and cemented the religious loyalties of devout Catholics throughout Antigonish County. The Sisters of St. Martha, living up to their namesake's ideal of self-sacrifice, were originally charged with the domestic management

MAIN STREET, ANTIGONISH, C.1937–39

of St. Francis Xavier University. The Sisters' field of service moved beyond the university laundry, kitchen, and dormitories when they established the county's first hospital in 1906.

In Antigonish County, economic transformation matched academic progress. Farms replaced forest clearings, frame houses superseded log cabins, and grist mills supplanted hand mills. Throughout the nineteenth century, the retreat of the forest made way for the familiar assortment of mills, stores, taverns, and blacksmith's shops. The economy relied on such traditional mainstays as fishing, lumbering, shipbuilding, and the coasting trade based extensively on the export of cattle, sheep, grain, butter, and pork. In 1829, T. C. Haliburton, author of *An Historical and Statistical Account of Nova Scotia*, penned this description of the budding community of Antigonish: "It is one of the prettiest villages in the eastern section of Nova Scotia, and the neatness and simplicity of its appearance amply compensate for the absence of bolder scenery. It has but one principal street which is serpentine, extending half a mile from east to west, and containing about 45 dwelling houses, exclusive of other buildings." Little more than a village at this time, Antigonish emerged as the county's main commercial and trading centre. It enjoyed the advantages of its new location, at the head of the harbour, approximately five miles (eight kilometres) west of Town Point, the site of the original settlement. The 1850s witnessed the laying of the foundation of wealth in the rising village of Antigonish. The economy benefited directly from the emerging class of Scots who were moving from subsistence to greater financial security. This same decade was marked by other important developments, most notably the arrival of the telegraph, the publication of the *Casket* weekly, the construction of a new courthouse, and the establishment of St. Francis Xavier University. Statistics for the 1880s testify to the steady economic evolution of Antigonish town and county. By then, the region's population had climbed to just over eighteen thousand, and men like H. H. McCurdy, Adam Kirk, C. B. Whidden and W. J. Beck held sway over the local mercantile elite. The county boasted thirty-eight sawmills, fourteen flour and grist mills, fourteen tanneries, fourteen carriage-making establishments, fifty-seven forges, five harness and saddlery shops, three carding mills and nine cheese factories. Weavers, carpet makers, tailors, shingle makers, shipwrights, tinsmiths, coopers, and brick and broom makers also contributed to the general prosperity. Antigonish County's native population carved out their own niche in the local economy as basket makers, lumbermen, and hockey stick manufacturers.

Technological developments in transportation and communication propelled both economic achievements and aspirations. As railway cars pulled into the Antigonish station in the 1880s, the days when residents travelled on foot, following blazed trails and wading through bogs and dense forest, were a distant memory. Doubtless few recalled the labours of the postman, John Carroll, who, during the early nineteenth century, trekked across the Keppoch hills with the mail for Antigonish and Guysborough counties tucked in his pockets. The early twentieth century witnessed the accelerating pace of change. The debut of the first motorized vehicle, a Model T Ford, in 1909, may have delighted onlookers in Antigonish, but it presaged the virtual extinction of the traditional conveyance of horse and buggy. The introduction of the telephone to Antigonish in 1888 and electricity the following decade had modern implications for both town and county. Although most parts of rural Antigonish were not electrified until the 1930s, it was clear that the inhabitants lived less and less in a world circumscribed by county boundaries.

The lives of nineteenth and early twentieth century Antigonishers were punctuated by various amusements and recreations. Picnics, church bazaars, and ploughing matches were popular events. Celts and Acadians alike revelled in the pleasures of "kitchen time," enlivened with fiddle music, storytelling, and dance. Clerical censure against the liquor vendors and the fleshly temptations of dancing did little to rob Antigonishers of their appetite for fun, although the clergy took a less grim view of squaredancing, which allegedly left its participants too weary for immoral behaviour. Many of these social entertainments provided some measure of nostalgic stability. They also provided an outlet for competitive impulses, along with such sports as hockey, baseball, curling, horse racing, and speed skating. Beneath the veneer of friendly rivalry lurked a powerful sense of ethnic and community pride easily roused to "fight to prove a thistle more fragrant than a rose." (MacLean 1991, 6) For the residents of town and county, politics also stirred passions. No less engrossing than a blood sport, it was a highly personalized preoccupation, heavily based on family, county, and traditional loyalties. The first Dominion Day celebration ignited a heated debate between the anti-Confederates who processed along Main Street with a flag at half mast draped in mourning crepe and the pro-Confederates who cancelled their cannon salute, closed up their stores and, according to the 8 July 1867 edition of the *Novascotian*, "stowed themselves away" for the day. Political passions showed no signs of abating in the twentieth century. In October 1908, over six hundred people crammed into

Antigonish's Celtic Hall to attend a nomination meeting. The Celtic Hall also attracted crowds as a dance hall and movie theatre until the construction of the Capitol Theatre in 1936. Local inhabitants were treated to the early cinematic productions of the Biograph, Edison's Kinetscope, and the Bioscope Company in the early 1900s. Talkies arrived in the 1930s. By the time the rock and roll group "Lloyd Arnold and his Rockin' Drifters" came to town in the 1950s, many entertainment tastes had become decidedly mainstream North American.

The history of Antigonish town and county is dotted with an unforgettable cast of people who rose to eminence as scholars, athletes, physicians, entrepreneurs, lawyers, and community builders. Many took on the qualities of legends in their time. There was the sports hero Ronald J. MacDonald of Fraser's Grant, the first Canadian to win the Boston Marathon in 1898; gold miner Alexander "Big Alex" Macdonald of Ashdale who made a fortune in the Klondike during the 1880s and 1890s; contractor Colin MacLean of West River, who constructed the base of New York City's Statue of Liberty; Mi'kmaw craftsman Tommy Young, who made the celebrated Swiper hockey stick at the turn of the century; midwife Jane Pushie, born in 1760, who attended the births of no fewer than one thousand Antigonish County babies; and her twentieth century equivalent, Margaret Ann Smith Ballantyne of Ballantyne's Cove, who was eighty-seven years old when she delivered her last baby in 1935.

The history of Antigonish town and county has been tinged with disappointments and setbacks. Since the late nineteenth century, the spectre of depopulation has cast a long shadow over the region. Statistics forcefully illustrate the impact of rural outmigration. Between 1881 and 1951, the total population declined from 18,060 to 11,971. The number of farms plummeted by more than half. By 1914, seventy-five per cent of the farms in Bailey's Brook had been abandoned over a twenty-year period. The fate of the Keppoch, once a thriving population with a church and school, was sealed by the 1930s. As its inhabitants dispersed, the wilderness reasserted itself. This bleak picture of rural decline was more pronounced in Antigonish County than in other Nova Scotian counties. Still, the region did not sink into lethargy. In the 1920s and 1930s, it was the birthplace of the Antigonish Movement, led by the charismatic visionaries Moses Coady and J. J. Tompkins. Their message of social betterment and economic redemption has had a transformative impact throughout the world. In the twentieth century, this region has continued to enjoy fresh transfusions of other cultural groups, namely Dutch, Asian, and Lebanese. It remains a place of ethnic diversity and human scale, where modern ideas coexist with traditional values, a close-knit society still bounded by kin, neighbours, and co-workers.

This photographic sampler of nineteenth and early twentieth century Antigonish town and county makes no pretence to completeness. The co-authors hope these photographs, like brush strokes on a broad canvas, will offer a multidimensional glimpse into the history of Antigonish town and county.

Chapter 1

Communities

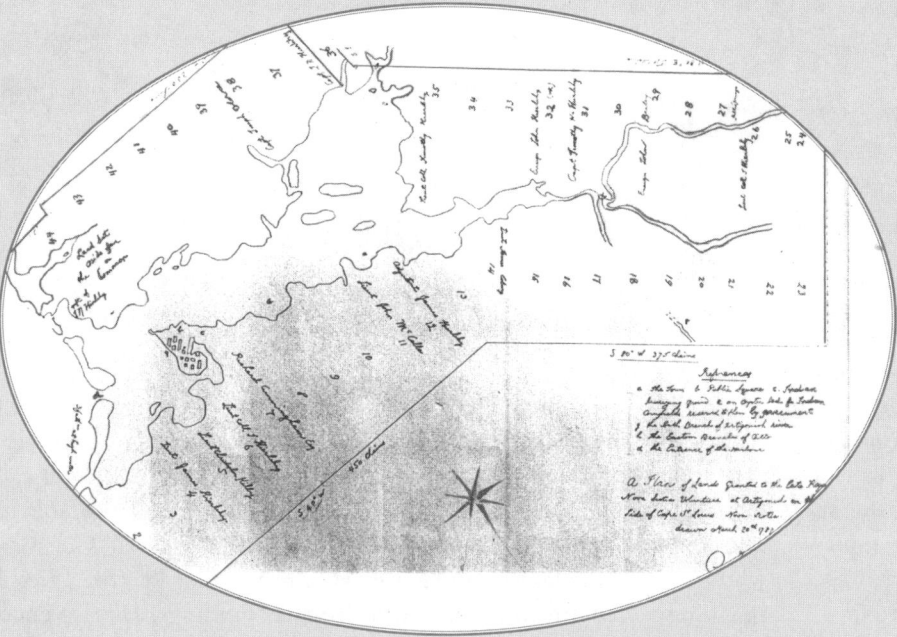

HIERLIHY TOWN POINT SITE, TOWN POINT MAP, 1787

This 1787 map shows the original site of the Hierlihy settlement at Town Point on a small peninsula on the west side of Antigonish Harbour. The tract of land granted to this group stretched from the harbour's mouth as far inland as Salt Springs on the West River. Here, Lt. Col. Timothy Hierlihy and a group of Royal Nova Scotia Volunteers, along with some wives and children, erected log cabins and planted crops. The land grant called the "Soldiers' Grant" comprised a generous 21,600 acres (8,740 hectares). Hierlihy received 2,200 acres (890 hectares) for himself. Officers were assigned an amount in proportion to their rank, while privates were allotted 100 or 200 acres (40 or 80 hectares). They were also given an assortment of agricultural implements and provisions for three years. Some land was set aside to be used as a commons and town square for the settlement. There were also areas reserved for the local Mi'kmaw population for corn fields, a burying ground, and an oyster bed.

VILLAGE OF ANTIGONISH FROM THE COURT HOUSE HILL BY JOHN ELLIOTT WOOLFORD, 1817

During his September 1817 visit to Antigonish, in the company of Governor Dalhousie, Maj. John Elliott Woolford sketched this early view of Antigonish from the vantage point of Court House Hill, later called Baptist Hill (currently Acadia Street). The trip proved memorable for Dalhousie. He met many of the local worthies, including Maj. Cunningham, who provided the horses, and Capt. Hierlihy (son of Lt. Col. Hierlihy) much respected for his age and vast property holdings. He also encountered Nathaniel Symonds, a local tavern owner with an ample girth and strong Yankee accent. In the early nineteenth century, Antigonish, referred to as the "Intervale," was little more than a rough clearing surrounded by dense groves of birch, maple, elm, and ash. Still, Symonds, who brought his family to Antigonish from New Hampshire in 1804, saw its potential. Within three years, he built the first general store on present-day East Main Street. Shortly after, the Harrington mill was erected in close proximity to Symonds's store. In 1811, Symonds began a trade in farm produce with Newfoundland, thus initiating a practice that would be pursued in succeeding decades in Antigonish. By the 1820s, the village of Antigonish boasted a growing population, a wider network of roads, schools and churches, a courthouse, an agricultural society, and a rapidly developing self-confidence. It was a pivotal decade in the growth of the community for the village was becoming a focal point for the adjoining rural areas in the matters of commerce and social exchange.

BIRD'S-EYE VIEW OF TOWN OF ANTIGONISH, C.1916

This panoramic photograph of Antigonish was probably taken from Chestnut Hill. This view is a far cry from that of 1801, when the town had only three houses. The cathedral spires of St. Ninian's dominate the skyline and the middle ground is packed with houses and business establishments, including a lumber mill. Much of the land around the mill was owned by the Whidden family, who also farmed extensively in that area. Lumbering, in all its phases, was a major factor in the economic life of the town and surrounding communities well into the twentieth century. In 1916, a brochure, co-published by the Town Council and Board of Trade, boasted almost fifteen miles (twenty-four kilometres) of "well graded streets" and a macadamized Main Street; they also noted with pride that the town had only one policeman.

Named after John Morris the surveyor, Morristown (formerly Morris-ton) welcomed settlers as early as the 1780s. Among them was Benjamin Ogden, a loyalist soldier, who was only twenty when he arrived in Antigo-nish in 1785. At one time, he had the only wagon in the area; this was when travel by horse and saddle was considered an uncommon luxury. Around 1800, the Highlanders started to make inroads into this area, most notably the MacGillivrays from Arisaig in Scotland. Donald, Angus, and Alexander MacDonald, sons of Angus MacDonald of Knoydart, Scotland, were among the first settlers in Lakevale. The availability of timber and the riches of the sea prompted them to remain. During the early nineteenth century, transportation along this section of the coast was fraught with great peril, especially during the winter months. The beach did not pro-vide a viable alternative—it was dangerous in the winter and impassable in the summer. The road near Morristown followed the cliff top with a precipitous drop to the sea. Dr. Alexander MacDonald, one of Antigonish County's earliest doctors, discovered this hazard first-hand as he navigated a narrow path drifted in with snow en route to Cape George. He narrowly escaped death as he and his horse plummeted over a precipice, a distance of sixty feet eighteen metres). Cribbons Point was named after Thomas Cribben, a former captain in the Royal Navy, who retired on half pay with his family at Cribbons Point around 1789. In 1891, Cribbons Point was fitted with a new wharf. It was a great convenience for the local lobster factory operated by Brophy and Gerard as well as the *Hamblin*, a little steamer that called bi-weekly. By the turn of the century, Morristown had a population of 160, along with one store and one lobster factory; Lakev-ale reported a population of a comparable size along with three stores, one sawmill, and one grist mill.

VIEW OF BALLANTYNE'S COVE, C.1930S

Although one time called Cap St. Louis, Cape George, the point of land jutting into St. George's Bay, was settled mainly by Scots. Some of the early settlers in this region were from Barra and had fought alongside other Barra soldiers serving with the British during the American Revolution. This district was named after the English patron Saint George, and gradually became shortened to Cape George. The two prominent fishing and farming communities are Livingstone Cove and Ballantyne's Cove, both named after early residents. Traditionally active in trading and fishing, the local inhabitants established trade with the West Indies and overseas. One of the most prominent citizens at Cape George was Robert MacDonald, nephew of Squire MacDonald of Lower South River. For five years, Robert clerked for his uncle before relocating to Cape George. By 1891, this merchant boasted a number of important local appointments including postmaster, church deacon and justice of the peace. In 1887, a Halifax newspaper reported that "the old Squire" of Cape George had served as postmaster and presided over provincial and federal elections longer than any other official in the province. By the turn of the century, Livingstone Cove reported one store and a population of 100; Ballantyne's Cove, with its population of 200, had one store and a cold storage facility; Cape George Point was by far the largest community with a population of 550, along with one store and one lobster factory.

POSTCARD VIEW OF MALIGNANT COVE, C.1940S

The origins of this unusual placename are shrouded in colourful mythology. The most popular interpretation suggests that during the fall of 1779, a British man-of-war, called the *Malignant*, was shipwrecked near the cove that came to bear its name. The crew members who survived the ordeal allegedly trudged as far as Pictou where Squire Patterson extended them hospitality through the harsh winter months. The other versions of this story are far more exotic, belonging to the realm of pirate ships and buried treasure. However implausible, this latter account has captured local imaginations and attracted a steady stream of beachcombers and adventurers hunting for prizes of gold. Around 1860, Antigonishers were all abuzz about the arrival of man in the village of Antigonish with gold-laden pockets and the rumoured discovery of an El Dorado near Malignant Cove. Eager fortunehunters poured into the area only to realize that they had been duped by a confidence man. The fate of the ship, buried under layers of sand, has been less glamorous. Periodically, its much-decayed hulk has been exposed by stormy weather and the souvenir seekers have plundered its remains. Angus MacLean, one-time carriagemaker and blacksmith at Malignant Cove, made a walking stick for the Hon. W. A. Henry, one of the Fathers of Confederation, from a piece of its white oak planks.

The history of the early settlement of Malignant Cove is more straightforward. Soldiers from the 82nd Regiment numbered among the earliest inhabitants of the farming and fishing community at Malignant Cove, most notably John MacNeil Brown and John MacNeil Breac. During the 1790s and early 1800s, a steady stream of immigrants from Barra, Skye and Eigg—the MacNeils, MacDonalds, MacLeans, Ballantynes, Livingstones and MacEacherns—followed their countrymen along the rough trail dubbed the Old Gulf Road. By 1800, the rugged coastline was dotted with small settlements from Merigomish around to Ballantyne's Cove on the eastern side of Cape George. Just over one hundred years later, Malignant Cove boasted one store, one saw mill, one grist mill, one lobster factory, and a population of two hundred. One of the most celebrated (albeit temporary) residents of Malignant Cove was John Boyd (Printer), founder of the *Casket* newspaper. In 1850, while teaching at Malignant Cove, Boyd set up a small printing press in Hugh MacGillivray's house. Here he honed his printing skills and produced some of his earliest publications.

ARISAIG ON SHORE ROAD
NEAR ANTIGONISH, NOVA SCOTIA.

POSTCARD VIEW OF ARISAIG, C.1920–1923 Arisaig is situated on the Northumberland Strait, northwest of Antigonish. It is renowned for its fossil-rich sea cliff dating back some 400 million years. It is also known for a large rock formation nicknamed Frenchman's Barn. Arisaig enjoys the distinction of being one of the first settlements established by Highlanders in Antigonish County. It was named by pioneer Angus Gillis MacDonald, who came from Morar, Scotland to North America with his kinsman, the Laird of Glenaladale and Glenfinnan, John MacDonald. After serving with the 84th (Royal Highland Emigrant) Regiment at Quebec City during the winter of 1775–76, Angus MacDonald eventually retired to a land grant at Merigomish, a reward for military service. MacDonald owned a five-hundred-acre (two-hundred-hectare) lot at Arisaig, but he opted for the security of the more established community at Merigomish. The first permanent European inhabitant was John Ban Gillis, who settled there along with his wife and son in 1785. He was soon followed by other Scots, particularly disbanded soldiers of the 82nd Highland Regiment, who fanned out eastward from Pictou to settle alongside their fellow Roman Catholics in what would become the oldest Highland Catholic mission in Nova Scotia. They were drawn to a landscape that offered opportunities for fishing and subsistence farming. The region, strongly reminiscent of the western coast of Scotland, was soon punctuated with familiar placenames such as Knoydart and Moidart. Among these Highland pioneers were John Smith, Dugald Dan MacDonald, Malcolm and Martin MacDonald, and Donald MacDonald. For mariners, the settlement of Arisaig—particularly its pier, constructed in 1811—was a welcome sight along a shoreline that offered little refuge during a storm. Early on in the next century, Arisaig was home to two hundred people as well as two stores, one lobster factory and one fish drying and salting factory.

ON THE ROAD FROM ARISAIG TO ANTIGONISH, 1873

Early on this locality was known variously as Glenuig, Glen Hide or Rear Malignant Brook. However, by the early 1860s, the name Pleasant Valley gained currency. Northwest of Antigonish, in the shadow of Brown's Mountain and Eigg Mountain, Pleasant Valley offered early inhabitants two attractive features—fertile soil and a thick forest of trees. Some of the earliest families in this district were Irish immigrants, most notably the Carters and the Delaneys, who arrived in the early 1820s. Among the first Scottish pioneers were Donald MacGillivray, Allan Gillis, John Smith, and Allan McDonald (Double Hill). For the Delaneys, the arrival of neighbours was heartening; their solitude was lessened by the comforting sight of wreaths of smoke rising in the wilderness. These early settlers probably arrived at Arisaig before wending their way over the mountains toward Pleasant Valley. According to local lore, some early trees measured as tall as eighty-eight feet (twenty-two metres). These were hauled by oxen to Malignant Cove and sold for spars to the Pattersons of Merigomish. Eigg Mountain was named by settlers who came from the isle of Eigg in western Scotland during the 1820s. The Mountain was a rough place to begin a new life from scratch. It required remarkable will to clear the land of the stones and dense forest growth; to fend off the depredations of the bears and endure the long winters that sometimes left the mountain roads buried under three feet (ninety-one centimetres) of snow as late as June. In 1888, the county school inspector reported that Eigg School had not operated for the year, for the region was "poor and very sparsely settled." Settlement in Pleasant Valley fared much better. By the 1850s, this district had two sawmills and weekly mail service. Around 1896, Ronald Angus (Merchant) MacDonald operated a successful general store at the junction of the Maple Ridge and Pleasant Valley roads; he was also local postmaster and mail carrier.

VALLEY OF THE WEST RIVER, 1909

During his trip to Antigonish in 1817, Governor Dalhousie was impressed by the dramatic vistas around Antigonish, especially West River, remarking: "… we could not help admiring the magnificence of the woods thro' which we passed, and the extreme rich sward of which clover thick as a carpet grew up on every little spot cleared enough to admit the sun to it. The soil is most uniformly red loam, light, sandy & gravel with now & then a tract of red clay. The trees are Beech & Maple, fir, Spruce & Hemlock of very large size…" Alexander Fraser enjoys the distinction of being the first "permanent settler" in this locale. He moved from Pictou to West River around 1795. He realized its agricultural potential while travelling with some local Mi'kmaw hunters who also introduced him to the Ohio and Lochaber regions. Fraser was joined in the summer of 1805 by John Smith, a native of Moidart, Scotland, as well as Nathan Pushie and Zephaniah Williams, who were among the older inhabitants first settling at the harbour and Williams Point. The West River, with its headwaters at St. Joseph's Lake, snakes about sixteen miles (twenty-six kilometres) before emptying into Antigonish Harbour. Not surprisingly, it was one of the first districts settled when colonists turned their attention inland. With its extensive intervale land and timber resources, West River had irresistible appeal. It was soon settled and enjoyed a brisk timber trade between 1812 and 1819. In later years, this farming district was also well known for its brickyard at Salt Springs, Lower West River, which employed as many as fifty men on a seasonal basis. One of the last local structures built with Salt Springs bricks was StFX's Mockler Hall.

St. Joseph's, c.1920

This panoramic postcard view of St. Joseph's dates from the 1920s. The focal point of this community was the white frame church, built in 1868, which stood on the hilltop overlooking St. Joseph's Lake (once called Loch Mór) until the church was lost to fire in 1926. The adjacent glebe house, a handsome architectural specimen of Second Empire, still stands today. According to oral tradition, the congregation was once summoned to worship by the clarion call of a conch shell, brought from Scotland by Angus Fraser. The first chapel and glebe house, originally called St. Bean's, was built in a small clearing in the woods. At that time, there was little more than a footpath connecting Gaspereaux Lake and St. Joseph's. The local population was composed of emigrants from Strathglass, Moidart and Ireland; "a more social, kindly, generous people I have never come across," remarked Father Ronald McGillivray in 1892. The church served a wide constituency, including the Ohio (once nicknamed Pinkietown), which was first settled around 1800 by the Scottish-born Andrew MacInnis, Angus MacGillivray, and Donald McPherson. They came to the densely forested area via Pictou and Cape George. As well, the parish included settlers in Beaver Meadow, which earned its name from a feud between local residents and some persistent beaver who were eventually bested and driven off the prized marshland. The first permanent inhabitant in Beaver Meadow was Hugh Fraser, who arrived in 1800. James River also fell within the boundaries of St. Joseph's Parish. It was most likely named after three pioneer settlers, James Miller, James Nichols, and James MacDonald. In addition, St. Joseph's served the people of the Keppoch, renowned for its long winters, wild bears, rough terrain and ghost stories. The ascent to the Keppoch, wrote Father McGillivray, was "steeper than the winding stairs that lead to the top of St. Peter's in Rome."

VIEW OF SOUTH LOCHABER, C.1900

In 1830, the British military officer Capt. William Moorsom sketched the pioneering settlement of Lochaber for his book, *Letters from Nova Scotia*. Although the foreground in his engraving is littered with stumps, Lochaber Lake shimmers like the promised land in the distance. One-time politician and newspaper editor, Joseph Howe was also charmed by the "sylvan enchantment" of Lochaber and waxed eloquently about its scenic beauty during his travels in 1831. About 1810, Malcolm MacMillan, Hugh MacMillan, John Cameron (Red), and John Cameron (Squire), natives of Lochaber, Scotland, were attracted to the intervale land near Lochaber Lake. The region offered fine soil for oats and potatoes and lush pasturage for cattle and sheep, while the lake promised a bounty of salmon, trout, and smelt. At that time, there was no road, only a blazed path between the head of Lochaber Lake and the Ohio River, which served as a portage route for the Mi'kmaq. The early colonists came primarily from Perthshire, Inverness, and Lochaber in Scotland, but there was also a steady influx of Irish immigrants, with John Duggan leading the way in 1818. Lochaber was originally called College Grant owing to a sizeable five-thousand-acre (two-thousand-hectare) lot allocated to the Anglican-run King's College, Windsor in 1813, affirming the Church of England's privileged status in the colony. By the early 1900s, Lochaber, with a population of 360 people, was a bustling economic centre with its two stores, two sawmills, one grist mill, and two carriage factories.

Upper South River offered early residents good farming country with much intervale land. Most of the early settlers were of Highland descent and came to Upper South River in the first two decades of the nineteenth century; some of their descendants still occupy the original homesteads. Two of the more prominent families were the MacGregors from Rannoch, Perthshire, Scotland, and MacMillans from Lochaber in Scotland. Other early settlers there included MacPhees, MacDonalds from Morar and Moidart, Cummings from Rannoch, Kennedys, and MacPhersons, the latter from Moidart. The well-known family of Allan (Ridge) MacDonald had first settled on the Ridge, Mabou, in Cape Breton in 1816, but moved to Upper South River in 1847. Another grant was taken up by Michael Horahan, a native of Kilkenny, Ireland, who settled there in 1820. These early settlers developed prosperous farms throughout the picturesque Upper South River. Perhaps the best known descendant of the first arrivals was A. S. MacMillan, premier of Nova Scotia, 1940–45. Some of the Mac-Gregors had stayed with relatives in the Merigomish area before coming to Upper South River. Settlers in Upper South River also moved into areas we know today as Springfield and Loch Katrine. By 1904, Upper South River had a population of 150 people, along with one cheese factory and one store.

This fine agricultural area, named after the South River, which flows into Antigonish Harbour, was settled shortly after 1800 by MacIntoshes, MacGillivrays, Chisholms, Frasers, and Grants. At one time, the area east from Antigonish was denominated "The South River." This designation was far too sweeping, and more precise names—Lower, Middle and Upper South River—were adopted to capture the subtleties of settlement patterns. As early as 1816, John MacGillivray started a school in Lower South River. By the 1820s, Squire Hugh MacDonald of Lairg, Sutherlandshire, opened a store there. This Scottish Presbyterian merchant started out in business with a horse and wagon, selling goods to farmers in Antigonish and Guysborough counties. He went on to become a successful entrepreneur, operating a number of mills, a carriage shop, and a cheese factory, and overseeing his own personal estate, called Elmbank. Reputedly one of the wealthiest men in Antigonish County, he entered into a financially ruinous partnership with a Halifax wholesale dry goods business. By the 1870s, the community had developed a thriving local economy. This main intersection was a hub of activity, around which clustered the South River School, a carriage works and blacksmith shop, cheese factory, and store.

ST. ANDREWS VILLAGE, C.1875 Named for the patron saint of Scotland, the community of St. Andrews received large numbers of Scots in the first decade of the nineteenth century. The first European settlers in the St. Andrews area came on the *Nora*, whose sixteen-week crossing in 1801 was a nightmare voyage beset by storms and smallpox. Among the early arrivals were Angus MacDonald (MacBride), John MacDonald (Borradale), Roderick Chisholm, and five MacIsaacs, namely John, Duncan, Angus, Hugh, and Archibald. Those who followed in their wake gradually spread out to help form new communities such as Marydale, Springfield, Pinevale, Glen Alpine, Frasers Mills, Caledonia Mills, South River, and Meadow Green. Blessed with tracts of good intervale land, those settlers developed good farms and a thriving beef industry. Irish immigrants with surnames liked McGrath, Shaunessy, Foley, McGuire, and Power also came into the region, most notably the Springfield area. The arrival of some Dutch farmers during the 1950s gave an important boost to agricultural development. A grammar school was established in St. Andrews by Rev. C. F. MacKinnon in 1838. The church in St. Andrews was a towering presence that enjoyed both prestige and power. It provided the essential qualities of stability and continuity. This photo shows St. Andrews Church, a large wooden structure, completed in 1845 (on a site adjacent to the present church), and the glebe house built in 1853. By the 1860s and 1870s, St. Andrews was riding a small crest of progress and prosperity. At the main intersection (locally known as The Cross) of the Post Road and the road leading to Tanner's Bridge, there sprang into existence four stores, a blacksmith shop, and two beer and ale establishments, one called The Nuns and the other MacLean's. By 1904, the community of approximately 160 persons contained two stores and one carriage factory.

Ten miles (sixteen kilometres) east of Antigonish is the village of Heatherton, the name given by an act of the Nova Scotia legislature in 1879. Previously it had been known as Pomquet Forks. The new name was given in memory of the ship *Heather*, owned by Christopher MacDonald, a local merchant who had other trading vessels that operated out of Bayfield. Included in the parish of Heatherton are the districts of Summerside, Fraser's Grant, New France, Bayfield, Glassburn, and Black Avon. Although these rural communities seem to run into one another, each has its own distinctive features and its own identity, particularly noticeable in athletic competitions. By 1898, Heatherton, with a population of about three hundred, was a flourishing locale with three stores, one hotel, two sawmills, a cheese factory, and a railway station.

VIEW OF AFTON, C.1914

The name for this pastoral community is believed to have been taken from the Burns's poem, "Flow Gently Sweet Afton." Initially settled by people of Irish extraction in the late eighteenth century, these settlers and their descendants eventually built some mills, a tannery, and at least one black-smith shop. Located on the main railway line to Cape Breton, the village had its own school and post office. Around 1900, this community of 150 people had one store, one sawmill, and one grist mill. Agriculturally, they carried on mixed farming but many of the young people in the nineteenth and twentieth centuries had to seek employment elsewhere because of limited opportunities. In 1820, one thousand acres (405-hectares) were officially set aside for the Mi'kmaw inhabitants in the Afton and Pomquet areas. Throughout the nineteenth century, these lands were under constant pressure from the encroachment of outsiders. By 1896, the Mi'kmaw reserve had lost much ground to this assault and consisted of approximately four parcels of land: 110 acres (forty hectares) of Pomquette Forks (at the head of Pomquet Harbour); 100 acres (forty-hecatares) at Summerside (on the east side of Pomquet Harbour); and Afton where two separate lots contained 344 acres (139-hectares). Today, the Paq'tnkek First Nation occupies Pomquet and Afton No 23, Summerside No. 38, and Franklin Manor No. 22 (part), totalling around 1,105-acres (447-hectares).

There were other areas adjacent to the village of Antigonish that, because of early settlement or geographic advantages, were also increasingly active and growing. Bayfield was an important port during the nineteenth century, particularly for the Whidden ships. Known originally as Little River, the settlement was given the name Bayfield in 1864 in honour of Henry W. Bayfield (1795–1885), who surveyed and charted, among other places, the coastline of Nova Scotia from Halifax to the Strait of Canso. The first permanent white settler was Elisha Randall, born in Preston, Connecticut, the son of David Randall, reputedly a United Empire Loyalist. Some of the earliest settlers in Bayfield, including Elisha Randall, had initially settled in what is today Guysborough County and gradually moved northward. A few were descendants of the Planters who had moved into the Annapolis Valley from the New England area and occupied the land vacated by the Acadians during the 1755 Deportation. Interestingly enough, the Highland Scots were conspicuously absent in the settlement of this small village. The Randalls, in particular, had a decisive impact on this community and through intermarriages with other families in the county, influenced trade, religion, and education throughout the entire region. In addition to an extensive shipbuilding and sea-going trade, Bayfield also had at one time three tanneries, a water-powered mill, an extensive lobster and salmon fishery, three schools, sawmill, a grist and carding mill, carriage works, and a cheese factory, as well as several stores. Some of the other early settlers whose names are still common today were the Taylors, Cunninghams, Connors, Irishes, and Hulberts.

Prior to European settlement, Pomquet, situated on the coast of St. George's Bay, was a popular Mi'kmaw camping site. The placename itself has native antecedents, with several possible translations, including "sand beach" or "a good place for landing." Historical evidence suggests that the earliest Acadian settlers in Antigonish County were refugees from the 1755 Deportation who fled eastward to escape the savage destruction of the Acadian settlements along the north shore of Nova Scotia and found a safe haven among the local Mi'kmaq. The consensus is that the earliest permanent Acadian settlement in this region dates back to the 1770s. In that decade, five families from St. Malo, France, following a circuitous path back to Acadia after the Deportation, landed on an island near Pomquet. They came to this sheltered spot bearing such surnames as Broussard, Doiron (Durant), Duon (also DeYoung), LaMarre, and Vincent. Between 1789 and 1792, the community expanded with the arrival of more families, namely the Boudreaus, Landrys, Melansons, and Rosias (now Rogers), drawn back to Acadia by a powerful allegiance to kin and homeplace. By the early 1800s, other surnames appeared on the local census such as the Wolfes (DeWolfe) who migrated from Chezzetcook, near Halifax, and the Venedams and Renyrimbeaus (Rennie) who came directly from France. The economic life of the community revolved around fishing, farming, and shipbuilding. By 1827, James Taylor of Pomquet operated a shelling mill and kiln for oats and barley. Even the woods provided a livelihood as lumber, shingles, and barrel staves were shipped to Halifax, Arichat, and Newfoundland. Pomquet became famous for its ship carpenters who ranked among the best in Nova Scotia, and worked as far afield as Maitland and River John. Around 1900, this community of about four hundred people boasted three stores. During the 1920s and 1930s, Pomquet was one of Nova Scotia's most successful egg producers.

**View of
Tracadie,
c.1945**

Tracadie, the nearest Acadian village, followed its own distinctive pattern of development. About 1772, a small cluster of Acadians, including Pierre Benoit, took up residence in the Tracadie area. Benoit has been described variously as adventurous, brave and hardy. He was fortunate to escape the horrors of deportation and owing to his fluency in native languages, he enjoyed a singular rapport with the Mi'kmaq population. Benoit built a log house on the eastern point of the harbour called "La Point du cimetière." Over the next ten years, families who came via Quebec, the Jersey Islands, St. Pierre and Miquelon, and along the Gulf Shore gravitated toward Tracadie, including the Gerroirs, Myettes, Pettipas, Coties, Perros, Deloreys, and Fougeres. By the early nineteenth century, the Tracadie area was a fascinating microcosm of multiculturalism. Along both the west and east sides of the Tracadie River (commonly called Black River) were lands allocated to the Black Loyalists. Wedged between this enclave and the Acadians was a cluster of Irish and Scots—most notably the Macdonalds, Trambles, and Grants. By the 1820s, T. C. Haliburton observed that Tracadie residents were employed on a seasonal basis, working in the fishery or plying the coasting trade during the summer, and shipbuilding or making hoops and staves during the winter months. Almost eighty years later, this farming settlement consisted of four stores, one church, and a population of around two hundred. Its large oyster beds were particularly renowned.

The Acadian village Havre Boucher is situated northeast of Antigonish on a harbour opening onto St. George's Bay. The placename has been attributed to Captain François Boucher of Quebec who wintered there during the late 1750s. The precise date of permanent European settlement is still a matter of speculation, although it occurred sometime during the 1770s. The original settlers had such surnames as Boucher, DeCoste, and LeBlanc. Included among the residents was also a family called Bellefontaine, who migrated from Chezzetcook near Halifax. The area just east of Havre Boucher originally bore their name, although the region is more commonly called East Havre Boucher. In the early nineteenth century, some Irish families migrated to the region. In 1812, Havre Boucher consisted of no more than thirty families; by 1858 this figure had climbed to more than one hundred. The livelihood of this compact settlement depended extensively on such traditional mainstays as farming, fishing, and shipbuilding. In 1904, *McAlpine's Gazetteer and Guide* reported that this community of about eight hundred people had seven stores, one hotel, one lobster factory, and one fish canning factory. It is interesting to note that from the early years of settlement, the three communities of Pomquet, Tracadie, and Havre Boucher were linked to Arichat and Cheticamp by economic and cultural ties. In fact, throughout the nineteenth century, there was a steady stream of lumber, shingles, and barrel staves from Pomquet and Tracadie to Arichat.

Chapter 2

House and Home

MI'KMAW WIGWAM, ANTIGONISH LANDING, C.1924

The residents of Antigonish County displayed considerable ingenuity in the construction of their early dwellings. The traditional Mi'kmaw wigwam was constructed primarily from spruce poles and layered sheets of birchbark. It was waterproof and easily erected, well suited to the seasonal movement of hunters and gatherers. Some of the earliest white settlers' dwellings were lean-tos of poles and brush, temporary expedients until something more permanent could be erected. The next stage was usually a log cabin or hut, roofed with bark and caulked with moss. One early inhabitant in North Grant built a house with the corner posts fashioned from tree trunks standing in their original position. Within a couple of years after their arrival at Town Point in 1784, some of the more comfortable families actually constructed frame houses. The distinction of owning the first frame house in Antigonish belongs to Dr. Benjamin Sterns, who came to Antigonish in 1804. With the introduction of sawmills, the one-and-a-half storey frame house with its clapboard or shingle cladding became more commonplace. Affording more space and comfort, it tended to be economical in design, and plain and utilitarian in its appearance. Wood was the dominant medium of construction in nineteenth- and early twentieth century Antigonish, Nova Scotia. In the latter part of the nineteenth century, the architectural landscape of Antigonish town and county became more complex as homeowners were influenced by the explosion of styles during the late Victorian period.

SYMONDS HOUSE, LINWOOD, C.1920

This clapboard house also exemplifies the Maritime Vernacular tradition. It has asymmetrical lines, a plain exterior, low ceilings and wide plank walls. This distinctive architectural form was one of several subtypes that retained their popularity among working class Maritimers well into the nineteenth century. This house was originally the home of Joseph Symonds, a well-connected resident of Linwood (Little Tracadie). He was the son of Nathaniel Symonds and husband of Sarah Randall, only daughter of Elisha Randall, the pioneer. Linwood boasted fine tracts of arable land and in 1826, Joseph Symonds purchased two hundred acres (81 hectares) in the area from Randall. In this small community, Symonds became a man of many parts, including merchant and postmaster. His house operated as a telegraph and post office, as well as a stagecoach stop, one of many stops in the service between Antigonish and Cape Breton operated by Thomas Snow Lindsay.

MacDonald House, McArras Brook, with Mary McAdam MacDonald, and John F. MacDonald (Johnny Joe) c.1900

The one-and-a-half storey shingled MacDonald house, built around 1830, is a typical example of local architecture. It projects a classical plainness and functional simplicity. The kitchen extension housed the summer kitchen, which was closed off during the winter months. The MacDonalds were a prominent local farming family and their house served as the local post office for almost fifty-three years, from 1899 to 1947. The position of postmaster passed from John A. MacDonald to his wife and finally to his son. The house also served as a stopover for the frequent influx of Canadian and American geologists who came to the region to study the famed rocks and fossils. One of their visitors was Hugh Fletcher, who extensively mapped Nova Scotia's geological landscape for the Geological Survey of Canada.

BLANCHARD HOUSE, ANTIGONISH, C.1889

This vernacular-style house, with its five-bay symmetrical façade, was built by John W. Blanchard, an Antigonish tanner, around 1834. Originally situated on Main Street, it projected a classical simplicity with its pitched roof, simple gable dormer, and familiar construction. By the mid-nineteenth century, the house was occupied by William R. Cunningham, who married Blanchard's widow, Charlotte Frances Symonds. This one-time ship captain and later shoemaker and tanner is best known for his courageous role in the capture of the mutinous crew of the *Saladin*, a British barque, in 1843. This Main Street house was later owned by Cunningham's son, Rupert Cunningham, who became the first town clerk when the town was incorporated in 1889.

HOUSE AND HOME   **25**

STONEHOUSE, HEATHERTON, C.1890S

The Stonehouse, situated at the junction of the Black Avon and Pomquet rivers, was a well-known landmark. Equally celebrated was one of its earliest owners, Alexander Chisholm (Donn) who was renowned for his cheer and hospitality, extending shelter and food to those who came to his door. His first dwelling on the property was a log house on the left bank of the Black Avon River. When Chisholm moved into the new stone house, Patrick Power converted the log homestead into a store. The Stonehouse was a popular stopover for clergy on their pastoral visits. In its sturdy appearance, the house echoed Scottish architectural prototypes and stood out conspicuously alongside its wooden neighbours. Around 1900, the house was torn down to make way for a more fashionable two-storey structure built by Duncan A. Chisholm best known as Duncan Stonehouse. Many local residents did not lament its demolition, believing that the dampness of the Stonehouse was directly responsible for the ill health of some of those who had lived there.

SINCLAIR
HOUSE AT
NORTH
LOCHABER,
C.1907

Left to right in this photograph are: George Sinclair, Roberta (Kirk) Sinclair, Maria (Inglis) Sinclair and John Sinclair. The Sinclair house was built around 1865, just in time for the newly married couple, George and Maria Sinclair, to move in. A blacksmith by trade, Sinclair engaged in a partnership with Alex Manson who operated the local carriage works; after all, blacksmithing and carriagemaking complemented each other perfectly. The household was renowned for its hospitality, their lives governed by the maxim, "Let me live in a house by the side of the road and be a friend to man." This one-and-a-half storey clapboard house had the spartan appearance typical of so many vernacular renditions of neo-classical architecture in early nineteenth century Antigonish County. However, the house's exterior was not completely plain. The central doorway was embellished with sidelights and a graceful fanlight. The Sinclair house was lost in a flue fire in 1912. Neighbours rallied to rescue the furniture from the main floor. One bold friend ventured into the upstairs bedroom to rescue an unpacked barrel of china recently arrived from Germany. The barrel was thrown out the upstairs window and the twelve-piece tea set survived intact without any damage.

MACDONALD HOUSE, MARYDALE, C.1880

This farmhouse was the residence of Big Angus MacDonald and Janet "Jennie the Widow" of Marydale. A native of St. Andrews, Angus was descended from the MacDonalds (McBrides), who numbered among the earliest Scottish residents on the Manchester Road, now Marydale. This one-and-a-half storey wooden frame house was clearly the home of an established farmer who boasted ownership of 140 acres (57-hectares) and four conveyances in 1871. His residence can also be categorized as Maritime Vernacular, for it embodies New England, Scottish, and classical influences. The five-bay façade and the symmetrical simplicity of the main section of the house are all traditional features of this genre. It is also adorned with corner boards, a square-headed transom, and two Palladian-style dormer windows, all pleasing neo-classical accents. The photo shows members of the MacDonald family posed in front of their home in the early spring. The snow has virtually melted away, but the boughs on the fenced garden remain. The MacDonald household was a productive one, and the womenfolk made a substantial contribution to the overall output. The 1871 census reveals that in that year alone they manufactured 480 pounds (218 kilograms) of butter and sixty-five yards (fifty-nine metres) of cloth.

RIVERBANK, MACMILLAN HOUSE, ANTIGONISH, C.1880

This spacious Church Street residence, overlooking Antigonish's salt ponds, was constructed by John MacMillan around 1870. Originally from Cape George, MacMillan was at one time a storeowner and superintendent of the way office and post office in St. Andrews. In 1868, after the death of his wife Isabelle Chisholm, he moved with his young family to Antigonish where he became a leading Main Street merchant much admired for his honesty and integrity. In the 1860s, he built two impressive Greek Revival–style stores on Main Street on an acre (0.4-hectare) of land across from the Presbyterian Church. One of these stores served as the headquarters of John MacMillan and Company until 1899. Constructed around 1870, Riverbank contains elements of both Classical and Gothic Revival. This convergence of styles typified much Maritime architecture. The steeply pitched Gothic dormer combines beauty and functionality. After all, it was designed with Nova Scotia's harsh climate in mind.

**HOUSE
OF JIMMY
"THE KING"
CHISHOLM,
CALEDONIA
MILLS, C.1900**

This Caledonia Mills L-shape residence with its off-centre main entrance on the gable end is a simplified mixture of Classical and Gothic Revival. The house displays the conservatism that pervades local Antigonish County architecture. The sensibility of the people, especially their frugality and practicality, was reflected in their highly functional structures. This establishment was the farm of Jimmy "The King" Chisholm, who is shown seated on his horse-drawn hay mower, justifiably proud of his outbuildings and mechanical farm implements. Chisholm was a carpenter and casket maker as well as a farmer. He lived up to his nickname by being the virtual monarch of all he surveyed. Mechanized farming greatly lightened the labours of farmers like Jimmy Chisholm. It is alleged that it took twenty hours to harvest an acre (0.4-hectares) of wheat in 1830 while by the 1890s it took less than one hour.

**DADEAU HOUSE,
TRACADIE,
C.1930**

In this photograph, Joseph Dadeau, a mason, and his wife, Sarah Delorey, are shown standing in front of their Tracadie home. This house was built around 1878 for Joseph's mother, widow of Joseph Dadeau Sr., who was a farmer and master mariner. Joseph Dadeau drowned in September 1870, when the schooner *Mary Catherine*, en route from Boston to Tracadie, was shipwrecked in a gale off Taylor's Head, east of Halifax. Almost all the crew lost at sea were from the parish of Tracadie. This one-and-a-half storey house represents a simplified version of Gothic Revival. Its centred gable and verandah with modest trim are hallmarks of this style and project a simple, rural grace.

ARCHIBALD HOUSE, ANTIGONISH, C.1884

In the late nineteenth century, some of Antigonish's rising merchant elite scorned traditional architectural designs. They opted for more fashionable, modern styles. In 1880, Leonard Archibald, local entrepreneur and first mayor of Antigonish, built himself this spacious house on South River Road. It is a fine example of Second Empire and is clearly the home of someone who aspired to far more than comfortable subsistence. Leonard Archibald started clerking with the Dickson Brothers in Antigonish during the 1860s. After a short-lived partnership with Norman Randall, Archibald took his future in his own hands and established a bustling merchant tailoring business. Epitomizing the hopeful economic mood of the time, he also expanded into the production of cheese and condensed milk, earning the reputation as one of Canada's leading makers of cheese. By the 1890s, he operated cheese factories at Black River, Lochaber, Dunmore, and Pinkietown. His product was first class; three of his cheese makers, Angus Cameron, William Fraser, and J. R. Stewart scored well at the World's Fair in 1893. In the late nineteenth century, Archibald, a well-established commercial presence in Antigonish, turned his hand to civic politics and threw his weight behind the town's incorporation. He was Antigonish's first mayor, serving from 1889 to 1890.

McCurdy House, Antigonish, c.1897–99

This impressive Antigonish residence, built around 1880 for Henry H. McCurdy, owner of McCurdy and Company, epitomized the rising fortunes of Antigonish's mercantile elite. This house reflects many of the key characteristics of Italianate with its long windows, low pitched hip roof, wide-bracketed eaves, and windowed tower. Inspired by the early villas of the Italian Renaissance, this design had romantic appeal to affluent mid- to late-nineteenth-century Canadians. In 1902, the Swiss-born engineer Gustavus Bernasconi purchased the residence for $3,250. From 1914 to 1924, it served as the House of Providence run by the Sisters of St. Martha; it was Antigonish's first maternity hospital.

WHIDDEN HOUSE, ANTIGONISH, C.1895

The prominent Antigonish merchant C. B. Whidden also found architectural expression for his worldly status. Around 1890, he built an elegant house on Acadia Street on the former site of the first poor asylum in Antigonish. The architectural style of this residence was Second Empire with its characteristic mansard roof and blocky dimensions. Stately in its proportions, Second Empire projected stability, wealth, and dynastic ambition. The round-headed windows and wide eaves with brackets were of Italianate derivation. Inside, the Whidden house had high ceilings.

INTERIOR VIEW OF WHIDDEN HOUSE, C.1910

The house, owned by Charles Edgar Whidden after his father's death in 1902, was typically Edwardian with its richly patterned carpet and luxurious upholstery. The design aesthetic for this era called for a less cluttered interior, an eclectic mix of dark-stained furnishings and lighter bamboo and caned furniture, as well as a teaming of floral wallpapers and sumptuous fabrics. The Whiddens were clearly up-to-date in their tastes, for displays of flowers complementing floral fabrics and wallpapers were *de rigueur*.

The commercial success of the Kirk family was also manifested in their handsome Antigonish residences. For his dream home, Brierdene, Antigonish merchant D. G. Kirk, retained the architect William Critchlow Harris, and opted for the more fashionable design, Queen Anne. The two-and-a-half storey house was built in 1904 close to the original site of Nathaniel Symonds's store. Brierdene marked a sharp break from traditional Maritime Vernacular designs. It was emblematic of turn-of-the-century North America with its vast appetite for opulence, eclecticism and ornamentation. Queen Anne was especially popular with late nineteenth century American plutocrats who regarded their homes as "personal castles." The house's most distinctive features are its corner turret fitted with carved glass, and conical roof, as well as its hipped dormers, one of Harris's trademarks. Also eye-catching is its fanciful juxtaposition of decorative chimney pots, bay windows, verandah, buttress, and dentil trim. One of D. G. Kirk's leading commercial interests was the hardware business. D. G. Kirk Woodworking Company, the Palace Clothing Company, branch stores at Tracadie and Bayfield Road, and a department store in North Sydney were also part of his business empire. Around 1944, Brierdene suffered extensive fire damage but the timely interventions of the local fire department saved the house.

LANDRY HOUSE AT TAYLOR'S ROAD, POMQUET C.1922

Left to right here are Alex R. Landry, William Landry, Celeste Landry, Loretta Landry and William John Landry. The Landry property at Pomquet was first owned by Elisha Randall, Sr. of Bayfield who erected a sawmill and mill yard on the site. In 1819, he sold the land and buildings to James Taylor, a carpenter who expanded the operation to include a shelling mill and kiln for oats and barley. Taylor's business thrived with the export of lumber, shingles and barrel staves to Halifax, Arichat, and Newfoundland. In 1903, William and Celeste Landry, after being married sixteen years, purchased the hundred-acre (forty-hectare) property along with the house, mill, and other outbuildings. A farmer and carpenter, William aspired to build for his family a new dwelling. He adopted the Four Square style, a popular design in rural and urban Canada from 1900 to 1930. (In 1919, Eaton's advertised pre-cut Four Squares in its catalogue, *Plan Book of Ideal Homes*.) At this time, late Victorian ostentation was jettisoned for house styles that projected solidity, dignity and middle class prosperity. The Landry house with its spacious veranda was a striking departure from nineteenth century examples of Maritime Vernacular. Its generous and comfortable proportions made it a popular place for teachers to board. For the Landrys, the house with its five bedrooms, Douglas fir mouldings, pantry, and maid's room, was a proud achievement.

Chapter 3

Living off the Land and the Sea

HAYING AT FRASER'S GRANT: SIMON PERRO (ON THE WAGON), JOHN BAILEY AND ALLAN LOUIS PERRO, C.1925

The natural resources of Antigonish County received favourable comment in Nicolas Denys's authoritative description of the coastal regions of Acadia, published in 1672. They also impressed Father Antoine Gaulin, based in Antigonish around 1720, who reported that the land fronting the harbour was thickly covered with large trees, some as large as "six brasses" in circumference. At his instigation, the Mi'kmaw residents sowed some corn, peas, beans, and cabbage, and abundant yields testified to the land's fertility. For most of the nineteenth century, agriculture, fishing, lumbering, and shipping were the main economic thrusts in Antigonish town and county. The village and county produced quantities of timber for export, along with hay,

WHARF AT HAVRE BOUCHER, C.1940S

sheep, cattle, horses, cheese, and butter. Agricultural production, however, focused extensively on livestock. The cultivation of both wheat and oats increased in the 1820s, stimulated in part by the impact of the Sydney County Agricultural Society and government financial incentives awarded oatmeal mills. By the 1830s, the picture is one of small farms and small business ventures with few extremes of wealth or poverty. In the following decade, the immigrant tide was ebbing away. In Nova Scotia, the best land had been occupied or claimed by speculators; rural life in Antigonish, as elsewhere, could mean long periods of isolation despite the fact that a rather extensive network of roads had been established from Pictou eastward by the 1830s. Still, productivity increased substantially by the 1870s, boosted by increased land clearing and improved farming technologies. For example, the county's grain output (not including wheat) climbed from 28,400 bushels (1,022 cubic metres) in 1827 to 254,000 bushels (9,144 cubic metres) in 1871. Agricultural activity peaked during the early 1880s; by that time, the number of farms had tripled since 1827. In the following decades, the prospects for farming communities looked bleak as the pace of rural depopulation gathered momentum. In the early twentieth century, the cause of agriculture was actively championed by the Forward Movement, the Antigonish County Farmers' Association, and the *Casket*, which reported regularly on scientific farming methods, fall fairs, cattle exhibitions, and horse shows. Leading the assault against the alarming exodus of farming population was Dr. Hugh MacPherson of StFX Extension Department, who promoted crop and livestock diversification, improved soil management and breeding practices, and local agricultural cooperatives. The fishing communities of Antigonish County were also under strain during the early 1900s as fishermen struggled to compete against the increased number of steam trawlers encroaching on their fishing grounds. They also worked hard to accommodate changes such as the growing prevalence of frozen bait, frozen fish lockers and motorized boats. No one was going to get rich at that time: in 1903, lobster fishermen were paid little more than three dollars a hundred weight. By the 1920s, the Antigonish Movement, with its message of marketing cooperatives, offered more than a glimmer of hope for those earning their livelihood from the land and the sea.

HARVESTING POTATOES, POMQUET, C.1890S

The Acadians were remarkably self-sufficient in the preservation and production of foodstuffs. Most families provided their own milk, beef, and pork, kept a few hens, and grew potatoes, turnips, cabbages, carrots, green peas, onions, and beans. The Acadians were particularly fond of those vegetables that were hardy enough to survive the frost. The potato was a staple for most early settlers; it was well-suited to climatic conditions and easily planted in the rough ground among the rocks and stumps. In Acadian Nova Scotia, potatoes were usually planted in the springtime after the first frost and harvested around mid-October, after the grain was brought in. Turnips could always wait until the first major frost. Both women and children participated in the potato harvest; children were also put to work picking off potato bugs during the summer months. This photograph comes from a stereopticon slide originally owned by Mary Anne MacDonald, one-time schoolteacher at Heatherton.

FIVE HORSE TEAMS AT A PLOUGHING FROLIC, CROSS ROADS OHIO, C.1900

Here, left to right, are Tommy (Big Duncan) MacInnis, Rory MacDonald, Charlie (Big Duncan) MacInnis, John MacLean, Alex MacLean and Sandy Chisholm. Co-operative labour was an integral part of farming in early Antigonish County. Local farmers banded together to share the burdens of cultivating, harvesting, and threshing with their neighbours. The ploughing frolic was usually held during late October. The plough teams and ploughmen arrived at daybreak along with some helpers carrying pickaxes and hoes. The host farmer usually geared up for their visit by ploughing a few furrows to mark the field's boundaries and to help guide the formation of the rows. Driving a team of horses while manoeuveing a hand-held plough was no small feat; coordinating the procession of ploughs also took special skill. Every district had farmers who were renowned for their skill in turning a furrow. They took enormous pride the evenness of their freshly sculpted furrows. After the last sod was turned, the horses were fed and the hungry crew retired for a meal prepared by the local womenfolk. Oftentimes, the party continued into the night with swinging hands, Gaelic songs, and dancing to jigged tunes; the barley beer flowed freely from the barrel. Ploughing frolics were usually organized to assist widowed women. Similarly, chopping frolics were arranged to ensure that they had an adequate supply of wood for the winter months. Ploughing matches were popular diversions with local residents. A crowd of twelve hundred people attended such an event in October 1917. The champion of the day was John J. Chisholm of Brierly Brook who honoured the tradition of his grandfather, Valentine Chisholm whom the *Casket* of October 12, 1939, described as "famed in his native Scotland as a plowman."

THE MACGILLIVRAY FARM AT BROWN'S MOUNTAIN, C.1910

From left to right are Charlie MacGillivray, Lauchie MacDonald, Mary Gillis MacGillivray, Gregory MacDonald, and Jenny MacGillivray Mac-Donald. The horse was pivotal to the economy of nineteenth-century Maritime communities. Carriage, harness, and saddle makers as well as tanners, blacksmiths, and livery operators were indebted to the horse for much of their livelihood. The horse was also a vital member of the farm household, helping with the backbreaking work of farming and providing transportation. In this photograph, descendants of the Vamy MacGillivrays, who settled both Pictou and Antigonish Counties in the early 1790s, pose proudly with their three horses. "Peg Leg" Charlie MacGillivray, who lost his leg in a lumbering accident, and his two brothers went to the United States to earn enough money to pay off their deceased father's debt to a Bailey's Brook merchant. The threat of a lien on the family homestead, a common practice of the day, hung over their heads until the outstanding account was settled. By the 1890s, Charlie farmed the property along with his brothers, Alexander and Duncan, while his sisters, Jenny and Ann, worked as tailoresses. They were the second last family to move off Brown's Mountain; the last being Cutie MacDonald and his two sisters, all three unmarried.

Simon Perro (left) and John Bailey take the sheep to market. Fraser's Grant was named after four Fraser brothers, Colin, Thomas, John, and David, who were among its earliest residents. This small rural settlement, dating back to the 1820s, had a population of fifty people in 1871. Although the primary occupation was working the land, these typically one-man operations were increasingly supplemented during the late nineteenth century by lumbering or even temporary employment in the United States, Ontario, or Western Canada. In the 1920s, John Bailey, born in 1864, was a thoroughly seasoned farmer in a community that numbered around one hundred people. In this photograph, he is shown driving a wagon of sheep, probably to the railway station, which was about three miles away. Throughout the nineteenth century and into the early twentieth century, rural communities in Antigonish County endured the ruinous effects of out-migration. They also continued to struggle against the limits of transport and communication. However, it was still a far cry from those days when cattle from the St. Andrews area were rounded up by drovers travelling on foot and taken to Lochaber, where they followed a route along the old Guysborough road through Trafalgar. Their trek took them down the Musquodobit Valley to the Enfield area before reaching their Halifax destination. The railway connection completed between Halifax and Truro during the mid-1850s shortened the run; the drivers only needed to travel as far as Enfield before heading back home. By 1911, the county shipped out ten thousand lambs on an annual basis.

GUS FOUGERE
AND HIS
SISTER, AGNES
FOUGERE,
AT EDWARD
FOUGERE'S
FARM,
FRANKVILLE,
C.1930S

The ox was an indispensable part of the farmer's work force. Although slow moving, a trained team was well-suited to heavy tasks. They were used to haul wood and water and pull ploughs, sleds, sleighs, and carriages. In fact, many farmers considered them far superior to the horse in terms of dependability, strength, and ease of care. Despite the pervasive mechanization of late nineteenth century farming, the Acadians stuck to traditional farming practices, with a decided preference for oxen, especially when tilling rough land. Edward Fougere was one of the last people in the Frankville area to employ oxen for regular farm use. Agnes is holding a typical Mi'kmaw splint basket.

LENNIE
MacPhie
AND THE
COMMUNITY
BULL, CAPE
GEORGE,
C.1940

By 1910, Antigonish County was dotted with sixteen agricultural societies. Some of the earliest organizations sprang up in Morristown, Arisaig,
St. Andrews, and Antigonish. These local societies were dedicated to the
promotion of improved purebred livestock and frequently kept purebred
rams and bulls for breeding purposes. In 1908, for example, the Fairmont
Agricultural society charged fifty cents and one dollar to members and
nonmembers respectively for the services of its Hereford bull, George.
They even built a special paddock for exercising their prize animal. The
community bull was often a celebrity in rural areas. Some even carried
high-flown names like Kilburn 2nd, King Harold, Lord Clarendon, Lord
Napier, and Prince Charlie. The prize bull owned by Bayfield's Agricultural
Society had a singular moniker—2nd Gwynne of the Forest. By the 1940s,
stud fees rose to around two dollars. At that time, the Nova Scotia Department of Agriculture undertook to subsidize sixty percent of the costs of the
bull's upkeep, but only if he was a purebred. All the bulls in Cape George
were deemed purebreds and they were kept at the farm of Kate and William McPhie. The introduction of artificial insemination made the community bull obsolete. The official charged with this new responsibility was
puckishly dubbed by locals "the bull with the hat."

Along with the church, school, blacksmith's forge and general store, the grist mill was an essential institution in nineteenth century Antigonish County. According to Sagart Arisaig, the early settlers in the Keppoch ground their oats "with a hand quern, or perhaps carried it on their backs twenty miles to the nearest mill" in Lochaber. The Hulbert water-powered grist mill and sawmill in Lochaber were located at Hulbert's Brook. The Hulberts came to Antigonish County as early as 1788. Following commonplace practice, the Hulberts fortified their local position through intermarriage with other early families, most notably the close and interwoven Pushies, Symonds, Randalls, and Irishes. As old families, or first-comers, they enjoyed a measure of seniority that gave them distinct advantages. The Hulbert name is inextricably linked to the history of Lochaber and Bayfield as well as Antigonish. Sometime in the 1850s, Alexander Hulbert secured "rights of use" to the southern side of the brook. He erected a stone and concrete storage dam above the falls, and capitalized on this source of water power for his two mills. He even had a kiln to dry the oats before they were milled. This photograph also shows storage pens for pigs in the foreground. Evidently, they were fed some of the middlings from the mill. The grist mill attracted a steady business as customers brought in their home-grown oats, wheat, and buckwheat. The Hulberts did most of the custom work processing the meal and flour for their area. In exchange for their labour, they kept a one-tenth portion—"toll wheat"—as payment. In 1871, there were three family members, Alexander, the father, and his two sons, John and William, involved in the two businesses. The grist mill operated seven months, while the sawmill ran for two. At this time, Lochaber had a thriving cluster of local businesses including six sawmills, four tanneries, two carriage factories, two grist mills, two blacksmith forges, one tailor shop and one turner shop. The Hulbert mills operated into the twentieth century and its third-generation owner, Howard Hulbert, installed a generator and electrified the premises. In the 1880s, there were thirteen grist mills operating in Antigonish County. Fifty years later, there were only three: Angus McGillivray's mill at Malignant Cove; James Penny's mill at Sylvan Valley; and Howard Hulburt's at Lochaber.

In the early 1900s, Antigonish County's dairy industries had a fine reputation. The Hygienic Fresh Milk Company of Antigonish was a pioneer in the production of homogenized milk in Eastern Canada. The County also boasted four cooperative creameries, namely the Antigonish Dairy Company, the South River Creamery Company, at Loch Katrine, the Intercolonial Creamery Company at South River Station and the Millburn Creamery Company at Malignant Cove. The bulk of the shareholders in these operations were farmers. The Millburn Creamery formally opened on 6 July 1915. A picnic was held to mark the occasion and speeches were delivered by agricultural experts. There were 150 patrons in its first year of operation, during which it manufactured 35,000 pounds (15,876 kilograms) of butter and 140,000 pounds (65,503 kilograms) of cream. The creamery's output was sold largely in Halifax, Sydney, and Glace Bay. In addition to the production of butter and cream, the creamery also produced milk, skim milk, and cheese. Local farmers purchased much of the skim milk to augment the diet of their pigs. Angus Cameron, a native of St. Andrews, was the manager of the creamery. In 1915, Malignant Cove was renamed Millburn, referring to "a mill by a brook." Ironically, however ominous sounding the place name "Malignant Cove," the local residents preferred it, and never adopted this new designation.

NORTH SHORE MILLING COMPANY, MALIGNANT COVE, C.1921

Around 1800, a grist mill for wheat was built at Malignant Cove; the miller's name is believed to have been Taylor. In the ensuing decades, the farmers raised barley and oats; the miller, John MacDonald, provided a pair of shelling stoves and a kiln. By 1900, there was a population of two hundred at Malignant Cove; in addition to a sawmill and grist mill, there was a store, and a lobster factory. The North Shore Milling Company was established in the summer of 1920. The impetus for the establishment of this business came from Rev. Roderick MacNeil of Georgeville, Rev. Duncan J. Rankin of Arisaig and William MacEachern of Livingstone Cove. In September 1920, a meeting at the Millburn Creamery was organized to discuss the plan. A managing committee headed by Angus MacGillivray was appointed to oversee work on the local dam. Residents of Arisaig, Dunmaglass, Maryvale, Cape George and Lakevale were canvassed for subscriptions to finance the construction of the grist mill. About 250 people pledged around five thousand dollars and a government subsidy was secured. By January 1921, the grist mill was open for business and promised patrons "first class work." The co-operative, which continued until the 1930s or 1940s, was run by Dougald and Angus MacGillivray.

Lumbering was an important engine of growth and a way of life for many Antigonishers during the late nineteenth and early twentieth centuries. The lumber and pulpwood camps provided important seasonal employment for the men who headed to the woods of Guysborough, Antigonish and Pictou counties to work as choppers, sawyers, yarders, teamsters, cooks, and river drivers. The Mi'kmaq, who were renowned as woodsmen, were regarded as especially seasoned river drivers.

Depending on the weather, lumber camps typically operated from October or November until March or April. The size of the camps varied. They sometimes numbered as small as ten men or ranged upwards to forty, especially for company-run operations such as Grant and Campbell of New Glasgow or the Colonial Lumber Company. In the camps, the bunkhouse and cookhouse tended to be temporary structures, fashioned from spruce boards. The workday started early, with the men entrusted with the care of the horses waking at 5 a.m. Breakfast, which was ready by 6 a.m., helped fortify the workers for such arduous tasks as chopping, dynamiting, horseshoeing and building roads. Lumbering was demanding work that resulted in aching muscles and offered few comforts; there was little Sunlight soap, but lots of black flies and bed bugs. After payday, it was always a temptation to head to Antigonish or New Glasgow to pick up some Catawba wine in green gallon (four-litre) bottles. The woodsmen cut both softwood and hardwood with a crosscut saw and the logs were usually hauled by a team of horses to the sawmill. Percherons were the preferred breed for woods camps. The introduction of the portable sawmill permitted greater flexibility than the stationary sawmill, and cutting no longer required close proximity to the rivers and streams.

SAWMILL AT GLENROY, C.1900–1904

The latter part of the nineteenth century witnessed the proliferation of sawmills throughout Nova Scotia and the manufacture of wood products. The introduction of the portable, steam-powered sawmill was significant, for it proved compact and adaptable. Its popularity undoubtedly fuelled the fortunes of Nova Scotia's most prolific engine builder, A. Robb and Sons, who produced the region's most popular line of portable mill machinery. This view of the Glenroy sawmill operations shows some of the senior mill crew, including the owner, easily distinguished by his bowler hat. The children managed to squeeze into the photograph simply as curious onlookers; the youngest sawmill hands in Nova Scotia tended to be at least fourteen years old. Typical of most sawmill photographs, it is a posed picture, showing none of the crew actively engaged in their assigned tasks. To the left in the photograph, open to the elements, are the steam engine and boiler, the latter a popular place to keep the teakettle warm.

HAULING LOGS TO THE MILL, ANTIGONISH, C.1920S

West End, Main Street was a hub of economic activity and Kirk's Mill, located near Whidden's Bridge, was an established concern. D. G. Kirk purchased this woodworking factory from John Colin MacDonald and operated under the name of D. G. Kirk Woodworking and Contracting Company. By 1916, the company employed from ten to twenty people, and manufactured a variety of wood products, including sashes and doors. One of Kirk's specific interests was providing creosoted lumber for wharves and breakwaters. For several years, starting around 1912, W. E. Landry oversaw the day-to-day operations of this business. John F. MacLellan's mill at the western edge of town was also a local landmark for many years and John MacDonald's Sash and Door Factory was another outlet for wood products. One of the most important names in the lumber business was A. S. MacMillan, premier of Nova Scotia from 1940 to 1945, who lived for some years in the town of Antigonish. At different times, he controlled large tracts of woodland and was perhaps the main advocate of dredging Antigonish Harbour so that cordwood could be shipped by boat.

COLONIAL LUMBER COMPANY, WILLIAMS POINT, 1913

The history of Antigonish sawmills dates back to the 1780s. At that time, Dorchester had one of twenty-two mills in Nova Scotia receiving a government bounty of twenty-two pounds. Between 1810 and 1820, a number of settlers cut timber for the overseas trade. But these were small operations compared to the Colonial Lumber Company which was established in 1913 at Gillis Cove, Williams Point. The company which planned to specialize in flooring also leased woodlands at Polson's Brook, near Upper South River and Donnybrook, near Cross Roads, Ohio. This business reportedly employed about 125 men. In an area covering four acres (one-and-a-half hectares), this modern facility included a mill that cut ten thousand feet (3048 metres) of logs daily, a flooring factory, dry kiln, powerhouse, and lumberyard. There was even a boarding house equipped with a kitchen for fifty employees. For its supply of hardwood lumber, the company drew predominantly upon the West River area as well as the Keppoch, and the logs were floated down the river to the site. Local customers were able to purchase flooring from the mill for ten dollars per thousand feet (304 metres). By the end of the First World War, the Colonial Lumber Company was bankrupt, largely because of gross mismanagement. Its American investors sustained some punishing financial losses. The equipment was dismantled and the buildings were razed to the ground.

Pulpmills started operating in Nova Scotia in the 1880s and provided an important market for spruce and fir pulpwood. Companies such as the Sonora Timber Company, which operated from 1924–1931, relied on farmers and woodsmen for their vast supply of pulp. The Sonora Timber Company, based primarily in Guysborough County, extended its reach into Cape Breton and Halifax and Antigonish Counties. They set up a pulp operation at Sherbrooke and Sonora and established several steam-powered rossing mills for barking pulpwood. The output at these two mills was significant; they exported pulp in twenty-five to thirty steamships annually. In places like Lochaber Lake, the log drive officially began as soon as the ice went out of the rivers and lakes. It was wet, cold work for the men who navigated the logs along the winding route to St. Mary's River and the head of the tidewater. In its heyday, the Sonora Timber Company offered its workers and suppliers good pay. Choppers and teamsters received anywhere from thirty to fifty a month. Farmers and woodlot owners sometimes commanded as much as $3.50 per cord.

MAKING HOCKEY STICKS IN LOCHABER, C.1890S

One of the most interesting economic activities in late-nineteenth-century Antigonish was the manufacture of hockey sticks. Little is known about this enterprise except that it was dominated by local Mi'kmaw craftsmen. Much of the wood for the sticks was likely obtained in the Keppoch. Throughout Nova Scotia, aboriginal craftsmen produced such items as axe handles and brooms. In Antigonish County, the Young name was synonymous with hockey sticks. Around the turn of the century, Charlie Young, who lived at The Landing near Antigonish, manufactured the celebrated "Swiper" hockey stick. He made upwards of three hundred each year and sold them throughout Nova Scotia. He used only the finest hardwood, with the root forming the blade so that the stick was fashioned from a single piece of wood. Charlie Young also made wooden crosses for the graveyard, while his son, Tommy carried on the family woodworking tradition, producing hockey sticks, lawn chairs, and boats. It is believed that some of Antigonish's legendary hockey players used the "Swiper" for their games.

UNIDENTIFIED
GROUP OF
MI'KMAQ AT
ANTIGONISH
LANDING,
C.1900

Antigonish Harbour was a popular seasonal camping site for the local Mi'kmaq. The area once teemed with eagles, muskrats, wild cats, and foxes and served as a vital base for hunting and fishing. Well into the twentieth century, Mi'kmaw families maintained their attachment to The Landing. They came on a seasonal basis, drawn by the twin needs of hunting and fishing. The area's proximity to Antigonish was also advantageous. It was close to a source of such staples such as flour, salt, sugar, and tea. Moreover, in town, the men found a ready market for their sturdy baskets, porch furniture, and children's rocking chairs. They also found employment as day labourers and gardeners, while the women often sold their basketwork and services as housekeepers. This photograph shows a traditional wigwam, a frame of poles, covered with sheets of birch bark and canvas sail cloth; sometimes skins and tarpaper were used to cover the frame. The ladder permitted accessibility to the opening at the top, which could be covered over during inclement weather. This shelter was easily erected and well adapted to a lifestyle of semi-mobility. The older man stands proudly with his winter eel pole, a multipronged pole that enabled the fishers to spear for eels through the ice. Throughout the nineteenth and twentieth centuries, the local Mi'kmaw eel fishery focused on the Antigonish and Pomquet harbour estuaries and watersheds. The eel was an important source of food for the Mi'kmaq year-round. For this fishery, the natives relied on such apparatus as eel pots and eel racks as well as eel spears; there were two different models of spears depending on the season. However, the significance of the eel went far beyond the realm of food gathering. The eel has played a diverse cultural role in Mi'kmaw life for over four-thousand years. Imbued with medicinal properties, it was utilized for such ailments as cramps, rheumatism, and headaches; eel skin could also be fashioned into bandages or braces to relieve sprains. The eel served other practical purposes—it could be employed for bait or adapted for use as bindings for sleds and moccasins. The eel also played a central role on ceremonial occasions, especially during feasts and community gatherings like funerals. Owing to its potent spiritual powers, it was used as an offering to express thanks or ensure good fortune in the hunt.

BAYFIELD WHARF, HAULING COD, C.1912

During the second half of the nineteenth century, Bayfield was a flourishing community, boasting a customs house, several mills (a grist mill, carding mill, and three sawmills), a cheese factory, three tanneries, and a carriage works. Shipping was the backbone of the local economy and the Bayfield wharf was its focal point. The Pomquet Island lighthouse and the breakwater provided a safe harbour. C. B. Whidden's fleet, which ran from 1864 to 1914, operated out of Bayfield during the summer months. Christopher MacDonald, a Heatherton merchant, also had ships based in that port. Vessels travelled from Bayfield along the coast, delivering and picking up goods in local ports. Captain James Keay of Bayfield often ventured as far afield as the West Indies, carrying a cargo of fish and returning with sugar, molasses, and rum. There was also a booming shipping trade with Newfoundland, focusing primarily on cattle as well as farm produce, grain, lumber, and socket stones used for tombstones. The transport of cattle was a highly competitive business and was pivotal to the local economy. Cattle were herded from neighbouring communities to the Bayfield wharf by men like Lauchie "the Drover" MacDonald. In the early years of this trade, the cattle were driven into the water where, secured with ropes, they were hoisted on board. Local men frequently accompanied them on the run to Newfoundland as cowherds. In the summer of 1876, the County of Antigonish shipped no less than 1,800 horned cattle to St. John's, Newfoundland. Similarly, in 1884, Bayfield sent a sizable shipment of horses and milch cows to St. John's. Fishing was also a vital economic activity. Vessels from Gloucester, Massachusetts came every summer and fall to fish mackerel off Bayfield.

BAYFIELD WHARF, LOADING CATTLE, C.1912

BALLANTYNE'S LOBSTER CANNERY, LATE 1930S

The wharf was a popular spot for a Sunday outing. It was the setting for courtships, business rivalries, and the occasional fight. The lobster fishery in Antigonish County commenced around 1870 and lobster canneries appeared shortly thereafter. Lobsters continued to be big business in the 1920s to 1950s. Canneries dotted the shoreline, situated in places like Bayfield, East Tracadie, Blue Rock, Linwood, and Havre Boucher. These businesses employed both men and women, often as many as eighty, some of whom were transient workers from parts of New Brunswick and Cape Breton. They were usually boarded in bunkhouses provided by the company. In 1902, Burnham and Morrill Company of Portland, Maine came

BALLANTYNE'S
COVE, FACTORY
WORKERS
ON SUNDAY
OUTING AT
BALLANTYNE'S
WHARF, C.1910

to Cape George and opened a lobster factory at Ballantyne's Cove; they already had operations at Arisaig and Morristown. In 1917, the company paid fishermen 41/2¢ per pound for lobsters. Within the cannery there was a distinctive hierarchy of jobs. For example, there was a great disparity in the summertime bi-monthly wages paid some of the male employees ($133.78) and the young women ($22.00–$28.00). It was hard work and the girls' hands were frequently raw from opening the lobster claws and tails. Nevertheless, the cannery provided local women with regular wages, which were often surrendered to their parents to contribute to the upkeep of large families. At this time, the local options for female employment were limited to such roles as dressmaker, laundress, domestic servant, and cook. In 1936, the fishermen rented the cannery from Burnham and Morrill. That year, they received 191/2¢ a pound for live lobsters and 9¢ a pound for canners. A meeting at the schoolhouse at Cape George in July 1935 led to the decision to form a co-op to run the lobster factory.

FISH HOUSES AT BALLANTYNE'S COVE, C.1920S

In the nineteenth century, fishing and seasonal trade in livestock with Halifax and Newfoundland stood at the centre of economic life at the Cape. Cape George was also an active participant in Maritime Canada's wooden shipbuilding industry. Moreover, this locality produced a singular number of sea captains in the late nineteenth century. In fact, at one time the parish church of Cape George boasted seven sea captains on its rolls. By the 1860s, there were two fishing companies operating at the Cape: one business was run by Aden Babson and Company of Boston at South Side Cape George while the other, owned by J. C. Hall, was based at Ballantyne's Cove. Although these operations provided employment, the fish merchants' control over the fishery was almost feudal in its scope. This pattern of exploitation changed little when Burnham and Morrill Company of Portland, Maine, established a lobster factory at Ballantyne's Cove. The prices paid the lobster fishermen for their catches promised little more than a meagre existence. Despite such hardships, the lobster fishermen were a hardy and resourceful lot. Many of them made their own boats, as well as their fish houses, which stood weathered near the shoreline. These structures, often heated by stoves, were used for storage and provided shelter to fishermen while repairing equipment during inclement weather. Some of the men even slept in them. With such deflated prices for their catches, it was difficult to get ahead financially. Survival demanded thrift, resilience, and practicality. Contributions, especially boxes of clothing, from family members working in the United States were always welcome gifts. The "box from Boston" or the "barrel from Detroit" became everyday expressions in the community.

EMMA E.
WHIDDEN AT
LIVERPOOL,
1907

The *Emma E. Whidden*, a 249-ton schooner built in Liverpool, Nova Scotia in 1907 was just one of the many vessels operated by the Whiddens over a fifty-year period. It is estimated that between 1864 (when C. B. Whidden purchased their first vessel, a small schooner called the *Lady Havelock*) and 1914 they owned approximately twenty-eight vessels that travelled regularly to St. John's and the West Indies, transporting horses, sheep, cattle, and cheese to the former destination and lumber to the latter. The return cargoes of sugar, molasses, rum, and spices helped "replenish the bins and shelves of the general stores throughout the countryside." The firm, C. B. Whidden and Son(s), was synonymous with shipbuilding and ship owning. The name most closely linked to shipbuilding in Antigonish County was Captain David Graham, who lived at Harbour Centre. He established two shipyards, one at Fennel's Point and another near Seabright, where he produced around thirty sailing vessels. Graham not only built vessels, he sailed them as well. This sea-going tradition was perpetuated by his sons, who also became sailing masters. The last vessel built by Captain David Graham was the schooner *Graham*, which was shipwrecked at Canso in May 1863. The Antigonish merchants felt the loss acutely, for the vessel was carrying their spring merchandise. Shipbuilding was not restricted to the Grahams. Other operations sprouted at locations along both sides of the harbour. Captain Angus MacDonald once estimated that over one-hundred vessels had been produced in Antigonish Harbour. According to local historian Tony MacKenzie, about 243 ships (schooners, brigs, or brigantines) were built and owned in the County of Antigonish before 1878. In Bayfield, for example, E. W. Randall and Captain James Keay constructed vessels for the highly competitive coastal trade between Antigonish, Halifax, and Newfoundland. Farther down the coast at Pomquet, the Crispos, DeCostes, Andersons, DeLoreys, and MacDonalds, to name a few, distinguished themselves as shipbuilders. In Tracadie, the Deloreys, Flynns, Landrys, and James Hall were prominent owners and builders.

The most memorable ship launching in Antigonish was that of the *Sea Bird* in 1849. This schooner was built in North Grant from timber hewn from Captain John MacDonald's property. On the day of the launching, the vessel headed towards the sea, transported on a platform with rollers and hauled by sixty head of oxen. "Fully rigged and flags aflying," this singular spectacle attracted wide-eyed attention all along Hawthorne and Main streets as it proceeded towards the Lower Landing. Here was gathered the "largest crowd to ever attend a launching in Antigonish County." (MFM #15099 67) The *Sea Bird* operated as a packet between Antigonish and Halifax. The launching of Captain Richard Cunningham's seventy-five-ton paddle steamer, the *Wellington*, was also an awe-inspiring moment for local people. It was built at a temporary shipyard on South River Road. The vessel was constructed by foreman builder Charles Kennedy, ironworker Hugh MacDonald and some ship carpenters from Pomquet. During the winter of 1877, the 120 foot-long (37-metre-long) vessel, cradled on sleds, was dragged by oxen over a carpet of snow to Gillis Cove; the distance was around one-half mile. The *Wellington* started its career carrying freight, but later operated as a tug, towing lighters. The steamer, which could accommodate over two hundred passengers, was a popular vessel for coastal excursions. The local band usually came along to provide musical accompaniment for the dances.

**WHARF AT
ANTIGONISH
LANDING, 1923**

The harbour was an attraction for the early settlers, for there were no roads and travelling to newly settled areas was done mainly by sea. However, the harbour has never been a haven for commercial shipping for any long period of time, as the depth of the water fluctuates. Furthermore, as the forests have become more denuded, silt flowing into the harbour from the several rivers that drain into it has made it distinctly unnavigable for any large-scale boats. In the 1820s, a tow path, stretching from The Landing up the West River to a wharf situated on Brierly Brook (at the end of present-day Court Street), served as the main route for transporting merchandise into the village. Scows were also used to transport farm animals to vessels in the harbour. As late as the 1920s, small schooners carrying fish, coal, or produce would also bring cargoes to the Landing Wharf. The goods would then be transported into town by horses hauling truck-wagons. This, of course, increased transportation costs and the price of goods. The most serious impediments to harbour navigation, however, were the sandbars and silting. Dredging was carried out there in 1864, 1878, and in later years; at one time, with the harbour dredged, vessels weighing as much as sixty tons could enter and unload their goods at The Landing. But this provided only temporary relief for the problem. Various efforts to extract the rich gypsum deposits lying inside the harbour had to be abandoned because of the sand bars. Proposals made by some involved in the lumber industry to have regular dredging of the harbour were considered to be too expensive and were therefore abandoned.

COPPER LAKE COPPER MINE, C.1910

There was interest in copper mining in the Copper Lake area as early as the 1860s. Over the next few decades, there were sporadic attempts at mining in the area. In the early twentieth century, the arrival of the Lake Copper Mining Company occasioned much excitement. It brought to the community the prospect of economic stimulus. In 1908, the company even opened an office in Antigonish, where officials prominently displayed samples of the mine's copper ore in its front window. That year, the *Casket* reported that the "The percentage of copper…is phenomenal." This photograph documents the extent of the operation, with its main shaft, the Red Shaft-house, located just behind the man holding the horse. Nearby was the white slag heap, the mound created from white slag emptied from box cars. Below the Red Shaft was the company's mine office and post office. In the centre of the photograph can be seen the cookhouse with a ladder on the roof; the extension served as a bunkhouse. Owners encountered much disappointment with their mining venture at Copper Lake. The lower shaft, The Grey Shaft, dug below the level of Copper Lake, was designed to provide access to rich veins of copper ore under the lake. However, the underground tunnels flooded with water and the equipment could not be salvaged. It is difficult to determine whether this serious blow or poor transportation connections contributed to the collapse of the company. Mining operations were suspended around 1911. This photograph was taken by John Hattie of Two Mile Lake, a teacher and photographer, who extensively documented life in Antigonish and Guysborough counties at the turn of the century.

Despite extensive mineral exploration in Antigonish County, few people associate this region with mining activity. However, there were other mining enterprises, most of which were short lived. As early as the 1850s, Rev.

Donald Honeyman, a keen geologist, reported significant outcroppings of iron in the Arisaig district. By the late nineteenth century and early twentieth centuries, there was intermittent prospecting at Doctor's Brook and its tributaries, Iron and McInnes Brooks. For a short period of time in the mid 1890s, the New Glasgow Iron, Coal and Railway Company (later amalgamated with the Nova Scotia Steel Company) shipped several tonnes of ore from the Arisaig, Ross and Iron Brook mines. The ore was transported to the Arisaig Pier by a pole tramway.

Around 1910, a company, excited by evidence of coal deposits, dug several shafts at Big Marsh; their potential was never fully determined because of inadequate capital. In the late nineteenth century, news of a gold strike in Pinkietown (Ohio) generated a buzz of excitement. A local newspaper correspondent wrote, "The day is not far distant when we shall hear the snort of the iron horse re-echoing along the green valley of Ohio." These high hopes were quickly dashed, as were the objectives of the Nova Scotia Gypsum Company at its short-lived gypsum plant in Harbour Centre. Some of the earliest gypsum exports from Maritime Canada came from Ogden's Cliffs. Little wonder that the Nova Scotia Gypsum Company considered its business venture in Antigonish a sure thing. However, in August 1928, operations were suspended, some eighty men were dismissed and the company removed its equipment to Cheticamp; even the half-mile (0.8 kilometre) standard-gauge railway, which connected the plant to a loading shed and pier, was pulled up. Interestingly enough, Antigonishers had better luck at mining outside the region. In the late nineteenth century, James M. McNeil of Malignant Cove, William Fraser of South River, Hugh McGillivray of Bailey's Brook and Ronald D. Fraser and Hugh McDonald, both of West River, realized their dreams of success in Colorado mining camps. Some even pursued careers with mining companies in South Dakota and Arizona. Of course, in a class by himself was Ashdale's Alex MacDonald, the "Klondike King," who made a vast fortune in the Yukon gold fields.

Chapter 4

Trades, Businesses and Industries

STAFF AT ANGUS MCDONALD'S FISH STORE, ANTIGONISH, 1904

Little is known about economic activity in early Antigonish County. Undoubtedly, the region and its Mi'kmaw residents fell within the commercial orbit of Nicolas Denys, the fisherman and trader who received a vast trade monopoly stretching from Gaspé to Canso during the early 1650s. Around

1659, he built a fishing post at Chedabouctou (Guysborough). Trade connections with the region were further enhanced between 1717 and 1720 with the establishment of France's Île Royale colony and Father Gaulin's efforts to consolidate the Mi'kmaq of peninsular Nova Scotia at a large mission at Antigonish. Although his achievements fell short of his objectives, the region, which was under English jurisdiction, must have profited from its proximity to Île Royale.

By the end of the eighteenth century, one of the leading businessmen in Antigonish County was Edward Irish, who operated the main store at Town Point around 1798. At approximately the same time, John Wright traded furs with the local Mi'kmaq. The contribution of these two men to the local economy was more distinguished than that of Lieut. John Wheaton, who established Antigonish County's first grog shop in the late 1780s. In the early nineteenth century, Nathaniel Symonds, a native of New Hampshire, found a niche for himself on the Main Street of Antigonish when the community was barely more than a few scattered small farms and rough clearings. He was an enterprising resident, who ran a shop, manufactured potash, and carried on a cattle trade with Newfoundland. His son, Joseph, became a prominent storeowner in Little Tracadie, where according to his business ledger, he did a bustling trade in rum and moccasins.

"The Main" has long been the commercial heart of the town and county. According to local lore, Antigonish's winding Main Street was initially carved out by Zephaniah Williams and his native guide, Joe Snake, blazing a path from Williams Point to Hartshorne Grant around 1798. However implausible the story, it is interesting to note that Snake does appear on the 1817 census as a resident of Afton. Over time, the footpath became a bridle path and eventually a cart road along which houses and businesses clustered. Main, Church, and Court streets were the focus of much of this early development.

The period between 1820 and 1880 may fairly be described as one of economic expansion and consolidation even though it was uneven in certain respects. The early economic history of Antigonish was dominated by a network of English-speaking merchants and tradesmen, many of whom were related and attended the Presbyterian church. Their financial and cultural power enabled them to dictate business practices. Although many of their customers were Gaelic- or French-speaking Catholics, English prevailed as the language of most mercantile activity. For local businessmen, language barriers were the least of their concerns. The scarcity of cash was the bane of all merchants. According to local historian Ronald MacDonald, there were more than five hundred actions for collection of debt in Antigonish County in 1837 alone. For workmen, payments for services were often in kind. Local carpenter Alexander MacPherson, for example, was routinely paid throughout the 1840s with everything from tobacco to oatmeal, butter, and cows; blotters and a pair of shoes sufficed as payment on several occasions.

During the second half of the nineteenth century, Antigonish town and county were dotted with a host of small businesses and trades. By the early 1880s, this lively economic scene included thirty-eight sawmills, fourteen flour and grist mills, fourteen tanneries, fourteen carriage works, fifty-seven blacksmiths shops, five harness and saddlery establishments, three carding mills, and nine cheese factories. The census also recorded one hundred and 186 people employed as weavers, 70 as carpet makers, 24 as milliners and dressmakers, 30 as tailors, 25 as shingle makers, and 30 as boot and shoemakers. As well, there were those who earned their living as shipwrights, tinsmiths, fish dealers, coopers, brick manufacturers, and broom makers. By the early 1890s, the town alone boasted tailoring, dressmaking and millinery shops, two carding mills, one woodworking factory, one milk canning plant, a brickyard, and several blacksmith shops. The increased number of carriage factories, as well as hotels and boarding houses, signified heightened mobility and expanding economic networks. The town also had an impressive roster of store proprietors who manifested an aggressive commercialism. The prominent merchants of the day did not sit idle. Many, like the Kirks and Whiddens, invested in a diversity of enterprises. Some even demonstrated remarkable innovation—J. H. Stewart, for instance, mastered a technique for shipping fresh eggs to Britain.

The population of town and county grew to over 18,000 in 1881, but thereafter showed an unhealthy decline, sinking to 10,073 in 1931. With the termination of reciprocity in 1866, the decline in wooden shipbuilding and a general depression in the 1870s, an increasing number of people left the town and county. The railway, which was completed to the Strait of Canso by 1880, was heralded as an economic stimulus, but it served instead as an iron highway for out-migration. The forces of industrialization that transformed so many Nova Scotia communities—like Amherst, Sydney, and New Glasgow—bypassed Antigonish. Despite temporary outbursts of prosperity, especially during wartime, Antigonishers in the early twentieth century continued to beat a well-worn path to the "Boston states" or other parts of the United States and Canada seeking to improve their lot as domestics, nurses, clerical workers, factory labourers, linemen, and railway and construction workers. One part of Cambridge, Massachusetts, was nicknamed "Little Pomquet" because of the number of expatriates from Pomquet there. In August 1905, no fewer than one hundred men boarded a harvest train in Antigonish to head to the Canadian west. This human drain affected other areas such as Havre Boucher where in 1909 at least fifty-five men made the journey westward to assist with the harvest.

ANTIGONISH TANNERY AND THE OWNER, JAMES O'BRIEN, ANTIGONISH, C.1870S

The tannery was an integral aspect of most nineteenth century small town economies. Unlike some of the seasonally-based grist mills and sawmills, they operated year-round. They also took in hides from all over and kept the harness makers, saddlers, and cobblers supplied with leather. In the heat of the summer, the tannery's presence was conspicuous by the swarms of houseflies and pungent odour. Here is the bearded James O'Brien during the early 1870s standing in his leather apron in front of his rambling Church Street tannery. O'Brien, one-time clerk at Thomas Somers's store, plied his trade as a tanner as early as 1838 and eventually built a large tannery close to his house. The proximity to the West River was an attractive feature for it provided access to waterpower. By 1871, his successful year-round business had two employees. He paid six hundred dollars a year in wages, reflecting the growing shift even in small towns toward the market-oriented medium of cash, rather than the traditional payment in kind or labour. When O'Brien died in 1876, his son, John, took over the family business. He introduced several innovations, such as a leather spinning machine and a steam engine, that substantially mechanized what had been a hand-run operation. As well as catering to local needs, he also manufactured leather for export.

In the 1890s, there were over sixty blacksmiths shops in Antigonish County. Few communities could survive without a blacksmith. He played a vital role in the rural economy well into the twentieth century. Specialized industries—most notably shipyards, mining operations, lumbering companies, printing trades, and railway firms—also relied extensively on his services. In rural areas, much of the blacksmith's time was devoted to shoeing horses and oxen, which were so vital to transportation and work. The routine of work was year-round with little respite during the winter months. After all, there were always sleds, axes, and crosscut saws to be repaired. The blacksmith could turn his hand to almost anything, making or fixing all forms of tools, farm implements, nails, sled runners, wagon wheel spokes, chains, or skates. William J. Levangie of Havre Boucher plied his trade as a blacksmith during the 1930s and 1940s. His business was a small but bustling operation. Among his varied tasks was sharpening picks for local road crews.

HEATHERTON LINEMEN AT UNIDENTIFIED LOCATION, c.1890s

As early as the mid-nineteenth century, Nova Scotia ranked as a leader in the development of telegraph and cable systems. According to historian Tony MacKenzie, this business came to be dominated by eastern Nova Scotia which "supplied line workers for half the continent." Many of these linemen came from Roman Valley, Guysborough Intervale, Heatherton, St. Andrew's, and Antigonish and the surnames of Farrell, Rogers, Chisholm, Grant, MacDonald, Forbes, Kelly, Carroll, Bonvie, Long, Doyle, Fraser, Purcell, and Glenn figured prominently in their ranks. This trade was so much a family and community tradition that it was long joked that the baby boys in Roman Valley "cut their first teeth on a pair of Klein pliers," an indispensible piece of lineman's gear. It has been estimated that at one time, thirty-two members of the Valentine Chisholm family could be found working on the lines somewhere between Montana and New England. This job, which promised regular pay, demanded dexterity, physical strength, perseverance, and teamwork. Some of the linemen took on legendary qualities during their lifetimes. There were Alex C. P. R. MacDonald and Peter Carroll who could each single-handedly erect a twenty-five-foot (seven-and-a-half-metre) pole, and "Little Joe" MacDonald, as agile as a mountain goat, who bounded down the poles in ten-foot (three-metre) jumps. One of the most celebrated linemen in North America was "Holy Angus" MacDonald of Antigonish who provided heroic service to the New York Telephone Company after the great blizzard of 1888, patrolling their lines on snowshoes. Telegraph and telephone lines transformed not only North American lifestyles but also landscapes. By the 1890s, there was a mesh of lines throughout Antigonish County. The Commercial Cable Company operated a line from Hazel Hill through Heatherton and Antigonish to New Glasgow where it joined up with the Canadian Pacific Telegraph line; conversely the Western Union's line ran from Canso through Guysborough and St. Andrews, connecting with their line at South River. At least five men in this photograph can be identified: Ranald A. MacDonald, John D. MacDonald, and Dan Kennedy, all of Black Avon, Alex A. MacDonald of Fraser's Grant, and John A. Mills of Farm Road, Heatherton.

RAILWAY WORK CREW AND WATER TOWER IN ANTIGONISH COUNTY, C.1880S

Railways gave a stimulus to the local economy, especially local lumber mills. They also meant more money in the tills of merchants, as well as short-term construction jobs clearing the road and laying the tracks. The railway also introduced some distinctive landmarks, ranging from the railway station to the ubiquitous water tower, usually located near a pond at ten-mile (sixteen-kilometre) intervals. Here the train would stop and the firemen, nimbly handling the hinged iron spout, would refill the tank behind the locomotive. In December 1880, the Eastern Extension Railway opened its line from New Glasgow to the Strait of Canso. There followed a flurry of station-building at various locations, including James River, Brierly Brook, Antigonish, South River, Taylor Road, Pomquet, Heatherton, Afton, Tracadie, Giroirs, Little Tracadie and Havre Boucher (Frankville).

HEATHERTON HOTEL, C.1882

By 1879, the village of Pomquet Forks looked forward to a prosperous future. The leading citizens decided to rename the community Heatherton and were excited by the prospects of increased business with the arrival of the railway in 1876. In December 1880, the Eastern Extension Railway from New Glasgow to the Strait of Canso opened for business. It was during this period that Duncan MacDonald began building the two-and-a-half storey Heatherton Hotel, which offered guests ten rooms and also housed a general store. The post office was situated there for many years. A livery stable was conveniently located next door and across the street was William C. Chisholm's store. The appearance of a hotel was prompted by the building of the railway and signalled the increased mobility of a travelling public. After MacDonald sold the business, the hotel continued to be a fixture in Heatherton until its demolition in the 1990s. During that period it served variously as a store, dwelling, and venue for fund-raising dances. In 1893, a former resident reported on Heatherton's economic progress, noting its impressive roster of merchants, blacksmiths, carriage-makers, carpenters, and prosperous farmers. He also made special reference to some private boarding houses and the Heatherton Hotel, a "first-class hotel," where good square meals could be obtained at all hours.

MERRIMAC HOTEL, C.1887–89

In late nineteenth-century Antigonish, there was a variety of establishments on Main Street which provided accommodation for travellers and lodgers. The selection included Smith's Hotel, Cunningham's Hotel, Revere House, Ronan House, and Central House; two of these were run by women. One of Antigonish's best known hoteliers was Rufus Hale, a native of Newburyport, Massachusetts, who originally came to Nova Scotia during Guysborough's gold boom in 1880. He moved to Antigonish in 1885, where he eventually took over the Central House and served as hotelkeeper at the Merrimac Hotel, formerly Cunningham's Hotel, a two-storey wooden structure with twenty-five rooms. At the turn of the century, Hale promised guests such amenities as a telephone, hot and cold baths, electric lights, "commodious sample rooms," and "good stabling." He assured potential clients that the premises catered to the needs of commercial travellers. Conditions in town lodgings often left something to be desired. Even as late as the 1920s, some of the local hotels offered nearly frigid conditions for guests during the winter months: the stoves were banked at night and the toilets were frozen solid by morning. Little wonder that the Royal George when it was built in 1906 seemed luxurious by comparison. The author Beckles Willson recalled his memorable visit to Antigonish's Queen Hotel, a "quaint little inn," around 1910. He was rudely awakened one morning by a man closing his closet door. The following exchange transpired: "'What do you want?'" I demanded. 'Nothing,' returned the intruder calmly. 'But what are you doing in my room? I locked the door last night.' 'What am I doing in your room? How else do you think I am going to get out of mine?' He jerked his thumb in the direction of the closet in an aggrieved manner…"

SEARS'S HOUSE AND HOTEL, LOCHABER, C.1900

In the nineteenth and early twentieth centuries, the Sears family was closely involved in Lochaber's economic development. The main road through Lochaber, which served as the principal route for coach travel between Antigonish and Sherbrooke, helped shape the early community as well as the Sears's fortunes. Their property was conveniently placed to provide lodging and refreshment to travellers. "Squire" John Sears quickly capitalized on its location and built a general store and a livery establishment. Their house, which met the requirements of a large family, was also expanded to serve as a hotel called the Half-way House by mail drivers. Here, they would stop for a meal or accommodation en route between Antigonish and Sherbrooke. Thomas J. Sears took over the family business and his wife, Martha, was a hostess at the popular country hotel. By 1901, the Sears household included, in addition to family members, a store clerk, mail driver, and servant. Starting in 1923, the hotel was operated by John Wall and his wife; she was renowned for her Christmas cake and dandelion wine. The Walls also ran the store, livery, post office, a forge, and a gas station along with a dance hall. Under their management, the hotel expanded to twenty bedrooms.

In 1906 construction of a new hotel building began. The Royal George was managed and later owned by James Broadfoot, the proprietor of the Queen Hotel, located on the north side of Main Street, between Church and Court streets. The building itself was erected by C. E. Gregory, local barrister and son of C. C. Gregory, engineer and barrister, who lived on the property known locally as Mount Cameron, which he renamed Fernwood. It was designed by an architect from Prince Edward Island, William Critchlow Harris. The new edifice was to have electric lights, indoor facilities, and a dinner menu the equal of any in the province. With its flat roof, two-storey veranda, and a hexagonal tower-shaped gazebo, the building was an eye-catching landmark for the town. It was equipped with steam heat, telephone services, a lounge room, and a dining room to seat sixty guests. Some rooms had a private bath and fireplace.

With the opening of this new structure, Antigonish had a hotel to be proud of. Not only did it serve many prominent Nova Scotians, especially politicians, but many of those who travelled to Guysborough, Sherbrooke, and points in between. Sunday dinner at the Royal George was, reputedly, a treat to be remembered. In 1913, ownership of the hotel was transferred to John Kennedy and A. K. MacDonald, who were formerly engaged in railway and highway construction. MacDonald's son, John "Beaver" MacDonald of Beaver Meadow, took over the management of the hotel. Perhaps the individual best known to the traveling public was Gregor Myette, who would drive hotel customers to and from the railway station at any time of the day or night and in all kinds of weather, initially with horse-drawn carriages or sleighs.

After the Second World War, the business was purchased by George Armour, the grandson of James Broadfoot, the former manager of the Royal George. Mrs. Armour helped in operating the hotel. With the great expansion of automobile traffic on improved highways and the growth of motels along those highways, there was a noticeable decline in the small town hotel business and the Armours retired from the Royal George.

**THE DINGLE,
SOUTH RIVER,
C.1940S**

In the early 1920s, Les Cunningham, a bricklayer by trade, and his wife opened a roadside stand in Lower South River. It was situated near the main highway, where the Cunninghams hoped to capitalize on tourist traffic. Selling pop, candy, and hot dogs was replaced by a more ambitious plan to build overnight cabins. The Dingle had an inauspicious beginning, starting with one leaky, unheated cabin lighted by oil lamps. However, it expanded with the introduction of electricity and running water, and the addition of a restaurant where Mrs. Cunningham prepared the meals. In 1929, the owners advertised ladies' rest rooms, cigars and tobacco, temperance drinks, ice cream, meals and lunches, gas, oil, fruit, and confectionery: "The Dingle is not a road house, but a place where you get good eats and good service." The Dingle catered largely to summer guests and hired a number of young women from Pomquet who worked as domestics. The Depression and the Second World War dealt a serious blow to the Cunningham's business fortunes. After the war, they returned from a brief stint in Pictou and revived the Dingle by building a lodge and new cabins. These modernized facilities, equipped with hot and cold running water, could accommodate no fewer than eighty-six persons. In 1950, novelist Will R. Bird described the establishment as an "unusually fine cabin colony." Antigonishers were quick to appreciate the monetary benefits of tourism. As early as 1905, the local board of trade lobbied for special railway rates for tourists, especially for former residents from Massachusetts. Expatriates usually returned during the Christmas season and summer break; "home for the hay" was the popular local expression for these summertime homecomings.

Frank Sylliboy sits alongside his sister, Matilda Paul, on the doorstep of Ben Paul's house near Heatherton. Nearby rests his summer eel pole. During the nineteenth century, Mi'kmaw society faced the devastating challenges of disease, declining supplies of fish and game, destitution, dislocation, and land encroachment. Despite their precarious subsistence, they demonstrated a remarkable drive for survival and resourcefulness in their struggle to straddle old traditions and new values. They supported themselves

FRANK SYLLIBOY AND MATILDA (SYLLIBOY) PAUL, HEATHERTON, C.1945

as coopers, basket makers, fishers, and trappers and manufactured lobster hoops, butter tubs, buoys, pick handles and axehandles, and moccasins. Both men and women showed great skill in their fancy beadwork. Frank Prosper's handiwork won a medal and honourable mention at the International Exhibition in Antwerp in 1885 and the Colonial and Indian Exhibition in London in 1886. The native fishers also enjoyed commercial success fishing mackerel at Bayfield, some of them regarded by government officials as "being the most successful of any engaged in that industry." (Dept. of Indian Affairs 1896, 56) The Indian agent in Antigonish County routinely chided local Mi'kmaw inhabitants for their lack of diligence in farming. Only once did he concede the obvious: "The lands reserved for them are not sufficiently extensive to admit wider agricultural operations." (1889, 43) In the 1890s, he did single out their efforts in growing potatoes and gave special mention to James Prosper, a successful farmer, who had realized a "considerable amount upon the products of his dairy." (1884, 44) By the turn of the century, an increasing number of young Mi'kmaw men left the county seeking employment, some heading for lumber camps while others migrated to New Glasgow, Trenton, and Cape Breton mining towns. Some went farther afield to Maine to find work as blueberry pickers and lumbermen.

THE
MERCHANT'S
BANK OF
HALIFAX
(LEFT: JOHN
MACISAAC,
MANAGER),
C.1880–1883

Originally chartered in 1869, the Merchant's Bank of Halifax opened a branch in Antigonish in 1871; the bank retained that title until 1901 when it became the Royal Bank of Canada. The Merchant's Bank was Antigonish's first financial institution. In the early 1890s, it lent money at the rate of five-and-a-half percent. T. M. King, a local merchant, acted as agent for the bank when it opened and housed the branch in his store. Soon after it was moved to another office located in the C. B. Whidden building at the west end of Main Street on Whidden property. This arrangement was not satisfactory, for King felt that the bank was too far removed from the more numerous business establishments on Main Street. Therefore, another move was made to the Adam Kirk building, later Palace Clothing on Main Street. By the early 1880s, John MacIsaac was bank manager at the Merchant's Bank; his fluency in Gaelic was one of his chief credentials for this position.

Business was carried out in that location for some time before there was another move, this time to the Kirk Block at the corner of Main and Church Streets. The bank manager lived in an apartment above the bank. This move was made in 1884, a year after the imposing Kirk structure had opened. The bank remained in that building until 1906 when it was moved to Antigonish's first permanent bank building, a brick edifice on Main Street, halfway between College and Sydney streets. The Merchant's Bank was the site of Antigonish's first attempted bank robbery in March 1887. The gun-wielding bandit was restrained until the policeman arrived, but not without the young teller sustaining two bullet wounds.

In late-nineteenth-century Antigonish, Main Street's typical workday began with the removal of wooden shutters that were replaced when the stores closed at night. The shutters, either iron screens or wooden folding panels, could also be hastily put in place whenever a street fight seemed imminent. These two gable-fronted frame stores were built by John MacMillan during the 1860s on a one-acre (0.4-hectare) lot across from the Presbyterian church. One building was used by John MacMillan and Company from 1862 to 1899, while the adjacent structure was owned by businessman Robert Dickson from 1868 to 1888. It was then sold to Charles N. Wilkie, a former clerk of Dickson, and William P. Cunningham. They opened a small grocery store employing three people and gradually expanded into a general store selling dry goods and groceries. By the late 1890s they sold everything from bicycle boots to saratoga rockers. When the store first opened, business transactions often involved barter rather than cash. In this photo, Wilkie and Cunningham (with top hat) are posed in the doorway, while Tom Bonner, a general bookkeeper, who shortly after started his own grocery business, stands proudly in front of them.

TURNBULL BAKERY, 1884

The Turnbull Bakery was located on College Street, just north of St. Mary's Street. It was established in 1869 and was located in a house built by Samuel Turnbull, a baker in his mid twenties. That section of the town tended to attract a number of tradespeople who moved there to serve the needs of a growing community. Some of the houses were small and were built as winter residences for those who moved into town during the winter months. Around 1876, the Turnbull Bakery moved to the corner of Main and Church streets where they sold an eclectic mix of bread, cakes, crackers, fancy cakes, syrups, beer, confectionery, and "Lunches at all hours." During the 1870s, they also catered several events for the Antigonish Highland Society, including a picnic at Gaspereaux Lake in July 1878. Their business continued to operate into the early 1900s.

Sugar Loaf Bakery, c.1940–1943

Pictured here beside the Sugar Loaf Bakery truck are, from left to right, Reg Glencross, David Glencross, Parker Glencross, and Joyce Glencross. In the 1890s, Mrs. McNeil came on the scene with her Main Street bakery and restaurant; she was as well known for her fine pastry as her oyster stew. By the 1920s, Antigonish had at least two bakeries. The Antigonish Bakery, operated by G. A. Barter, offered customers fresh bread, cakes, and pastry baked daily. Mrs. Rod McDonald on Main Street also sold home baking, along with cigarettes, tobacco, and confectionery. The Sugar Loaf Bakery, which was operated by Parker Glencross, opened for business on Main Street in the mid-1930s before relocating to the old curling rink on Victoria Street. On this site they also ran dry-cleaning and candy-making operations as sidelines. The family used a van to deliver their baked goods, such as hot cross buns and oatcakes, to customers in Antigonish, Guysborough, and Pictou counties, as well as to Cape Breton. The business, which had around ten employees, was eventually destroyed by fire.

THE *CASKET*
OFFICE,
C.1890S

Since 1956, the *Casket* office has been located on College Street, just north of Main Street. This weekly has had a number of locations since it was founded in 1852, the first one being in a house on the present site of the Atlantic Save Easy store on College Street. It was later moved to a location between Church and Court street, just east of St. James United Church. In 1862, it was in Alex MacDonald's store, on the present site of the Capitol Theatre. On the Ambrose Church map of 1877, the business was shown as located on Church Street. For a short time in 1888–89 it was housed in the original StFX residence known as the Big House which was later moved, in two parts, to West Street. There may be some connection between this new location in 1888 and the fact that the publisher, Angus Boyd, resigned in the same year. He was succeeded by Joseph Chisholm, later chief justice of the Supreme Court of Nova Scotia. The sixth location of this movable franchise was in a large wooden building on College Street just south of Main Street and usually referred to as the Knights of Columbus building. The final move was in 1956, to its present location where, over the past thirty years, the brick building has been modernized and up-to-date equipment installed. There is now a staff of more than twenty employed there.

The first issue of the paper appeared on 24 June 1852; the person credited with suggesting the name is Dr. William Currie of Antigonish. He put forth the name "casket" which, in its original meaning, referred to a box used to hold jewels. John Boyd, the first publisher, adopted the slogan, "Liberty, Choicest gem of the old world and fairest flower of the new." Boyd appreciated the openness, the freedom, and the lack of rigid class distinction in Nova Scotia. For over 150 years, this weekly has served as both a community and religious paper, reflecting the views of its mainly Catholic constituents, and chronicling much history in its pages.

Thomas Somers store, Antigonish, c.1900

This three-storey building was located on Main Street, on the present site of the Bank of Nova Scotia. The owner, Thomas Somers, was born in West River, the son of Hugh Somers and Mary Ronan. He was an extremely shy man and, when he married Annie Bridget O'Brien, he had the ceremony performed in the Bishop's Palace rather than at St. Ninian's Cathedral, which would have been open to the public. Somers's general merchandising business, which specialized in such dairy-related supplies as revolving churns and cream separators, was in operation from about 1880 to the early 1920s. His sister, Mary Somers, a seamstress, was situated on the third floor while her brother's business occupied the first two floors. From the early 1920s into the early 1950s, W. J. Ross carried on a general merchandising business in the building and later sold it to Sobeys, although he continued to operate a small tobacco shop in the building.

THE KIRK
BLOCK,
ANTIGONISH,
C.1900

In the nineteenth century, the Kirks were one of Antigonish's most prominent families. However, they had modest origins. Adam Kirk of Lismore,
Pictou County, started his apprenticeship at fifteen years of age with
the merchant John Cameron of Addington Forks. Kirk then clerked for
Duncan Grant, a leading Antigonish merchant, before striking out on his
own and building a store at Lower Barney's River. Grant lured him back
to Antigonish with the promise of a partnership. In 1859, Kirk purchased
the deceased Grant's interest in the business and quickly climbed the social
ladder in Antigonish. The Kirks became one of the town's leading merchant families and exerted enormous "ledger influence" at election time.
Adam Kirk and Company expanded and modernized, culminating in the
construction of a handsome three-storey brick building in 1883–84 on the
corner of Main and Church streets. Its design was typical of the Italianate
commercial architecture that dominated most main streets in late nineteenth-century Canada. The painstaking management of this large department store business, which extended to customers the guarantee that they
would "get their money's worth and the right change back," was shared
with Kirk's sons, Duncan Grant Kirk, Robert Dickson, and Aubrey who
became active partners.

KENNEDY AND MACDONALD COMPANY DRY GOODS DEPARTMENT, C.1916

In 1915, John Kennedy and A. K. MacDonald, retail and general merchants, purchased the Kirk Block; the two had formerly been railway contractors and later operated the Royal George Hotel for some years. Kennedy and MacDonald Company sold dry goods, millinery, ready-to-wear clothing, furniture, footwear, groceries, and general household goods. They also carried out an extensive mail order business in Antigonish, Guysborough, Inverness, and Richmond counties.

INTERIOR
VIEW OF J. P.
MCKENNA'S
DRUGSTORE,
C.1916

Drugstores were one of the many conveniences on Main Street, Antigonish. The first drugstore was operated by Charles Walden. Positioned prominently over the doorway of his business were the symbols of his profession, the pestle and mortar, as well as the nameplate, which read: "Charles Walden—Chemist and Druggist." In the 1880s, J. D. Copeland operated a prominent Antigonish drugstore. Most nineteenth-century pharmacists spent the bulk of their time "rolling pills, folding powders, and making suppositories." Copeland also offered his patrons an assortment of products, including dyes, horse and cattle medicines, trusses, eyeglasses, and fishing tackle. As well, his stock included perfumes, pipes, combs, and mirrors. By the 1920s, he offered his patrons a selection of Kodak film. The civic-minded Copeland sat on the committee that named the original streets of the town in 1877. He also taught chemistry at StFX. for a number of years and served a brief stint as inspector of schools for Antigonish. In 1896, Foster Brothers established a drugstore in Antigonish and sold a diverse selection of products, primarily toiletries, patent medicines, and cigars. One of their employees, John Patrick McKenna, a graduate of Dalhousie's School of Pharmacy, went on to establish his own business, McKenna's Drug Store in 1912, one door east of the Presbyterian church. As a dispensing chemist, he advertised prescriptions as his specialty, but stocked an eclectic mixture of cigars, perfumes, soaps, and Dr. Daniel's, Woodbury's and Gibson's veterinary medicines. According to his ads, the cold season could always be fended off with anodyne spruce expectorant, syrup white pine (with tar and codeine), and emulsion cod liver oil. This business catered to a widespread clientele throughout Antigonish, Guysborough, Inverness, and Richmond Counties. In the early twentieth century, C. M. Henry also opened a drugstore business, offering a rival selection of medicines, perfumery, and Dr. Daniel's veterinary medicines at "reasonable prices."

MCCURDY AND COMPANY STORE, ANTIGONISH, C.1890S

This handsome three-storey brick veneer building was built in 1882 by H. H. McCurdy who moved to Antigonish in 1869. He originally learned about merchandising while working in his father's store in Baddeck. The McCurdy store, once situated on the corner of Main and Hawthorne streets, was lauded in the August 24, 1883 edition of the *Morning Herald* as one of Antigonish's finest "commercial palaces," a striking contrast to the house-like wooden commercial buildings along Main Street. In its heyday it employed nearly sixty persons and sold everything from "a needle to an anchor."

The first floor housed offices as well as a large retail department; at the rear was a room specially devoted to the sale of footwear. The second floor showcased furniture and other home manufactured goods and contained the tailoring and millinery departments. The next floor featured a "vast variety" of agricultural implements as well as an assortment of trunks and valises. By small town standards, the store's interior was impressive. The handsome counters with their black walnut finish extended the length of the store, while the walls were ornamented with panelled plaster and elegant cornices. In 1901, Chisholm, Sweet and Company purchased H. H. McCurdy's business. The partnership of Kinsman Sweet and A. D. Chisholm, a longstanding McCurdy employee, proved profitable. Their business, with its slogan "The Store that Satisfies," became a leading Antigonish mercantile establishment. It sold men's clothing, ladies' ready-to-wear garments, children's clothing, crockery, furniture, carpets, leather goods, trunks, wallpaper, and rugs. A store flyer dated 1915 advertised such choice items as "Holeproof Hose" guaranteed to "not need darning for six months," health mattresses, gold oak buffets, Homestead rockers, English worsted, single-breasted men's jackets and a ninety-seven-piece dinner set for $8.75. Chisholm, Sweet and Company also operated an extensive regional mail-order business. The growing popularity of the department store signalled profound changes in lifestyles and merchandising. The Chisholm and Sweet building was a casualty of the 1939 West End fire.

JOHN MACPHERSON BARBERSHOP AND CONFECTIONERY, ANTIGONISH, C.1910

Here, left to right, are proprietor John MacPherson and his nephews Dan and John Angus MacDougall. As early as the 1880s, M. M. Dooley advertised his Antigonish hairdressing saloon, highlighting his specialty as cutting "Ladies' and Children's hair." By the next decade, the town of Antigonish boasted three barber shops. They were always popular spots where news was exchanged and politics debated. It was also a place where the barber, equipped with his straight razor, powdered soap, and aromatic concoctions like bay rum and Florida water, provided his male customers with the luxury of a fine shave and haircut.

"Jack the Barber" MacPherson also sold soft drinks, cigars, cigarettes, tobacco, and various confections in his barbershop and store located opposite the Queen Hotel. Note the two large notices in the front window of MacPherson's establishment, advertising an event at the Celtic Hall. Barbershop shaving waned with the emergence of such inventions as the safety razor and later the electric shaver.

C. B. WHIDDEN AND SON STORE INTERIOR WITH PAYSON CLARKE (IN DARK SUIT), ANTIGONISH, C.1917

Charles B. Whidden, son of the Rev. Blair Whidden and Harriet (Symonds) Whidden, started his flour and feed business in Antigonish in 1863. He took his two sons, Charles Edgar and David Graham into partnership in 1881. Nine years later, Charles Edgar withdrew from the business which continued to operate under the name C.B. Whidden and Son until 1928. C. B. Whidden and Son's grocery store and feed shop with its wide steps, decorative scalloped verge board, and large plate glass windows was one of Antigonish's major commercial landmarks. In keeping with new merchandising techniques, the store featured signs advertising brand names for Purity Flour, Red Rose Tea, and Jonas' Flavouring Extracts and stocked its store windows with abundant dry goods displays. Throughout the late nineteenth century, this business specialized in flour, meal and fish, and boasted such specialty brands of flour as Eastern Ray. The store also offered a wide range of goods from chop feed and middlings to kiln-dried cornmeal, sugar-cured hams, and choice winter apples. The Whiddens carved out a niche as the leading fruit dealers in Antigonish and by 1900 the store advertised such delicacies as bananas and oranges. The interior was crammed with barrels of molasses, some stacked five and six tiers high, tubs of butter, and shelves groaning under an assortment of canned goods. One of the store's most eye-catching features was the flagpole at the peak of the roof. From this mast flew the Union Jack or Canadian Ensign or the pennant of whatever Whidden vessel had safely arrived in home port. This building was lost in the West End fire of 1939.

D. R. GRAHAM STORE, ANTIGONISH, C.1920

In 1907, David R. Graham, who worked alongside his first cousin, Edward Whidden, at C. B. Whidden and Son, struck out on his own. He established his first grocery store at the corner of Main and Church. Three years later, Graham purchased the building depicted in this photograph from J. Frederick MacDonald, Collector of Customs. It was formerly the location of John MacMillan and Company. "Davy" Graham operated a grocery business until 1945. He sold a variety of goods, boasting such offerings as oatmeal, flour, "fine groceries," crockery, confections, and fruit, with "chocolates a specialty." He promised his patrons the "best quality at moderate prices." During the 1930s, visitors to Graham's store during lunch time were entertained by the lively tunes of two local black fiddlers, George and Davy Jackson.

BROPHY'S
STORE
INTERIOR,
MORRISTOWN
C.1911 (LEFT
TO RIGHT: K.
MACGILLIVRAY,
O. CAMERON,
J. BROPHY, H.
MACISAAC, AND
J. MACDONALD)

The country store was a vital institution in rural areas where trips into town were rare. The owner supplied food and goods as well as credit and communication. Gossip was traded over the counter or alongside the cheery fire in the wood stove. "Little Allan's" store at Cross Roads Ohio actually had a small room reserved for those who had the spare time for loitering and extended chitchat; some wag nicknamed the room "the senate." In most rural communities, the store also housed the post office. James Brophy's store at Morristown, which he operated from 1897 to 1916, served a dual purpose as a general store and post office. MacPherson's store at Upper South River was a favourite meeting place for many in the community. This general merchandise store with its steep-pitched gable roof was originally owned and operated by Alexander MacGregor. The second owner was John C. MacNaughton who carried on the business between 1900 and 1910.

MACPHERSON STORE, UPPER SOUTH RIVER, 1931 (LEFT TO RIGHT: JULIA DRUHAN AND ALLAN MACPHERSON)

John C. MacNaughton sold his store in 1910 to Angus Dan MacPherson who carried on for some time and was succeeded by his son, Allan MacPherson, who operated a canteen and gas station before closing the business; by then the hitching rail for horses was long gone. Country stores were not exclusively run by men. At Cross Roads Ohio, Anita Mac-Donald managed the country store and post office from 1929 to 1947; a nurse by training, she doubled as the local doctor, delivering babies, making house calls, and healing the sick.

MacDonald
Music Store,
Antigonish,
c.1916

The MacDonald Music Store on East Main Street catered to the musical needs of early twentieth century Antigonishers. It was established by Ida MacDonald, the semi-invalided daughter of Captain Alexander MacDonald. She acquired a taste for commerce while living with her uncle, Allan Denoon, and helping him sell musical instruments. The MacDonald Music Store had a unique niche in Canadian business. Its selection had a strong Celtic flavour, offering local patrons as well as mail-order clients a wide range of items including bagpipes, costumes, and Celtic sheet music, as well as novelties like clan postcards and maps of Scotland and Ireland. There was also an extensive assortment of volumes in Scottish and Irish Gaelic and English, including dictionaries, fiction, travel accounts and books about folklore, heraldry, dancing and poetry, along with an abundance of classical and modern sheet music, both American and British editions. The store featured musical instruments, most notably violins and mandolins, imported directly from Europe; Heintzman pianos were also available. In 1917, local historian William D. Cameron praised the store's service: "If you have a desire to speak, read or write Gaelic, you can get the works from No. 1 Primer up and get them as cheap, if not more cheaply, than you yourselves could import them from Edinburgh. If you want a violin, bagpipes or chanter here you find a choice selection. Take the Gaelic Books, anyhow, learn to speak it and enjoy life." The Celtic Music Store opened in 1932, following in the Macdonald Music Store's footsteps. It was established by Bernard MacIsaac, who worked in MacDonald's Music Store, before buying out the business. MacIsaac championed the cause of Celtic music throughout the county and even commissioned recordings of local artists including Lanark fiddler "Hughie Number Eleven" under his label "The Celtic Music Co."

EASTERN AUTOMOBILE COMPANY, ANTIGONISH, C.1916

This firm was first known as the Antigonish Garage Company and was the local service centre for Ford cars until 1946. The name Eastern Auto was adopted in 1916, three years after the company was first formed by T. J. Sears, T. J. Bonner, Nicholas Landry, and Alphonsus (Phonse) Sears. For a few years, the company sold several makes of cars including names no longer familiar, such as Grey-Dart and Hudson Essex; they also handled DeSoto and Studebaker. Since 1932, the firm has held a franchise for General Motors cars such as Buick, Cadillac, GMC trucks, and Pontiac. The firm carried a variety of auto supplies and catered to the counties of Antigonish, Pictou, Inverness, and Guysborough. Their building was a large one with a storage capacity for seventy-five machines. An elevator, capable of carrying cars to any of the four storeys in the building, weighed two -and-a-half tons. The company in its early years continued to repair sleighs and wagons, which were still in common use during the firm's initial period of business; the owners of the firm recognized that local horse owners would continue to need repairs and equipment and thus continued to carry the necessary supplies for some years.

At one time, Eastern Auto operated an outlet in New Glasgow and, according to the diary of T. J. Sears, either he or one of his partners made frequent trips there to check on that branch of the business. The building there was also a large one, with room for one hundred cars if such space was ever needed. The connection with New Glasgow lasted between 1919 and 1938, at which time Eastern Auto concentrated its attention on Antigonish and the business in New Glasgow became Vee-Eight Motors.

**ANTIGONISH
FIRE
DEPARTMENT,
C.1950S
(L-R) DONALD
MACLELLAN,
BERNIE
CLEARY, JIMMIE
DECOFF, WALLIE
MACMILLAN
AND CHARLIE
MACDOUGALL**

The Antigonish Fire Department was established in 1864. This was the village's first organized effort at fire protection. At that time, the first line of defence against fires was a hand engine, manned by sixteen men, eight on each side. The pumper was fed by puncheons filled by bucket brigades bailing water from either Brierly Brook or the Wright River. There were at least three cisterns constructed of hemlock staves situated at critical locations throughout town; there was one near St. James Church, another near Cunningham's forge on Court Street and another on the corner of Pleasant and College streets. By 1882, the men, who called themselves the Rescue Fire Engine Company, were equipped with hats and jackets, but lamented the lack of an adequate quantity of hose. They operated out of an Engine House located on Court Street. Despite meagre apparatus, the firemen served the town courageously in times of need and participated in drills, full dress parades, firemen's balls, public demonstrations, and even sports competitions. In May 1883, they demonstrated to Antigonishers the prowess of their equipment, especially their new Paragon rubber hose, by shooting two streams of water over Cunningham's Hotel, and another stream completely over the flagstaff of L. C. Archibald's store. In June 1892, fourteen local firemen headed to Charlottetown to participate in a hose-cart race. The original hand engine was used until the early 1890s, when the fire brigade was reorganized into two ten-man hose companies and one seven-man hook and ladder company. The catalysts for these changes were the town's incorporation and the introduction of a town water system in 1889. Around the turn of the century, the fire hall relocated to Sydney Street. Its most distinctive feature was the bell tower, from which hung a bell and the drying hose.

"Gorman, the Shoe Man," as he styled himself, operated J. P. Gorman's Shoe Store from 1910 to 1924; it had formerly been N. K. Cunningham's Boot and Shoe Store. He boasted an exclusive line of footwear, including Invictus, Slater, Classic and Just Wright shoes and promised his female customers oxfords, colonials, slippers, and "dainty and dressy" sandals. A full range of hockey boots, including the celebrated McPherson's Lighting Hitch Hockey Boots, rubbers, and overshoes was kept in stock. Gorman's local competitors were D. D. McDonald's Shoe Store, sole agent for Smarden Street and Hospital Boots, which advertised hockey boots, snowshoes, moccasins, and overgaiters, and J. A. Chisholm's Shoe Store, which offered repairs as well as "Better Shoes for Less Money." When Gorman's Shoe Store closed in 1924, he sold his stock to J. A. Chisholm, whose business was situated at the west end of Main Street. A native of East Tracadie, John Gorman for some time worked with Wilkie and Cunningham before establishing his own business and doing some commercial travelling. Quite active in local politics, he was the MLA for Antigonish during the years 1942–49.

OLD POST OFFICE AND BAND STAND, ANTIGONISH, C.1893–99

The first post office opened in Antigonish in June 1816, inauspiciously housed in a stage barn on Main Street. From there it moved to a more permanent location on the corner of Main and Court streets. Starting in 1882, the post office found its home in this temple-fronted Greek Revival structure erected in 1854. This two-storey wooden edifice was built by Alexander MacDonald, known locally as Sandy the Carpenter. It served initially as the first college building of StFX University, accommodating a public school as well as seminarians who would walk down from the campus to attend lectures there. Classes were held at this College Street location between 1855 and 1881 when the federal government purchased the building on the so-called College Lot and renovated it to serve as the local post office.

NEW POST OFFICE, ANTIGONISH, C.1920S

In 1905, plans were implemented to construct a major new post office building in Antigonish. The design was a generic one, used for post offices in many other towns and cities across Canada. According to original blueprints, the customs office was to be located in the basement, while the attic floor would accommodate the janitor and his family. The new brick building, capped with a clock tower, opened officially in July 1907, while its predecessor, the former college building, was shortly thereafter moved to the rear of the court house at the northwest corner of Court and Main streets. It was used as a municipal office until destroyed by fire in 1943.

GEORGE WONG AND HIS WIFE AND CHILD, MOLLY AND JENNY WONG, C.1931

In April 1930, George Wong leased a portion of the Kennedy and MacDonald store on Main Street as the site for his café. The former shoe department was transformed into a kitchen and the café was fitted with a dozen small tables and some cubicles. Patrons were impressed by the linen tablecloths, silver plate cutlery, and crystal. When the café opened, the first day's receipts went as a donation to St. Martha's Hospital. During the depression, the family-run business relocated temporarily upstairs, close to the Wongs' apartment. The need for a larger space prompted the move across The Main in the early 1940s. In the back yard, close to Sydney Street, was a garden, which supplied most of the needs of both the family and the restaurant. Here the café became a popular landmark, earning the reputation as "one of eastern Nova Scotia's best known eating houses." A devastating fire in 1961 claimed two lives, George Wong Jr. and countryman Charley Wong, and left ten people homeless and the restaurant in ruins. Rebuilding began almost immediately. From the 1930s on, George Wong's family formed the nucleus of a Chinese community in Antigonish. His restaurant served as the base from which he welcomed some of his kin and countrymen and re-established connections with his village in southern China. Other local Chinese families included the Mahs, who operated such Antigonish businesses as the Rex Café and Jack's Confectionery. The Joes (Chows), who ran the Moonlight Restaurant, came to Antigonish in the early 1960s.

BRINE'S LUNCHES, BOWLING AND BILLIARDS, C.1930S

In 1916, G. R. Brine opened his first ice cream parlour in the old Queen Hotel on Main Street. The rooms in the establishment were completely renovated and modernized. They looked quite sumptuous with their polished hardwood floors, oak fixtures, papered walls, and electric lighting. The earliest ice cream parlours in town were little more than improvised home-based operations with a few tables and chairs. Mary Falt, who moved with her family to Antigonish in 1907, recalled, "Ti and I used to love to go to a Mrs. Campbell's home, and, dressed up with our little pocketbooks and money coaxed from our mothers, we'd enter the parlour and there was Polly the parrot in her cage." Brine's was a much more elaborate affair, providing a wide range of ice cream flavours, as well as sundaes and ice cream sodas; these were served at marble top counters complete with wrought iron chairs. He also advertised other treats for his patrons such as hot chocolate, sandwiches, confectionery, fruit, tobacco, and cigars. By the 1920s, fancy stationery, greeting cards, banners, and novelty items supplemented his offerings. Around 1930, Brine's branched into another commercial venture, billiards and bowling, situated in a two-storey building on the south side of the street, adjacent to the Dingle restaurant. A young Gerry Cunningham was paid five cents a game to reset the pins. In the early 1940s, the Celtic Hall, billed as a "modern recreation centre," also offered clients facilities for bowling and billiards as well as dancing.

TOM PHEE (FEE), ANTIGONISH, C.1940

In the early part of the twentieth century, Tom Phee was part of the human landscape of Antigonish's Main Street. He was hired by the town as a sweeper, and patrolled the streets with his broom and handcart. Although his family roots were in Linwood, by 1891 Tom and his wife Annie, both in their early twenties, were living in Antigonish where he worked as a labourer. It is a little-known fact that he had a talent for performing light vaudeville. A soft-spoken man, with a distinctive curled moustache, Tom took special pride in the military service of his sons, Ernest and Norman, who served with the No. 2 Construction Battalion, Canada's only black battalion, in the First World War. Norman was a twenty-year-old teamster and groom when he signed up in 1916. Economic opportunities in the local area for black men were scarce and tended to be seasonal. Some eked out a living with mixed farming while others worked as farm labourers, sold ice, or cut pit props and pulpwood in the woods. In Antigonish, the Whiddens, who hired their workers without prejudice, provided welcome employment hauling coal or making deliveries by horse and wagon/sleigh or by truck in later years. Other black men were forced to seek employment outside the region in the New Glasgow steel plant, the Cape Breton mines, or on the railroad.

ZINCK'S TAXI, ANTIGONISH, C.1945

Zinck's Taxi Company started operating in Antigonish in 1941 with Donald Zinck, a former resident of Lunenburg, as the owner. A no-nonsense type of individual, Zinck was a hard-driving personality. At one time, the company had nine cars and two buses in its fleet, with the buses making daily runs to and from Pomquet and Cape George. There were few cars in the rural areas in the early 1940s and Zinck's provided a needed service in that decade; there were about eight car owners between Mount Cameron and Cape George. Zinck's buses also provided transportation for the StFX sports teams. In addition to the bus and taxi services, Zinck's also hauled cattle and lumber and provided the heavy equipment needed in construction jobs. One of his projects involved moving the presses and linotypes of the *Casket* from its old location to its present building in 1956; each of the machines weighed over a ton.

By 1948, there were approximately thirty-seven taxis operating in Antigonish town and county, some of them "fly by nighter." Zinck's, however, provided a more professional operation and outlasted most of its competitors. In the late 1940s the cab fare in town was twenty-five cents; the cost of a trip in the county was ten cents a mile. Driver Johnnie MacLellan, who started with Zinck's in 1946, continues to drive his taxi today, after more than a half century of service.

The Arsenault Monumental Works was established by Wilfred "Papa" Arsenault in 1936. This skilled craftsman learned his stonemason trade in Tracadie, New Brunswick. Arsenault established his business in close proximity to a quarry in North Grant. The original freestone for St. Ninian's had been hauled from this site, but by the 1930s the quarry had fallen into disuse. Arsenault cleared away the shrubbery and began extracting the famous "Scotch rock." His first significant commission was the local cenotaph erected in 1936. During the following two years, his firm built St. Ninian's Cathedral vestry as well as Gilmora Hall at Mount St. Bernard; the latter project required a work force of approximately sixty-five men. The quarry operation was an elaborate affair, requiring at least two full-time blacksmiths. Some of the workers employed by the Arsenaults came from neighbouring counties and were housed in nearby tents or shacks. The workday started with a steam whistle blast at 8 a.m. Hammers and chisels rang throughout the morning and afternoon, interrupted only when the workers stopped to take their meals at the cookhouse or drink a ladle of water during a break.

St. Andrews Co-operative, c.1940s

In Maritime Canada, the charismatic champions of the Antigonish Movement, Rev. Moses Coady and Rev. J. J. Tompkins, provided the publicity and enthusiasm that helped win support for the concept of consumer co-operatives among the farmers and fishermen of eastern Nova Scotia. The base of operations for this cause was StFX University, which gave Coady and Tompkins the facilities necessary for the promotion of their ideas. The *Casket* newspaper also played an important part in disseminating the ideals later incorporated in the Antigonish Movement, including the first People's School, which opened at StFX in 1921 and was attended by fifty students ranging in age from seventeen to fifty-seven. Throughout the 1920s and into the 1940s, those who attended the sessions of the People's School were given instruction in how to conduct meetings, make reports, and prepare financial statements. All of this helped to lay the groundwork for the formation of credit unions and co-operative retail and wholesale outlets throughout this region and beyond.

The co-operative stores proved to be of great benefit to the farmers, fishermen, miners, and steelworkers. Local people managed the stores and understood their constituents without having to resort to the bloodless efficiency of the chartered banks, headquartered in large urban centres. Prior to and during the depression years, the relatively small co-operative stores were to be found in many towns and rural communities. They proved to be of inestimable help in forging a bond of union among their supporters as well as providing an essential service. The accompanying photograph shows a typical co-op store in a rural setting. The St. Andrews Co-operative was established in 1917 and reorganized in 1937 under the Nova Scotia Co-operative Act. It is believed to be one of the first producer/consumer co-ops organized in Atlantic Canada. This three-storey building became the site of a thriving business. It purchased eggs, butter, tallow, and hides from its members, and even helped them find buyers for their lambs and cattle. Angus H. MacPherson was manager from 1918 to 1948 and remained secretary treasurer until 1970. Today, the small co-operatives face stiff competition from the large chain stores and for many it is a losing battle. This happened in St. Andrews where the co-op store closed in 1995.

Chapter 5

Women's Work

BARNYARD CHORES, ANTIGONISH COUNTY, C.1910

In many homes in nineteenth and early twentieth century Antigonish town and county, women's work encompassed both production and reproduction. They were an integral part of the informal economy and contributed extensively to the household's self-sufficiency. Men's work tended to be seasonal, but women's relentless cycle of work consisted of daily tasks performed year-round. These included caregiving, housecleaning, baking, knitting, weaving, dyeing, carrying water, milking, tending to the chickens, and sometimes even the livestock. The products of these labours, such as surplus butter and eggs, yarn and cloth, were often sold outside the household. Such work, however vital, was frequently undervalued and conferred little status, as evidenced by the story of Amelia (Stearns) Kinney of Linwood.

Her first home during the 1860s was meagrely equipped with furnishings; there was only one chair. Her husband remedied this situation by hauling a small stump into the house with the command "Amelia, you sit there." As head of the household, he was entitled to the privilege of sitting on the only chair. Still, stories abound of the amazing tenacity of the early women settlers in Antigonish County whose daily routine was an exhausting catalogue of labour. One account relates how Isobel MacPherson and her neighbour, Margaret Cameron of St. Andrews, trekked some two miles to Antigonish Harbour, each returning with a sack of herring, to supplement the supper time fare of milk, potatoes, and oaten bread.

The overall patterns of the female work world were irreversibly altered by industrialization. For example, many of the tasks traditionally performed within the home by women—such as carding, spinning and weaving—were among the first displaced by factory production. In the late nineteenth century, the lobster canneries that dotted the coastline of Antigonish County provided new opportunities for female employment. But it was not enough to stem the tide of Antigonish women heading to the Boston States to work as domestics, nurses, clerical workers, and factory labourers. Margaret O'Brien of Antigonish was typical of those who left the region. In the early 1900s, she found employment in a Boston factory. Here, notwithstanding the bleak conditions, there were opportunities for social interaction and camaraderie among her co-workers, many of them from back home. They often lifted their spirits by singing the following ditty: "We're the girls from Nova Scotia, We're the girls that skin the fish, Oh how we hate the Irish, We're the girls from Antigonish."

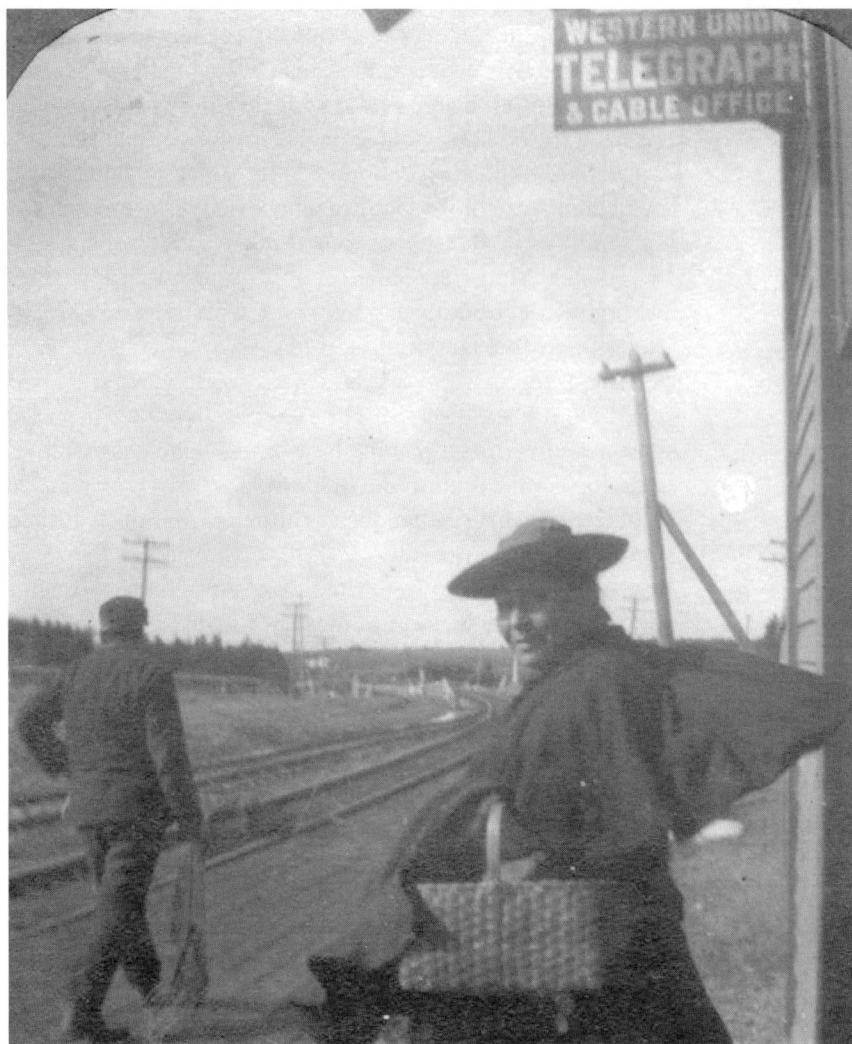

UNIDENTIFIED MI'KMAW WOMAN AT HEATHERTON RAILWAY STATION, C.1890S

In Mi'kmaw communities, native women supplemented family income with their handiwork. They made a wide range of practical items for local sale such as potato, apple, picnic, egg, and berry baskets. They also produced fancier work such as woven containers for gloves and handkerchiefs, scissor and thimble cases, sewing baskets, and hat baskets; many of these were aimed at the summer tourist trade. It was customary for Mi'kmaw women from the Afton Reserve (now Paq'tnkek Reserve), east of Heatherton, to travel to Antigonish via the morning "way freight" with its passenger coach. Their arrival at the Antigonish railway station seldom went unnoticed, for they arrived bearing baskets made of ash splints and sweet grass, which they sold door to door. Sometimes they came to town to work as domestics for a half day each week.

Haymaking at Giant's Lake, c.1927

From left to right are Mary, Catherine and Sarah MacLean, Mike MacIsaac, Ronald MacLean, and Campbell MacNeil. Haymaking was a labour-intensive family endeavour. Children were put to work tramping down, often in their bare feet, the hay in the hayrack and haymow. Some learned to make hay as young as five years old. Women kept the men fortified with hearty meals and cold drinks during the haying season. Many worked out in the fields alongside their men. In 1903, one visitor to the region was vividly impressed by the haymakers during her trip through Antigonish County, especially the women "with turned-up petticoats and bright handkerchiefs over their heads." Throughout the nineteenth century, local farmers relied almost totally on homemade farm tools, seldom purchasing implements except perhaps the Griffin scythe. The increased mechanization of farming, most notably the introduction of the horse-drawn mower around 1900, substantially transformed farm life, especially haying traditions. Although Giant's Lake is located in Guysborough County, its proximity to the county boundary line has always given its residents a distinctive Antigonish County orientation. The MacNeils, MacLeans, and MacIsaacs all had strong Antigonish County family connections. Campbell MacNeil, one-time health inspector for Antigonish County, later moved to Dunmore and eventually Lower South River.

REBECCA
KINNEY AND
HER HUSBAND,
G. H. CAMERON,
C.1907

Rebecca Kinney of Linwood was typical of many young Antigonish women who participated in the exodus of women to the United States during the late nineteenth and early twentieth centuries. For many this choice was motivated by the spur of family obligation, the lure of paid work and changing economic forces. Rebecca's experience is only one variant of the story of the single female leaving home. Her first job was in the dressmaking department of H. H. McCurdy and Company, Antigonish. In September 1890, she headed to Massachusetts with her older brother where, for almost sixteen years, she worked for wealthy families, initially as a lady's-maid or caregiver for invalids, and later as a private nurse. Rebecca's long exile from Nova Scotia did not end with her marriage to George Henry Cameron in 1907. They met in Boston for the first time, even though their original homes in Nova Scotia had only been twenty miles (thirty-two kilometres) apart. That year they headed to the Canadian west so her husband could pursue his career as a printer.

Left to right, in the first row: Reynolds MacPhie, Angus MacDonald, Harold MacPhie, (unspecified) MacDougal, (unspecified) MacDougal; the second row: Mary C. MacEachern, Peggy MacPhie, Sarah Beaton, Mary Roberts, (unidentified), Angeline MacEachern, (unspecified) Roberts, (unidentified), Christie A. Gillis; the third row: Alex Beaton, Bessie Malcolm MacEachern (teacher), Agnes MacInnis, Lewis MacInnis, Selina MacGillvray, Alice Roberts, and Christine MacInnis.

This is believed to be one of the earliest class photos taken at South Side Cape George. Bessie MacEachern, who was the daughter of Malcolm MacEachern, was just nineteen at the time. She taught briefly, and eventually headed to Boston to pursue secretarial work. As early as 1829, there were two schools in Cape George: one located at Cape George Point and another at South Side Cape George. The former had an enrolment of forty-four students, while the latter had twenty-four students registered. In 1912, the school at Cape George Point was closed; isolation and poor salary were cited as the reasons for its closure. Annie MacInnis, who graduated from the Cape School in 1912, returned to the Cape to teach after attending Mount St. Bernard and the Teacher's Normal College in Truro. She received an annual salary of a hundred a year. Several years later, when her career took her to Saskatchewan, she was paid four hundred annually, a princely sum by comparison. Mary Dawe of Sydney taught at the cape during the depths of the depression. She boarded locally and walked two miles (three kilometres) each way to the school. At this time, families in straitened circumstances were hard pressed to pay their school rates. In at least one instance, she was actually compensated with fish. Dawe's most indelible memories of the one-room school, which was heated by a potbellied stove, were the squirrels in the lobby and the scant teaching equipment.

**EMMA CLYKE,
BAYFIELD,
C.1912**

In the nineteenth and early twentieth centuries, women could use their domestic skills to find work outside the home. Domestic labour, however, held little value in either monetary or social terms. Here is a photograph of Emma Clyke, who was a servant in the Irish household in Bayfield for many years. She worked for Frederick R. Irish, a prominent farmer and one-time justice of the peace, municipal councillor, and warden of the municipality of Antigonish. For Antigonish County black women, there were few employment opportunities outside the home except in domestic service. There was, however, a strong tradition of midwifery among black women in Antigonish County. In fact, midwives were used well into the 1950s in Rear Monastery and Upper Big Tracadie. They received little compensation for their services, sometimes just household goods or vegetables or whatever money the family could spare.

MOUNT ST. BERNARD STUDENTS MAKING FUDGE TO SEND OVERSEAS, C.1916

However unglamorous the work, Antigonish town and county women on the home front made their own vital contribution to the war effort. They managed households, businesses, and farms during their husbands' absences. They spearheaded bazaars, bake sales, dances and concerts to raise monies for the Red Cross Society, Belgian Relief Fund, and Canadian Patriotic Fund. They prepared packages crammed with food, clothing, and other treats such as fudge to ship to military personnel at the front. Like communities all across Canada, Antigonish bustled with volunteers knitting socks, scarves, mitts, and sweaters. All knitting was scrutinized by a small group of women with a sharp eye to quality control. During the winter months of 1914, Antigonish town and county shipped on average one hundred pairs of socks to the Red Cross headquarters in Halifax. The efforts of this informal corps of volunteers did not go unappreciated. Archie MacPhee of Lochaber applauded the generosity of the Lochaber Red Cross, writing "If the good ladies could see the difference that dry sox makes they would feel amply repaid … Those big thick pairs from home are a great preventive of trench foot." The local Red Cross spared no energy assisting the Allied cause both financially and materially. In January 1916, the local branch sent five hundred dollars overseas to subsidize Red Cross activities. Four months later, they contributed two hundred dollars to the St. Francis Xavier Hospital Unit's fund. They further supplemented this donation with socks, sheets and feather pillows.

K. Gillis
L. D. Oper.

M. P. McKinnon
Dist. Supt.

B. Wilmot
Chief Clerk

M. McNeil
L. D. Oper.

M. B. McDonald
Chief Operator

V. Floyd
Asst. Chief Operator

L. Fraser
Local Oper.

K. McLellan
Night Oper.

C. McDonald
Local Oper.

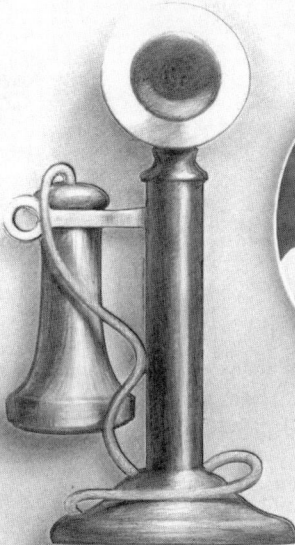

F. Lee
Local Oper.

M.T. & T. CO. STAFF
ANTIGONISH
1920

E. McDonald
Local Oper.

MT&T STAFF,
ANTIGONISH,
1920

From left to right, these people are F. Lee, K. McLellan, M. B. McDonald, M. McNeil, K. Gillis, M. P. McKinnon (district superintendent), B. Wilmot, L. Fraser, V. Floyd, C. McDonald, and E. McDonald. Despite the fanfare, the establishment of Antigonish's first telephone exchange in the late 1880s proved somewhat disappointing. The equipment was so primitive and service so erratic that it was suspended within the year. Local businessman Leonard C. Archibald purchased the defunct business in 1891 and introduced some improvements, including a switchboard that was capable of handling fifty phones. By July 1897, there was a telephone connection between the town and H. H. Crerar's lavish estate at the harbour. The residence of Captain McDonald, also at the Harbour, had a phone installed around the same time; he charged his neighbours "a small toll" for the use of this convenience. In 1901, the Antigonish Telephone Company, incorporated in 1898, entered into negotiations with the Nova Scotia Telephone Company to facilitate the implementation of long-distance service. The upshot of these deliberations was the Antigonish and Sherbrooke Telephone Company, which commenced operations in May 1904, having purchased its telephones and switchboards from the Nova Scotia Telephone Company. Within the year, the company boasted 170 miles (273 kilometres) of telephone lines and eighty-three telephones. The exchange was housed in a small building on College Street until 1919. The first manager was A. S. MacMillan, born on a farm at Upper South River; he went on to become premier of Nova Scotia in 1940. Maritime Tel & Tel eventually purchased Nova Scotia Telephone's assets and opened a brand new exchange on College and St. Mary's streets that served about 1,500 subscribers. Like switchboards across North America, which were dominated by the so-called "hello girls," women figured prominently on the staff of MT&T's exchange in Antigonish; as a general rule, supervisory roles were allocated to males. In rural Antigonish, telephone service was provided by a myriad of localized companies such as the South Lochaber Mutual Telephone Company established in 1913. Subscribers to this company were obliged to donate forty poles or free labour amounting to $30. In rural communities, women also enjoyed a monopoly as operators. Cassie Gillis, employed by the South Lochaber Mutual Telephone Company, held this position for thirty-five years. Her daughter then took over for three. In 1962, fourteen mutual telephone companies in Antigonish County, all of which were connected to long distance service through the MT&T Antigonish exchange, were driven out of business by the impending costs of modernization. The South River Mutual Telephone Company and the South Lochaber Mutual Telephone Company held on, even after dial conversion, until October 1974.

Three Acadian women at Pomquet, c.1920s

In addition to their regular domestic routine, Acadian women frequently laboured in the fields alongside the men. Even into the early twentieth century, their daily working attire tended to be simple and traditional. The most distinctive features of this style of dress were the black handkerchief or "cape normande," patterned cotton blouse, and plain skirt, all of which were rejected by a new generation of young Acadian women who regarded them as relics of the past.

ANNIE
BALLANTYNE
AND BELLE
MACPHIE
SIMPSON,
CAPE GEORGE,
SUMMER 1928

Women did their laundry at Wash Brook in Wilkie's Intervale at Cape George until the 1940s. Here they gathered with their cauldron of boiling water, corrugated washboards, and large cakes of soap. The washing of the heavy blankets, quilts and thick Stanfield's underwear was an annual ritual. When the water supply was low during the summer months, the women also gathered at the brook to clean their clothes. Here they washed, scrubbed and dried their clothes before hauling them home. Wash day was a sociable event where work and community overlapped, local news was exchanged and the value of cooperation was reinforced.

LUCY LEVANGIE, FRANKVILLE, C.1930S

This group of photographs captures the varied domestic tasks of women throughout the nineteenth and early twentieth centuries. Here Lucy Levangie can be seen churning butter in her Frankville home, one of the many tasks juggled along with raising a large family. Tuesday was normally churning day. In some parts of rural Antigonish, butter and fresh eggs were taken to town where they were traded for cotton cloth, tobacco, tea, sugar and other groceries. The other photo illustrates women's work outside the house in the farmyard, where the breeding and care of chickens, as well as the collecting of eggs, were relegated to the female members of the house. Here, Angelique Benoit, wife of John "La Loup" De Wolfe of Pomquet Head, and mother of twelve children, feeds her flock of chickens. Margaret Doiron, a hard-working woman, had dual responsibilities, running her own household and contributing to the smooth operation of the glebe house at Pomquet. She started working for Father Chisholm when she was about sixteen years old and could turn her hand to anything; milking the cows, tending the garden, and hauling the firewood were normal everyday activities for her.

ANGELIQUE
BENOIT
DEWOLFE,
POMQUET
POINT, C.1910

MARY
MARGARET
(LANDRY)
DOIRON,
POMQUET,
C.1940S

SPINNING FROLIC AT CASHEN HOME IN CLOVERVILLE, 1932

Depicted here are, from left to right, Maimie Cashen, Mrs. Walter Grant, Mrs. A. G. Stronach, Mrs. Annabell MacNeil, Janie Cashen, and Mrs. Mary Jane MacLellan. The frolic represented a distinctive attitude to work, for it turned a utilitarian task into an occasion for social interaction. Although women's work centred on the household, women's existence was not limited to the home. In many Scottish communities, work, community, and kinship converged as women shared the burdens of making blankets and winter clothing. The spinning frolic was usually held during the summer, between sowing and harvest time. The women would arrive at a neighbourhood home in the morning carrying their spinning wheels under their arms. As the wheels hummed, the women punctuated their work with lively conversation, song, and frequent cups of tea. By early evening, most of the rolls of wool were transformed into skeins of thread. Tradition kept alive the practice of home-based manufacture of cloth long after necessity was a factor. For women, the social dimension of the frolic and the opportunity to get out of the house must have had a definite appeal.

MINNIE FRASER, SOMERS ROAD, C.1943

For women, old age did not signal retirement from household chores. Here, Minnie Fraser, a farmer's wife living on Somers Road, is shown playing surrogate mother to neglected lambs. No farm was complete without some sheep, for many households produced their own wool. This multipurpose material could be used as batting for quilts, incorporated into hooked rugs and woven into homespun cloth. Every spring, there were always little abandoned lambs who required special bottle feeding. It was always hard on the poor owner whose lamb became a family pet before butchering time. Old age was no deterrent to the performance of other tasks such as knitting and spinning.

GRACE (STEWART) MACNAUGHTON, NORTH
LOCHABER ON WEST SIDE, C.1932

Amelia (Stearns) Kinney, who had ten children, knitted her last pair
of socks when she was ninety-one. Ohio-born Grace (Stewart) Mac-
Naughton, who lived for ninety-two years, is shown seated at her spinning wheel on the doorstep of her Lochaber home. She spent her lifetime
contributing to the self-sufficiency of her family. She spun all the wool
required for socks, mitts, vests, and other clothing. In addition to raising
ten children, she hooked rugs, pressed apples for bottling, prepared soap
from wood ashes and lard, managed a large garden, pickled and preserved
produce, made raspberry and strawberry vinegar, and cured beef and pork
hams for winter use. She also made cheese, which was then packed into
straw-filled barrels where it ripened over several months.

MARGARET ANN SMITH BALLANTYNE AND HER SON, C.1937

Margaret Ballantyne, known locally as "Namie," was renowned in the Ballantyne and Cape George areas as a midwife. Born in 1848, she was a schoolteacher by training, but served her community in the dual roles of doctor and nurse. It is estimated the she delivered approximately two hundred children between 1875 and 1927. At the advanced age of eighty-seven years, she delivered her last baby, a ten-pound (four-and-a-half kilogram) infant at Ballantyne's Cove. Ballantyne was an intrepid soul, seldom daunted by deep snow and rough roads. One story tells how she rolled down a steep hill in a buffalo robe coat so that she could reach the expectant mother in time. Margaret Ballantyne was part of a venerable tradition of Antigonish County midwives, the most celebrated being Jane Pushee, who delivered over one thousand babies. She also resorted to novel ways to reach her patients. Dreading the springtime freshets, she traversed them crouching in a large clothes basket borne by a couple of men. Most rural areas had their own midwives. In the early 1900s, Louise Benoit of Dagger Woods served the people of Pomquet as a midwife. As one source states: "She was almost as good as a doctor and sometimes better than some."

SARAH MACDONALD AND JOSEPH E. KENNY, LANARK, C.1940S

Fairmont native Sarah MacDonald, wife of Lanark farmer William Fraser MacDonald, was born in 1862. She is shown here seated at her spinning wheel alongside her foster son, Joseph E. Kenny, who used to help her tear up rags for her rugs. Her life reflects the multifaceted roles of the wife and mother. She was an accomplished rug hooker and knitter, and was renowned for her healing powers, ministering to people and animals alike. In her advanced years, she cared for three orphaned boys until she died in 1951 at the age of eighty-nine.

**TEA TIME,
ANTIGONISH,
C.1930S**

No day, however busy, was complete without at least several tea breaks. Here, on a social call to town, Christina MacLean (left) and her sister, Jennie Cameron, both bundled in their fur-collar coats, partook their tea outdoors. Tea drinking has long been an important social ritual for Maritimers. However, the actual art of making tea was highly valued. There was a particular protocol to be followed once the kettle was filled with cold water retrieved from the spring-fed dug well. The loose tea was measured out carefully (a teaspoon, or five millilitres) per cup and one for the pot) into the teapot warmed on a trivet on the stove. The water at full boil was then added, and the mixture was steeped for three minutes, no more and no less. If followed strictly, this procedure guaranteed a cup of tea that did not elicit the comment, "How long have you had that teabag on the clothesline?" Christina, who returned from Lowell, Massachusetts in 1929 to take over the family farm, was the postmistress at Cross Roads Ohio from 1938 until the post office closed in 1959. Her sister, Jennie, left widowed in 1920, supported her large family with her handiwork. She is reputed to have owned the only knitting machine in Antigonish and found a niche in the local market for her socks, hats, and mitts as well as knitted material in stocking stitch.

Chapter 6

Religion

AFTER THE MASS, ST. CROIX CHURCH, POMQUET, C.1900

Churches have played a prominent role in the history of Antigonish town and county and its early clerics such as the Rev. Thomas Trotter and Bishop William Fraser were important community leaders. Antigonish's first Roman Catholic church, later designated as St. Ninian, was located on Main Street almost midway between College and Church streets and was built as a mission of Arisaig in 1810. The name St. Ninian was suggested by Bishop Plessis of Quebec who visited the district in 1812; he had previously learned some Gaelic from Catholic Highlanders in Ontario. At that time the parish of St. Ninian also included many of the rural districts surrounding town including Lochaber, Heatherton, St. Andrews, Antigonish Harbour, and St. Joseph's. It would be another half-century before some of the outlying regions had their own pastors. Antigonish was officially named the seat of the Diocese of Antigonish in 1886; it had previously been in Arichat, Cape Breton, although both Bishops MacKinnon and Cameron spent most of their episcopal and priestly tenure in Antigonish. By the late nineteenth century, St. Ninian's Cathedral, completed in 1874, and the bishop's residence, known locally as "the Palace," appeared to preside majestically over the affairs of the town of Antigonish from their elevated position on the crest of Cathedral Hill.

Generally, the town and county have been predominantly Roman Catholic but other denominations have had their pockets of strength, such as the Anglicans in Bayfield and a small but steady number of Presbyterians in Lochaber, Upper South River, Cape George, and Beaver Meadow. The Presbyterians also had a firm foothold in Antigonish town. During most of the nineteenth century, their membership rolls incorporated some of Antigonish's leading merchants and tradesmen who held centre stage in the economic life of the community. Interestingly enough, the disparity between the numbers of Catholics and Protestants did not automatically lead to religious discord. There are some striking examples of ecumenism in the early history of Antigonish town and county. For example, Nathaniel Symonds, a Presbyterian from New Hampshire, built the second Catholic church in Arisaig around 1812. Similarly, the original contractor for Antigonish's St. James Presbyterian Church in the early 1860s was "Sandy the Carpenter" MacDonald, a member of St. Ninian's parish.

ST. NINIAN'S CATHEDRAL.
Antigonish, N.S.

ST. NINIAN'S
CATHEDRAL,
ANTIGONISH,
LITHOGRAPH
BASED ON
PHOTOGRAPH
BY COLIN
"THE CHIEF"
CHISHOLM
C.1874

The ambitious dream of a stone Roman-style cathedral for Antigonish, reminiscent of the Italian Renaissance, originated with Bishop Colin Francis MacKinnon, who became the second Bishop of Arichat in 1851. The land on which the cathedral was built was acquired from the college; construction lasted from 1866 to 1874. The old St. Ninian's Church, a wooden structure situated just off Main Street, was converted into the Main Street School. In the initial phase of construction, the cathedral received a boon from an illwind—a shipwreck near Morristown. Bishop MacKinnon bought the cargo of lumber salvaged from the wreck and within two days parishioners, using horse-drawn sleighs, hauled the wood to town. Parishioners initially pledged three days of labour each week gratis except during harvest season. They helped haul such essential building materials as stone, timbers, and slate. The women spearheaded a series of annual bazaars as revenue raisers; for several years the Antigonish Highland Games were held in connection with these bazaars. The bazaar in 1871 was especially memorable. At the rear of the church was a four-tiered amphitheatre designed to accommodate three thousand people. According to the *Acadian Recorder* on September 20, 1871, enthusiastic spectators witnessed examples of Celtic sports as well as some local Mi'kmaw residents "performing some of the defunct war exercises of their forbears." Huge blocks of limestone and sandstone, some weighing as much as two tons, were transported to the site by horse, oxen, and wagon from North Grant and Brierly Brook. Local inhabitants long recalled with extraordinary vividness "looking out over the various approaches to the Village to see endless caravans of horse-drawn vehicles in an unbroken chain to the site of their Cathedral."

INTERIOR
C.1920S

The building, dedicated on 13 September 1874, was a striking departure from the traditional small-scale wooden churches of rural Nova Scotia. It was a magnificent edifice with its Romanesque arches, thirty-foot (nine-metre) windows, and double colonnade of pillars with lush Corinthian capitals. The façade was embellished with sculptural niches, carved scrollwork, pedimented entrances, the armorial bearings of Pope Pius IX and Bishop MacKinnon, and the chiselled words "Tigh Dhè" (House of God). As a more whimsical touch, a carved cluster of shamrocks and two sprigs of thistle over the central entrance celebrated the Scottish ancestry of the parishioners and the Irish roots of the master builder, Sylvester O'Donoghue. Much of the interior decoration of the cathedral, especially the luminous frescoes, was carried out from 1899 to 1903 by the Quebec-born Ozias Leduc and his team of assistants.

The history of Antigonish's Anglican congregation dates back to the town's earliest beginnings at Town Point. Many of the Loyalist settlers, including Lieut. Col. Hierlihy, were Anglicans and they initially held services in their homes. They were called to worship by the bell-like tones of an iron pestle striking a heavy brass mortar. From approximately 1788 to 1829, the religious needs of this community were served irregularly by mission priests from Guysborough County and by members of the Hierlihy and Ogden families who acted as lay readers. In Upper Big Tracadie, the Anglican presence was reinforced by Thomas Brownspriggs, a Black Loyalist, who provided lay leadership for the church during the 1780s under the sponsorship of the Society for the Propagation of the Gospel. By the early 1820s, the Anglicans in Dorchester finally had a house of worship, its construction having been delayed by the scarcity of funds. Early records indicate that Trinity Church, which was equipped with a stove and vestry and featured regular choir music, bore an uncanny resemblance to a Methodist meeting house. In Little River (Bayfield), the growing Anglican community waited until the late 1830s for their chapel, while the congregation in Linwood had their own church by the following decade. As the main locus of settlement and commercial development shifted from Town Point to Antigonish, so did the activities of the Anglican church. In 1842, a new church, St. Paul-the-Apostle, situated on land donated by Thomas Hill, one-time lawyer, high sheriff and postmaster, was consecrated by Bishop John Inglis. This structure was replaced in 1898 by another based on a design submitted by Gustavus Bernasconi, a parishioner who was a trained civil engineer. The old church was purchased by R. D. Kirk and took on new life for a time as a tenement house.

**St. James
Presbyterian
Church,
Antigonish,
c.1920s**

In the early 1800s, local Presbyterians used to gather at the home of Nathaniel Symonds for religious services. Rev. James Munro became their first settled pastor in 1806 and his successor, Rev. Thomas Trotter served from 1818 to 1853. In 1805, Munro donated an acre (0.4-hectare) of land on the southeast corner of Main and Church streets, which served as the site for a schoolhouse, burying ground, and church; the latter was the first church erected in the village of Antigonish. The growing congregation struggled to support its early ministers. Trotter refused to be left in straitened circumstances and supplemented his income by teaching, farming, and eventually operating a grist mill, a carding mill, a fulling mill, and a woolen factory. In 1828, the Presbyterians built a new church on Main Street; it was equipped with a handsome wineglass pulpit and sounding board. In 1862, construction of the present-day church began under the supervision of Alexander MacDonald, "Sandy the Carpenter." The impressive structure, which combined classical and Gothic elements, was hailed by one contemporary visitor as unsurpassed "by any church of the same description in the three provinces." Shortly after the new building was opened, the congregation found itself wracked with dissension over the introduction of an organ and the threatened displacement of the traditional tuning fork. On 10 June 1925, the Presbyterians joined church union and adopted the name of St. James United Church. Despite doctrinal clashes between the Presbyterians and Catholics, friendships were occasionally forged between the clerics of these denominations. Rev. Mr. Trotter and Bishop Fraser were fast friends who fished trout together in Brierly Brook.

Left to right are Carmen Simpson, Shirley Whidden and Bill Simpson.
The Baptist church in Antigonish traces its roots back to 1823. In that
year, several pastors, including Rev. David Nutter, visited the town and
motivated followers to establish a local Baptist church. All members—initially there were no more than seven—signed a temperance pledge as a
condition of their membership. The Whiddens were pillars in this congregation. John B. Whidden, a carpenter and millwright, bore most of the
costs of building the first Baptist meeting house. Ordained in 1832, he
also served as its first regular pastor, ministering to local Baptists inter-
mittently between 1846 and 1864. In 1875, a larger Baptist church was
constructed on Court House Hill, later called Baptist Hill. It was originally
the site of Antigonish's first courthouse. The property was donated by Mrs.
C. B. Whidden. A large tank for baptisms was installed near the front of
the church and was covered over with flooring when not in use; this was a
decided improvement over the chilly waters of Brierly Brook that had been
employed for some of the earlier immersions. The original meeting house
on Hawthorne Street was eventually razed to make way for a parsonage
known locally as "The Hedges." In 1925, most of the Baptist congregation
joined the newly formed United Church.

St. Andrews parish was established by Bishop William Fraser in 1837. Its first pastor was Rev. Colin F. MacKinnon who, in 1842, began the construction of a new church. There had been a chapel built earlier at Garanach Hill; it was located in the old cemetery in a section known as MacIntosh Lane. The new church was positioned just north of the present edifice and was opened for worship in June 1846. Twelve hundred people could be seated in this new building and it served a wide area for many years. Rev. MacKinnon was instrumental in the construction of a new glebe house; he was also the moving force behind the establishment of the St. Andrews Grammar School. It was not uncommon for young people in the parish to carry their shoes in their hands while walking to church in the summertime. On arriving near the church they would put their shoes on. Horse-drawn carriages and sleighs provided one means of transportation well into the 1920s but walking, often from a considerable distance, was the most common way of going to and from worship.

Extensive repairs had to be carried out at certain periods and by the 1930s it was obvious that a new building was required. In 1934, Rev. John Angus MacPherson organized a drive for finances and by 1948 the foundation for a new church was laid. Dave Floyd, a former native of the parish, was the main contractor and the new stone church was dedicated in July 1951. The old church, pictured above, was dismantled in the same year; it had served the parish for 109 years and is still fondly remembered by the older residents.

St. Joseph's Roman Catholic Church, St. Joseph's, c.1923

In 1867, St. Bean's Church at St. Joseph's, built in 1841, was replaced by a new wooden church called St. Joseph's. It was situated on a hill overlooking St. Joseph's Lake. Within the year, the nearly complete structure was destroyed in a violent windstorm. The parishioners and local priest rallied to undertake the task of rebuilding. John Smith of West River was retained as chief contractor while Sylvester O'Donoghue, the master builder of St. Ninian's Cathedral, supervised the interior work. The new church welcomed parishioners in the fall of 1868, but the congregation waited until 1883 before hearing the peal of a bell from their church tower. A series of church picnics enabled them to raise sufficient funds to realize this dream. By 1911, St. Joseph's boasted one of the most impressive glebe houses in Antigonish County. This spacious Second Empire two-storey structure had many elegant features including bay windows, covered verandas, and a central tower affording a lofty view of St. Joseph's Lake. On 19 January 1926, the congregation lost their church in a devastating fire that left the structure in ruins within an hour. It is said that the bell tolled a requiem as it toppled to the ground. Once again, the parishioners and their priest rose to the challenge. Father George J. MacLean used the veranda of the big glebe house to celebrate his first solemn high mass at St. Joseph's in May 1926. Throughout the year, donations rolled in from as far afield as Boston and New York, and summertime dances and other forms of entertainment also generated necessary funds. By October 1926, a new brick house of worship stood on the old church site. During the depression years, the people of St. Joseph's Parish struggled with debt, but their faith was never shaken. The spiritual dedication of these people is exemplified by the stories about the early Keppoch residents who travelled on foot to attend mass in Antigonish every Sunday, and the women in the Ohio who sometimes trekked twenty-five (forty-kilometres) miles to attend mass in Arisaig.

PETIT CLAIRVAUX MONASTERY, PARISH OF TRACADIE, C.1900

Founded in 1825 by a Trappist priest from France, Rev. Vincent de Paul, this monastery was originally known as Petit Clairvaux; after 1938 it was called St. Augustine's Monastery. A contemplative order, the Trappists followed a life of strict separation from "the world, of union with God by prayer, mortification, study, spiritual reading and manual labor." (Schrepfer, 4) Their monasteries are normally located in secluded areas. Some of the early priests at Petit Clairvaux performed parish duties for there were no other priests available. Merland, for example, was named after Rev. Vincent de Paul (born James Merle), because of his work in that district. He also founded a small order of nuns, the Trappistines, composed of a few women from the Pomquet and Tracadie areas.

During the second half of the nineteenth century, a group of Trappists from Belgium kept alive the work begun in 1825. They suffered serious setbacks in 1892 and again in 1896 when fire destroyed the monastery and the large barn and mills. The monastery was forced to close in 1900 due to a lack of personnel but it was revived in 1903 by some French monks, driven by religious persecution from their homeland. The First World War reduced its numbers once again when six members were recalled to France to serve in the army and those left were too old to maintain the property. It was then sold to a Catholic corporation in Montreal and later bought by a group in Sydney, but nothing was developed and it remained closed until 1938 when a group of Augustinian monks, forced out of Germany, took up ownership and residence there. They too improved the buildings, built new ones and a chapel, and generally proved an inspiration for people throughout the county. The Augustinians, who will be long remembered for their spiritual values and their positive agricultural lessons, remained there until 2000. The monastery is presently occupied by a small group of Maronite monks.

In his journal of 1812, Bishop Plessis wrote that there was a small chapel in St. George's Bay "less than two leagues from St. Peter's Chapel at Tracadie" and located in the midst of thirty houses. The chapel may have been there since 1790, perhaps built by Acadian settlers who had started to trickle into the area in the 1770s. Although visited occasionally by missionaries, Havre Boucher

St. Paul's Church and Sisters of Charity Convent, Havre Boucher, 1914

was still a relatively new settlement in 1812. It was raised to the status of a separate parish in 1858 and the first resident pastor was Rev. Hugh MacDonald, who served between October 1858 and August 1860.

The cornerstone for a new church was laid on 30 June 1861, under the direction of Rev. Charles P. Martell, pastor 1860–1865; he was also the pastor at Tracadie and Pomquet for much of that period. Unfortunately, the church was destroyed by fire in 1916 but the parishioners mobilized that same year to build a replacement, under the direction of Rev. Moses M. Doyle. The contractor for this new church was W. E. Landry of Antigonish. As the years passed, there was noted deterioration in the building and it was renovated at a cost of $250,000, a huge sum for a small parish. The renovation did not halt the erosion and in 1995 the parishioners voted eighty-two percent in favour of a new church, the present St. Paul's in Havre Boucher.

For many years the convent adjacent to St. Paul's served as the village school. It was administered by the Sisters of Charity who arrived in Havre Boucher from the Motherhouse in Rockingham on 24 August 1891. They were met at the railway station by a contingent of carriages and a large crowd of people who hoped that the sisters would improve upon existing educational opportunities.

The Sisters taught primary, intermediate and high school classes; high school students living in other school sections of the parish could be accepted at the convent if deemed practicable. With the building of new and modern rural schools and the centralization of the educational system, the role of the sisters declined accordingly. In the early 1950s, the convent school was replaced by the Havre Boucher Consolidated School. The sisters remained in the community, however, until 1966. The convent was demolished in 1970.

AFTER THE MASS, IMMACULATE CONCEPTION CHURCH, HEATHERTON, C.1915

Heatherton was initially served by Rev. Alexander MacDonald of Arisaig who cared for the spiritual needs of the whole district. He visited Heatherton as early as 1802. Between 1815 and 1827, Heatherton was served from St. Ninian's in Antigonish. When St. Andrews parish was formed in 1827, Heatherton came under its jurisdiction until they received their own church in 1842; they remained as part of St. Andrews Parish until 1863. The church presently used by the Catholic population of Heatherton was built 1867–1869; the first pastor was Rev. John J. Chisholm who served during the years 1875–1892.

Immaculate Conception Church is best known for the notorious episode of the Heatherton Stampeders, which was precipitated by the federal election of 1896 and the dominant issues of the day, the separate schools controversy in Manitoba and the remedial bill. Shortly before the election a circular letter was sent to all parishes in the Antigonish diocese by Bishop John Cameron, a lifelong Conservative. Every pastor was to read that letter which, in effect, told people to support the remedial legislation. This meant voting Conservative. Lifelong Liberals simply balked at this sort of coercion and charged the bishop with overstepping the boundary between religion and politics.

When the letter was about to be read in the Heatherton church, forty-eight Liberal stalwarts, on a prearranged signal from their ringleader, William Chisholm, a young lawyer, walked out of the church. Locally, they became known as the Heatherton Stampeders. For almost two years, the Stampeders were refused the sacraments and four years would pass before the issue was laid to rest, but not forgotten. Eventually, a compromise was worked out between the federal government and Manitoba, and Bishop Cameron had his fingers rapped by Cardinal Ledockowski, Prefect of the Propaganda in Rome. Local lore relates that William Chisholm, who instigated the walkout, later slipped while boarding a train and had the toes of his foot cut off. Tories argued that this was his just punishment.

LICENTIATE
WILLIAM JOHN
ELMS, UPPER
BIG TRACADIE,
C.1917

John Elms enjoyed a long career as a religious leader at the Tracadie Baptist church where he served as a pastor for twenty-four years. He also acted as a clerk, treasurer, trustee, Sunday school superintendent, and delegate to the African United Baptist Association. His wife, Sadie MacPhee from New Glasgow, played the organ at the church. Elms was a devout man for whom the Bible was his moral compass. He was also a gifted preacher. His sermons, prepared Friday and Saturday nights around the kitchen lamp, were stirring, emotional discourses. For Elms, ministering was the central focus of his life. He would state emphatically: "I'm going to do it as long as the Lord gives me breath." He was an avid visitor of the sick and shut-ins. After Sunday services, he would walk from Tracadie to Lincolnville to bring spiritual sustenance to the dispersed flock. Music, as well, was an important expression of his faith and mission. He sang hymns such as "I'm a witness for my Lord" with great fervour. Throughout Tracadie, John Elms was also known as a First World War veteran, sheepshearer, and a gardener who shared with his neighbours his talent for cutting seed potatoes. The establishment of the Tracadie Baptist church owed much to David Nutter, an English-born Baptist preacher, who visited Tracadie in 1821; his circuit also took him to Truro, Guysborough, and Canso. His time in Tracadie proved pivotal for the black residents who felt marginalized by both the Anglican and Catholic churches. Nutter's evangelical message inspired them and became a powerful incentive to organize the Tracadie Baptist church, which is now regarded as "the second oldest to serve a black congregation in Nova Scotia."

ST. ANNE'S MISSION CHURCH, SUMMERSIDE, C.1890S

Among the Mi'kmaq, the Feast of St. Anne is an important ethnocultural event steeped in historical significance. Gathering at certain locales such as Chapel Island, Shubenacadie, Summerside, and Pictou Landing on July 26, clans throughout the region converged annually to worship their patron saint, Saint Anne, exchange information and participate in storytelling, song and dance. At St. Anne's Mission Church at Summerside, some families came at least a month in advance and erected birchbark tents as temporary dwellings; many of these were assembled near the scene of the celebration. Mi'kmaq from Pictou Landing travelled by boat to attend this spiritual and social occasion. The church was decorated in readiness for services of holy communion and confirmation. Even baptisms and marriages were held at this time. The Feast of St. Anne was a fascinating spectacle—both reverent and lively—attended by crowds of worshippers. It was accompanied by waving flags, bell ringing, intoned psalms and chants, bonfires, banqueting, and firing guns, all symbols of joy. Into the 1920s, some of the older Mi'kmaw residents turned out in their traditional attire: the women were outfitted in their pointed caps and jackets embellished with ribbon trim while the men wore blue broadcloth coats with beaded epaulettes and woven belts. The celebration's crowning moment was the solemn procession of chiefs, priests, young men and young girls dressed in white dresses and veils carrying aloft a statue of St. Anne. They were led along a route ornamented with flags and arches by a cross-bearer. Young children threw flowers before the image of their patron saint. The occasion was also highlighted by the election of a new chief when circumstances dictated, who was blessed by the bishop. This religious festival drew the attention of the white population who, motivated by devotion and curiousity, travelled by buggy and horse to observe the so-called Indian Walk or Indian Picnic.

FEAST OF ST. ANNE, SUMMERSIDE, C.1920S

JOE LANDRY AND ANGELIQUE VINCENT CROSS AT FEAST OF ST. ANNE, SUMMERSIDE, C.1910

GEORGE AND
CLARENCE
DeWOLFE, FIRST
COMMUNION,
POMQUET,
C.1920S

First Communion was an important rite of passage for many children in Antigonish County. It was a beautiful, edifying ceremony with the girls outfitted like miniature brides and the boys dressed in their Sunday best. Tradition dictated in some parishes that girls after their first communion join a society called "The Children of Mary" or "Les Enfants de Marie," pledging themselves to lives of piety and purity. These two brothers, George and Clarence, with their rosy cheeks, polished boots and impeccably combed hair, marked the occasion with a special photograph. The solemnity of this event is reflected in the boys' straight backs and grave demeanours.

In nineteenth and early twentieth century Antigonish town and county, the Church was not a compartmentalized entity but rather a dominant force that permeated everyday life. In Catholic households, religious devotions such as morning and evening prayer, mealtime blessings, and the family rosary during Advent and Lent punctuated daily routines. In many Catholic households, the family kneeled beside the kitchen chairs to recite the rosary before heading to bed. Homes were adorned with religious pictures, a crucifix, a holy water receptacle, and a piece of palm. The church was both a physical and metaphysical presence, looming in both foreground and background, keeping people mindful of where they were. Along with the Glebe house, it served as a bastion of watchfulness. The church bell rang faithfully three times of day, at 6 a.m., noontime and 6 p.m., signalling for adults and children to interrupt both work and play for the Angelus. In this photograph, the Pomquet church stands out clearly with its elongated spire, overlooking the henhouse with its numerous flock in a union of the sacred and the profane.

FATHER CORMIER, PASTOR AT NORTHEAST MARGAREE AND AGATHE BOUDREAU DOIRON, POMQUET, 1929

THE MAPLE HALL UNDER CONSTRUCTION, HEATHERTON, SUMMER 1927

Left to right, in the front row: (John Angus) Macdonald, Alex Dan Chisholm, Austin Tate, Charlie Perro, and William A. Chisholm; in the back row: Allan Cameron (Piper), Frank Grant, Angus (Cooper) MacDonald, Joe Rogers, Andrew Grant, and Rev. Hugh John MacDonald. The parish hall was the social epicentre of most communities. In August 1926, Father Hugh John Macdonald of Glenroy, who was pastor of Heatherton for forty years, mobilized his parishioners to build a parish hall next to the church. Construction began in October 1926, and parishioners banded together to haul sand and gravel to the site by horse and wagon. The men also provided the lumber as well as much of the free labour. The work was carried out as circumstances permitted, squeezed in between the spring planting and the fall harvest. Maple Hall, named after the row of maple trees planted at the front, was completed the following September. At the official opening, there was an address, supper, and grand march. A radio with a loudspeaker was also installed so that guests could hear the broadcast of the celebrated Tunney-Dempsey fight in Chicago. The Maple Hall became a popular venue for community meetings, dances and suppers; many of these events were fundraisers for the parish. In this photograph of the volunteers who helped build the hall can be seen Allan J. Cameron of Springfield, the renowned piper, who was official piper at the Nova Scotia-New Brunswick border for about fifteen years and later appeared on Sesame Street for a season.

ST. MARTHA'S
HOSPITAL
UNDER
CONSTRUCTION,
ANTIGONISH, 11
OCTOBER 1924

In 1905, around one hundred Antigonish citizens, both Protestant and Catholic, called upon the town council to address the desperate need for hospital care. Local physicians and college authorities supported their appeal. Apart from the StFX College Infirmary, there was no hospital to serve the area between New Glasgow and Sydney. In 1906 the Sisters of St. Martha opened a "cottage hospital," a six-bed unit in the Campbell house, located on St. Ninian Street West. This first building was used only for a short time and the sisters scouted around for a new location. They hoped to acquire the Harris property on Bay Street but it required renovations and for a time patients had to be accommodated at Mount Cameron, a college property. They moved into the Harris house in 1907, in the same year the sisters were incorporated. In 1911, a School of Nursing was opened in Antigonish. It was not long before the sisters realized that the Harris property was inadequate to the growing demand for hospital services. For two decades they worked with limited facilities and by the mid-1920s a vigorous financial campaign was launched to raise $150,000. It proved successful and a new four-storey brick hospital was opened in 1926 with a capacity of around 125 beds; the weekly rate for a private bed was twenty dollars. The new St. Martha's Hospital boasted state-of-the art apparatus in its operating rooms, laboratory, and radiology and physiotherapy departments. This building, augmented by a Tuberculosis annex in 1933, a new hospital wing in 1951 and a new nurses' residence in 1964, served for much of the twentieth century, but by the 1970s it was very evident that a larger and better-equipped facility was needed. All sectors of the four eastern counties, and all denominations contributed to the cause as they had done in 1906; approximately $7.1 million was raised from a population base of barely fifty thousand people for a new regional hospital opened in 1989.

Presbyterian pioneers in the region between Lochaber and Upper South River first attended church services in a log structure built around 1837, midway between Lochaber Lake and Loch Katrine, in an area dubbed "the Swamp." As a consequence of religious upheaval within the Kirk in 1843, another church was built nearby to accommodate the new members of the Free Church. The rival churches were within earshot of each other, the hymns in one frequently drowning out the sermon in the other. Owing to the persuasive influence of the Rev. John Forbes, the two factions united in 1869 and twin churches were built at Lochaber and Loch Katrine to mark this new era of co-operation. The Lochaber Presbyterian church, called Chalmers Presbyterian Church, was situated next to Mill Brook and faced the Lochaber Road. In 1925, this church remained within the Presbyterian fold serviced by student ministers while a new United Church, situated on the MacPhee property about half a mile (four-fifths of a kilometre) away, opened for worship in 1931. While awaiting completion of Lochaber United Church, Manson's carriage shop served as temporary quarters for the new congregation. Chalmers was reduced to rubble in a fire in the 1950s.

Chapter 7

Education

INTERIOR OF HARBOUR CENTRE SCHOOL, THERESA MACMILLAN (TEACHER) C.1952

One of the first schools near Antigonish was run by Rev. C. W. Weeks, an Anglican priest, in the year 1815. More than likely situated at Town Point, close to the Anglican church, this school operated sporadically. Rev. Thomas Trotter, second pastor of St. James Presbyterian Church, is credited with establishing Antigonish's first grammar school in 1818. By the mid-1820s, Trotter estimated that around one thousand children attended schools in Sydney County. In the late 1830s, there was a combined school of Protestants and Catholics taught by John Forrestall, brother of Richard James Forrestall, MLA. In 1841, the Antigonish Academy opened with Charles W. Leaver, an Anglican, as teacher; within two years there were seventy-nine students registered. Archival sources indicate that in 1854 Jessie MacPhie and Mary Irish both offered instruction to pupils in the village; twenty scholars attended MacPhie's School, while forty-one studied under

Irish's tutelage. A private school, taught by Louisa Harrington Pelton, located on St. Mary's Street between Court and Elm streets, was closed in 1865 after the introduction of the free school system. Lagging educational opportunities for female students enjoyed a real boost when Miss Narcissa Hooper opened her female school in 1858 in the lower storey of the College building. She promised her scholars "a good, sound English education" along with French, Italian, and pianoforte. By the early 1880s, Antigonish's local schools were on a much firmer footing, buttressed by such educational institutions as the Main Street School, St. Ninian Street School and St. Bernard's Convent School, all committed to a vision of scholastic achievement.

Schoolchildren did not fare so well in the county, especially during the log cabin beginnings of education. Admittedly, there were some important pioneering landmarks. Local tradition claims that the Arisaig district boasted a private school as early as the late 1790s. There were schools in Malignant Cove and South River by 1815 and 1816 respectively. In 1817, Neil MacKinnon was licensed to operate a school at Williams Point "for the instruction of youth in reading, writing, and arithmetic." By 1828, there were twenty-two schools in the county but only ten operated on a regular basis and only a small percentage of students paid fees. Some improvement came with the creation of a district board of commissioners in Antigonish in 1826. Providing some semblance of organization and promoting the establishment of schools, this board also increased the number of school districts, formalized school boundaries, and regularized the appointment of trustees to superintend and manage the school districts and examine the schoolmasters. The Free School Act of 1865 was also a turning point. That year, twelve schools in Antigonish County were repaired and thirteen new ones built. Still, improvements were sluggish, and school inspectors routinely despaired about teachers' paltry salaries, substandard teaching qualifications, and the inferior physical condition of the schools, some only large enough to hold seats, a teacher's desk, and a stove. In 1883, Roderick McDonald's education report stated bluntly that teachers' wages in Antigonish County were "considerably lower" than those paid in Guysborough County; even the salaries of male teachers with first-class licenses was "far below the wages of a common laborer." By 1910, eighty-two percent of all Antigonish County teachers held Class C and D licenses; those holding the D license, the lowest ranked qualification, typically received less than a dollar a day. In the 1930s, rural schools in Antigonish County enjoyed the benefits of study clubs, Arbor Day programmes, school fairs, Teachers' Institutes, and debating contests. School orchestras were started at Saint Andrews and Fraser's Mills. Even with these innovations, rural depopulation and the closure of schools continued. Yet, despite their faults such as leaky ceilings, crowded desks, smokey wood-stoves, faded maps, drafty privies and second-hand text-books, the one-room schools remain a cherished memory among older inhabitants.

ST. ANDREWS GRAMMAR SCHOOL, ST. ANDREWS, C.1916

Shortly after Rev. Colin F. MacKinnon arrived home from his years in Rome in the summer of 1837, he was assigned to the mission of St. Andrews by Bishop William Fraser. Many of his parishioners were illiterate. MacKinnon's early education was indelibly stamped by his classical training at East Bay College, an ecclesiastical school established by his first cousin, Father William B. MacLeod. MacKinnon resolved to replicate this experience in St. Andrews. In 1838 he opened a classroom in an old log house that was soon replaced by a newer building which, while not imposing, was an improvement. In addition to the regular students there were a number who busied themselves in studying Latin. The school proved to be very successful, mainly because Rev. Colin MacKinnon recruited some exceptional teachers. Besides John and Malcolm MacLellan, classical scholars from Scotland, others were: Dr. Alex MacDonald of Meadow Green, who studied medicine in New York; John MacDonald, who is credited with drawing up the plans for the old St. Andrews Church; John MacKinnon, brother of Rev. Colin MacKinnon and later an MLA; Dr. Hugh Cameron; Rev. David MacGregor; Rev. John Shaw; Rev. Ronald MacGillivray, the historian; John MacDonald (Ridge); Malcolm MacNeil; William D. Cameron (Drummer on Foot); and several others. This building was used by the school section until sometime around 1920.

The forerunner of the Main Street School shared quarters with St. Francis Xavier's seminary-college in a two-storey wooden building erected on College Street in 1854. Starting in October of that year, public school classes were held in the basement; the other two floors were allocated to the older pupils, including the college students. By 1856 the building accommodated twenty-three female students, ranging from six to eighteen years, as well as ninety-three male students registered in elementary, high school, college courses, and nine seminarians. This arrangement for the public school continued until 1880 when the new three-storey brick wing of Xavier Hall was completed. The College Street building, sold to the federal government, took on new life as a post office while the public school children were relocated to the extensively renovated old St. Ninian's Parish Church. This school, which opened in 1881, was attended by pupils from town and nearby rural areas within walking distances. Within two years, there were 292 pupils in attendance. Among the earliest teachers at the Main Street School were Helen Kenna Landry, Mary Belle Grant Ormond (the first organist at St. Ninian's Cathedral), and Sophie Grant Dickenson. The curriculum was the common one of the day with lessons taken from the Royal Readers, the memorization of popular poems, the use of slates and arithmetic tables found on the backs of scribblers.

Semi-annual examinations, attended by the school trustees, were held over a period of two or three days. Discipline was strict and one form of punishment was to have "prayerful meditation" among the headstones in the nearby graveyard. The old building grew increasingly dilapidated, even "squalid" in Bishop Morrison's opinion, and when Morrison School was opened in November 1917, the students marched triumphantly to their new quarters on Cathedral Hill. The distractions of Main Street may have been missed, but certainly not so the twelve-hole partionless privy.

ST. NINIAN
STREET
SCHOOL,
C.1960S

ST. NINIAN
STREET
SCHOOL,
C.1960S

CLASS
PORTRAIT, ST.
NINIAN STREET
SCHOOL, C.1910

After the introduction of the Free School Act in 1865, some Protestant ratepayers in Antigonish mounted a campaign to obtain their own "separate" school. Their lobbying resulted in the establishment of a four-room school on St. Ninian Street in 1872. Little is known about this local Protestant school during its early years. However, later on, classes were held at the St. Ninian Street School for primary, intermediate, and junior high school students. It is believed that in its early years, some high school courses were also taught there although it later became common for boys to take the higher grades at Morrison School while the girls attended Mount St. Bernard. In the early twentieth century, the classrooms at St. Ninian Street School differed little from those in other local schools, with their wood-burning stoves and large pails of water and dippers for thirsty students. At that time, the school lacked running water and the privies, one for the boys and another for the girls, were positioned out back, concealed by a lattice work fence. In 1935, there were thirty-six students attending the school; Mary Elizabeth Graham was responsible for teaching students registered in the "advanced department" while Annie Mac-Naughton taught the primary grades. St. Ninian Street School continued to operate until the 1960s when it was replaced by a new school offering primary and intermediate grades on Braemore Avenue. It finally closed its doors in the early 1980s, after serving as the temporary headquarters for the local Canadian Association for the Mentally Retarded (now Canadian Association for Community Living).

CLYDESDALE SCHOOL C.1905

WINNERS OF ANTIGONISH COUNTY SCHOLASTIC DEBATING COMPETITION, CLYDESDALE SCHOOL, 1933

From left to right are champion debaters Edith Smith, Marg Janet Chisholm, and Roland Eadie. The Clydesdale area was initially settled in the early nineteenth century by immigrants from New Hampshire and Scotland. They spread throughout the areas we identify today as the foot of Brown's Mountain, Pleasant Valley, and North Grant. For a time, Clydesdale was referred to as Yankee Grant because of the settlers from New Hampshire. Some of those early arrivals were Towns, Campbells, Browns, McPhersons, McKinnons, Cumstocks, and Ronans. One of the first schools in the district was established by Neil McKinnon, formerly of Williams Point, around 1824. The first school was a makeshift operation housed in his home. Those from New Hampshire as well as those from Scotland recognized the need for some educational instruction, regardless of how primitive the facilities were.

The whitewashed clapboard school was the focus of many community activities, including the meetings of the North Grant Agricultural Society during the 1880s. During the first half of the twentieth century, the Clydesdale School felt fully the crisis facing most rural schools—population loss and declining enrolments. Student numbers at the Clydesdale School fell from twenty-nine pupils in 1927 to ten in 1958–59. Academic standards at the school, however, did not decline, especially under the tutelage of dedicated teachers such as Jessie Smith (later Jessie Baxter), a native of Clydesdale, who later taught at St. Ninian Street School.

AFTON INDIAN DAY SCHOOL, C.1913

In the nineteenth century, there was no separate school for the Mi'kmaw students in the Heatherton, Summerside, and Afton areas. In 1907, it was reported that six children on these reserves were attending a neighbouring school. The Indian Day School in Afton opened in December 1913, at least seventeen years after local Mi'kmaq had expressed to their Indian agent, William C. Chisholm, their desire for a school. The plain painted structure with its porch, cloakroom, and single classroom was described in a government report as "centrally located and well equipped"; there was even a janitor and truant officer hired along with a teacher. Government officials applauded this development, voicing the hope that education would quell the Mi'kmaq's "spirit of independence" and accelerate their acquisition of the English language. They noted that attendance figures at the reserve school compared favourably with those at neighbouring schools; in terms of obedience, their record was often superior. Thirty-four pupils were in attendance during the school's first month of operation, although a few children on the Summerside reserve opted to go to the public white school. The first teacher, William J. Rogers, served at the school from 1913 to 1928. His successors included John L. McDonald, Christine Kennedy, Alice McKeough, and Jennie Forbes; the latter arrived in 1938. In the 1920s, the average attendance hovered around ten students. By the 1940s, the school was closed, possibly a tactic designed to expedite the official agenda of centralization; it re-opened early in the following decade and later burned down in the 1970s.

FRASER'S MILLS SCHOOL, C.1930S

Sources indicate that during the 1820s, a barn belonging to Angus Boyd, one of the first settlers, housed the first school in the Fraser's Mills area. It was typical of most early log schoolhouses, which were caulked with moss and heated with a primitive fireplace. The furniture was no less primitive, usually rough-hewn seats, three to four inches (seven-and-a-half to ten centimetres) thick, fitted with wooden legs. The only piece of furniture deserving the designation of desk belonged to the master, and usually traveled with him to his new postings. The curriculum focused on the three R's: reading, writing, and 'rithmetic. Penmanship was singled out for special attention so early teachers became quite proficient at sharpening their students' goose quill pens. The first native-born teachers at the Fraser's Mills school were John McDonald and Lauchlan McPherson. A second frame school was built around 1831 at Fraser's Mills, erected in a more central location conveniently serving residents on both sides of the river. A third schoolhouse, which was remodelled several times, served the community until 1926; it was replaced by a two-storey building that housed a community hall on the second floor. The school had an impressive success rate, producing by 1913 four priests, four medical doctors, two lawyers, one judge and no less than twenty "High Grade" teachers.

EAST TRACADIE SCHOOL, c.1930S

This school section was formed following the passage of the Free School Act of 1865. Small school sections were the norm at the time due to the lack of transportation. School sections were to be four miles (six kilometres) in diameter so that students would not have to walk more than two miles (three kilometres) to attend school. By May 1887, the East Tracadie school district encompassed "the eastern side of Tracadie Harbour," stretching from the Black Bridge around Barrio's Point to "Robert Kenny's north western line."

A problem common to all rural schools was the retention of good teachers for more than one term. Another drawback was the loss of good teachers to school sections that offered a higher salary. As late as 1910, a female teacher with a Class D license (which meant that the teacher had only completed Grade IX) received only $206 for a one-year term.

In an Acadian district like East Tracadie, after the passage of the Free School Act, the bulk of the instruction was given in English. This disadvantage was felt acutely in most French-speaking areas. According to A. G. MacDonald's 1886 education report, among the eleven teachers in the sections including Middle Pomquet, West Arm Tracadie, Big Tracadie, East Tracadie, Havre Boucher, and Back Settlement Havre Boucher only two "pretended to know anything of French." (MacDonald, 56) For that reason some students, boys especially, quit school early and busied themselves in learning a trade. The East Tracadie Schoolhouse operated from 1920 to 1966; it was torn down in 1970.

CLASSROOM INTERIOR, MORRISON SCHOOL, ANTIGONISH, C.1930S

Depicted here in the front row from left to right are Robbie MacDonald, Neil MacKenna, Donald Kell, Jackie MacLean, and Bill Murphy. Morrison School was built in 1917 by contractors Landry and MacGillivray and named after Bishop James Morrison. Originally an all boys' school, the three-storey brick steam-heated building had four classrooms on each floor. During the early years, the centre of each classroom was equipped with a large coal stove and coal box. The top floor originally had quarters reserved for the janitor and his family.

Located directly behind St. Ninian's Cathedral, Morrison School formally opened on 12 November 1917. With its large windows and gleaming hardwood floors and staircases, the new school seemed modern and spacious compared to its decrepit predecessor, the old Main Street School. Morrison encompassed all grades from primary to Grade XII, until the construction of a new high school not far from the Bishop's Palace. From that time until its closure in 1991, Morrison School served as an elementary school.

The first principal of Morrison School was Sister Mary Paula, Congregation of Notre Dame (CND); she also taught grades III and IV. Catherine Hogan was in charge of the intermediate department and Gertrude MacKenzie taught and supervised the primary grades. CND sisters continued to fill the position of principal until 1929. At that time, Sister St. Andrew Avellino was replaced by a layman and for the next twenty-six years, all principals would be male. Some of Mount St. Bernard's female students received their earliest teacher training at Morrison. They were sometimes called in to substitute when regular teachers were absent.

STFX
UNIVERSITY,
ANTIGONISH,
1908

Founded by Bishop Colin F. MacKinnon at Arichat in 1853, the college was removed to Antigonish, where he had always intended it to be, in 1855. In 1838 he had lent his support to the establishment of a grammar school at St. Andrews and the success of this venture, with its able staff, led him to enlarge his vision of higher education for his people. In 1866 St. Francis Xavier College was awarded the power to grant degrees; this boost also meant that it had to align its offerings with those of other institutions of higher learning. Priest-professors, teaching for minimal wages, carried the bulk of the teaching load, but there were some lay teachers as well. Classes were carried on in a building erected for that purpose in 1854–1855, located directly behind the present town office.

The 1870s were difficult due largely to a lack of funding, but matters improved in the 1880s and the first brick building on campus, the present Education building, was erected. In 1890–91, a Master of Arts degree was offered, an alumni association was formed and the first honours degree programme was part of the curriculum. It was also in this decade that the Sisters of St. Martha arrived on campus to care for the domestic needs of the college. Discipline was not only strict, it was also enforced and the college resembled a minor seminary in many ways. However, new societies in drama, music, debating, and athletics were organized in the 1890s and marked the beginning of a trend towards non-religious activities. By 1900 it was obvious that the college was having a significant impact upon the social, religious, and economic life of eastern Nova Scotia.

The twentieth century saw increased efforts to attract faculty from some of Europe's best universities, despite the lack of any great sources of revenue. Some alumni did give important donations but the major funding came from the people of eastern Nova Scotia who, despite limited resources, gave what they could. New buildings continued to be erected, some paid for by donors, and new curricula developed. A major development was the beginning of adult education in the 1920s and the establishment of an extension department, which eventually led to the Coady Institute. Both world wars had an impact upon StFX as did the depression of the 1930s. Despite such challenges, the seed planted by Bishop MacKinnon has borne much fruit.

STUDENT'S ROOM, ST. FRANCIS XAVIER UNIVERSITY, C.1918

The student's room was typically decorated with pennants, calendars, and a jumble of books. At this time, some of the on-campus StFX students were housed in the old main building in dormitories affectionately nick-named Broadway, The Gardens, Middle Dorm, Pie Alley, and Pig Alley. Each dormitory wing was closely policed by a priest-prefect. Mockler Hall, which was constructed in 1915, provided accommodation for over one hundred students. This functional-looking four-storey brick building was equipped with hot water heating, shower baths, a billiard room and a senior reading-room. There were single rooms as well as suites of two rooms, all finished in Douglas fir and birch. Out-of-town students who lived off campus were required to stay at "approved boarding houses." By today's standards, student life during the 1920s was restrictive. University regulations were stringent and discipline was enforced with parental firmness. Smoking and drinking were prohibited on campus, although there were always ways to circumvent these rules. At least one student became quite adept at flipping a lit cigarette into his mouth in order to avoid detection. There was an early rising on campus around 6:30 a.m. with classes beginning sharp at 8:00 a.m. The day's routine was governed by a rigid schedule that marked out specific times for meals, study, recreation and religious observance. The ringing of the bell in the university bell tower helped structure the pace of the day.

MOUNT ST. BERNARD, C.1890

Throughout the early decades of the nineteenth century, the education of girls in Antigonish and elsewhere was often neglected. Beginning in 1883, female students attended the newly established Mount St. Bernard. In 1882, Bishop John Cameron announced that he intended to build a convent at Antigonish, to be completed the following year. This convent would be under the direction of the Congregation of Notre Dame. The bishop, knowing of their excellent teaching success elsewhere, wanted them in Antigonish. The convent was opened on 5 November 1883, with a registration of eighty-six pupils; the academic program was supplemented soon after with courses in music, painting, and drawing. From its inception, St. Bernard's Convent School (shortly thereafter called St. Bernard's Academy) educated girls from primary to high school. The first formal graduation ceremony for high school students was held in 1886 when Janet Cameron of Mabou, a Grade XI student, received the Academic Diploma and Gold Medal. Many non-Catholic girls could attend high school classes there after completing their earlier studies at the St. Ninian Street School. The academy was best known for its art and music lessons; the latter included piano, organ, guitar, and mandolin. They even offered private tutelage to town residents in music and elocution. Until 1894, female education in Antigonish went no further than Grade XII. That year, the door to higher education opened when Mount St. Bernard became affiliated with StFX, which was the first Catholic college in North America to provide courses for women leading to a baccalaureate degree.

REAR VIEW OF
MOUNT SAINT
BERNARD FROM
MORRISON
SCHOOL, C.1918

THE READING
ROOM, MOUNT
ST. BERNARD
COLLEGE,
C.1910

In 1898, a disastrous fire struck the Mount, destroying much of the convent. With the generous help of Bishop Cameron, the townspeople, and other religious communities, the main building was rebuilt and an eastern wing added to it. Expansion continued throughout the twentieth century; Immaculata Hall opened in 1917, Gilmora Hall in 1939, the Pottery School in 1947, the Camden Marguerite Complex in 1961 and Lane Hall in 1967. The buildings that once constituted Mount St. Bernard are now owned by St. Francis Xavier University.

Antigonishers have long remembered the sight of young ladies from the Mount processing two by two along the town's sidewalks on Sundays and holidays. The so-called "parade of wild geese" was led by a group of nuns with two posted in the rear. With such vigilant chaperones, there was little chance for frivolity or flirtation. In their annual calendars, the Sisters of the Congregation of Notre Dame advertised the college's many advantages, including its "healthful surroundings," croquet lawns and the "many beautiful walks" throughout town. General regulations stipulated that boarders should come equipped with a "plain black costume" for Sunday outings, as well as a blue flannel blouse waist for calisthenics and a good jacket; they were to be outfitted as well with a sewing kit, complete toilet set, a table set, replete with cutlery, table napkins, and table ring. The Sisters at the Mount applied themselves with great diligence to moulding their female scholars into "true women," dedicated to Christian devotedness, order, and cultural refinement.

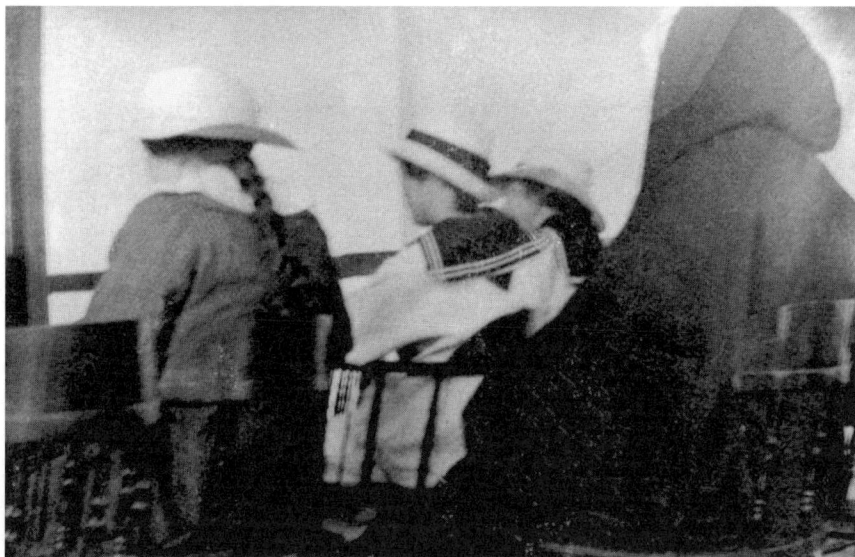

In the late 1880s, there were already promising signs of integration between St. Bernard's Academy and StFX. For example, college professors provided regular instruction to senior-level female students in English literature, physics, and chemistry. They were also given access to the college's laboratory facilities. By 1894, the doors of the college were finally opened to women, providing them with expanded opportunities for higher education. Three years later, four women graduated with BA degrees. St. Bernard's Academy's affiliation with StFX represented a significant turning point in the history of female Catholic higher education in North America. By 1902, there were thirty-three females and eighty-four males in the arts programme at StFX. Initially, female students in their freshman year attended classes at the Mount. By their sophomore year, attending regular classes at the college with the men became the norm. The intermingling of female and male students demanded certain adjustments; chaperoning was a critical issue. At the request of the priests at the college, the CND sisters acted as chaperones for the Mount St. Bernard resident students who attended co-ed classes. Conversation between the sexes while on campus usually drew a stern rebuke.

Chapter 8

Transportation

ROCKS ALONG THE ROAD, ARISAIG TO ANTIGONISH, 1873

Accounts of travel in nineteenth-century Antigonish County were often
a catalogue of horror stories. Sloops or schooners provided considerable
ease of movement of goods in coastal areas. However, travel by land was
a different matter. Well into the 1840s, Nova Scotia was crisscrossed with
rough, blazed trails, and stony bridle paths. Closer to the villages and towns,
the traveller was fortunate enough to encounter roads more conducive

to vehicular traffic. In the early nineteenth century, plans to survey and build a road between Antigonish and Manchester (Guysborough), running through Beech Hill, South River, St. Andrews, Marydale, Beauly, and Glassburn to the county line, were implemented. The so-called Old Manchester Road ran "up hill and down dale," an often arduous sequence of steep undulations (MacDonald 2000, 12). The principal highway was the Great Eastern Road, which led from Pictou to Antigonish via Arisaig and then proceeded along the Manchester Road to the Straits of Canso. Although the connection to Antigonish was the "only road beyond Pictou fit for wheeled vehicles" (Parks, 16) in the 1830s, the coastal route via Ferry Point and Pomquet Ferry through Pomquet and Tracadie to the Straits was little more than "an infamous track covered with rocks and loose stones." (Moorsom, 334) For more venturesome travellers, there was also an alternate route, across the Antigonish Mountains, but it was "scarcely fit for carriages." (Patterson, 393) It required considerable skill to navigate the narrow, rough and lonely stretch between Brown's Mountain and Bailey's Brook even on horseback. Little wonder that the spirits of the residents were lifted when they heard the horn announcing the arrival of the mail from Pictou. The horse trails that served as transportation links to Sherbrooke, County Harbour, and Cape George were not much better. They were choked with roots, proving treacherous for even the most sure-footed horse. In the 1840s, another road connection between St. Andrews and Guysborough was established via Marydale, Caledonia and on into Roman Valley. By mid-nineteenth century, the post road to Antigonish by Marshy Hope Valley was opened to traffic; it was considerably shorter than the long Gulf Shore Road.

Despite these improvements, travel was a bone-shaking, tooth-rattling experience for passengers as the stagecoaches lurched and swayed through muddy ruts, washouts, and sharp turns. Although this means of travel was restricted in the winter months, early accounts relate how the ice on St. George's Bay was so thick that it formed a bridge facilitating contact between Cape George and Cape Breton. It is told that Angus McInnis and his best men walked from the Cape across the ice to Judique on a matrimonial mission—a feat perhaps more foolhardy than heroic.

Well into the late nineteenth century, the horse remained an important cog in both the economy and systems of transportation. However, the advent of the railway, which freed travellers from the constraints of time, space, and weather, sounded the death knell for many traditional forms of transport. So too did the introduction of the automobile, which released a flood of changes. Still, well into the 1940s, road conditions in Antigonish County continued to be primitive. Even cars were regarded as novelties on some back roads. Children in these rural areas delighted in counting the number and models of cars that passed by.

Coastal excursion near Bayfield, c.1910

Second from the left here is Mazie (Cunningham) Irish; second from the right is Ada Parker. Before the arrival of the railway, Antigonishers relied extensively on coastal transportation. Much of the merchandise was transported by vessels, many of which were locally owned and manned. The smaller schooners were able to unload their cargoes at the Landing. The larger vessels, which anchored at such locations as Mahoney's Beach, Jimtown, Monk's Head, Red Point, and Town Point, transferred their goods to lighters or scows. These flat-bottomed boats, propelled by long oars or sweeps, shuttled merchandise to the Lower Landing where it was then unloaded and trucked to town. It was an expensive, time-consuming process. In the early nineteenth century, local inhabitants routinely complained about the upkeep of the tow path as well as the gravel banks, sand banks, brush and trees deposited during flooding. These deposits obstructed the main channel, impeding the movement of boats and rafts, many of which could only pass at high tide. Well into the 1920s, small schooners carrying coal, fish, or produce still came to the public wharf at the Landing, but the costs of truckage to town made this method of transportation unprofitable.

STAGECOACH STOP ON ST. MARY'S STREET, ANTIGONISH, C.1870S

In the early settlement years, most residents travelled on foot. According to popular folklore, the first wheeled carriage visited Antigonish in 1816. As prosperity increased, horse paths replaced primitive blazed trails, eventually evolving into roads traversed by ox carts, farmers' wagons, and the mail driver's two-wheel cart. Antigonish town and county residents keenly felt the lack of regular communication before 1817. They depended on the services of a postman who stopped in the village in February en route to Sydney. It was considered a singular feat when John Macdonald of Williams Point trekked from Antigonish to Halifax and back with a packet of letters in five days. In the 1830s, J. W. Blanchard offered patrons a weekly stage service between Pictou and Antigonish via Arisaig and Malignant Cove. The one-way fare was set at twenty shillings. By 1844 there was year-round, semi-weekly service. In 1852, Hiram Hyde held the contract for carrying mails between West River and Port Hastings as well as Antigonish and Guysborough. On the Guysborough end of the run, he relied on a small and shabby horse-drawn wagon. The mail connection between Cape Breton and the mainland was tenuous at best. Sometimes, mail delivery was delayed by as much as a week. In 1853, Donald McDonald, the ferryman at the strait, ventured out on the floating ice pans, risking life and limb, to meet the mail boat half way.

STAGECOACH
STOP AT
CALEDONIA
HOTEL, MAIN
STREET,
ANTIGONISH,
C.1867–69

Thomas Snow Lindsay, who started out as a manager for Hyde, soon dominated the Antigonish stagecoach business. In June 1860, he was awarded the mail contract to cover the areas between West River (Pictou County) and Antigonish, Antigonish and Sydney, and Antigonish and Guysborough; the entire service was daily by 1865. Lindsay ran a tight operation, headquartered on St. Mary's Street, Antigonish, where he had a stage barn and residence. Passengers awaited the arrival of the stagecoach at the Caledonia Hotel as well as Cunningham's Hotel, later called the Merrimac. Lindsay engaged "good, sober, and careful drivers" and employed no less than forty-six horses. He also purchased several Concord coaches, retired from the Truro-Pictou route, for his run between New Glasgow and Antigonish. These coaches usually required from four to six horses. According to D. G. Whidden, two horses were "generally sufficient to carry, practically, all the passengers and mails" to Cape Breton. The service to Cape Breton boasted few comforts. One American tourist heading for Baddeck in 1873 wrote, "The wagon was drawn by two horses. It was a square box covered with painted cloth. Inside were two narrow seats facing each other, affording little room for the legs of the passengers and offering them no position but a strictly upright one." By 1880, there was a train connection between New Glasgow and Port Mulgrave. The expanding presence of the railway signalled the demise of stagecoaches. They were reduced to "a minor auxiliary service" as travellers increasingly opted for rail service (Evans, 134).

MAIL WAGON EN ROUTE TO SHERBROOKE WITH JOHN ANGUS MACDONALD (THE DRIVER) AND JACK CARROLL, C.1910

In the 1880s, there was a daily stage connection from Antigonish to Sherbrooke via Lochaber. At the same time, the mails were transported to Addington Forks, Cross Roads Ohio, Ohio, and West Side Lochaber twice a week while Cape George, Georgeville, Morristown, Harbour Road, Maryvale, Malignant Cove, Lakevale, North Grant, and Antigonish Harbour had four scheduled runs each week. There was also a semi-weekly stage run from Antigonish to Morristown and Georgeville. Starting in 1901, T. J. Sears operated the stage line between Antigonish, Sherbrooke and Goldboro, and kept coach horses for his business. His Antigonish livery was among the largest in the county, with over forty horses. The daily mail delivery between Antigonish and Sherbrooke by horse and wagon as well as horse and sleigh continued until the late 1930s. According to *McAlpine's Gazeteer and Guide*, the fare for the run between Antigonish and Lochaber Lake in 1904 was $1.25; the trip to Sherbrooke was $2.50. After 1938, mail was transported by car and the once full day's trip was reduced to one-and-a-half hours. In 1939–40, Bruce MacDonald of Sherbrooke made the run in a bus. During the late nineteenth and early twentieth centuries, Alexander Manson's house and carriage shop in North Lochaber was one of the popular stops on this post road. At this location, horses were changed and refreshments obtained. Originally called Oakdell, it was known among travellers as Fourteen Mile House, the approximate distance from the Antigonish Railway Station. Manson served as postal way-office keeper and later postmaster until his death in 1925. The postmaster's home was one of the key centres of community life, a busy spot where people gathered to hear the latest news. In some Antigonish County communities, certain families dominated this occupation for extended periods of time. At Williams Point, the Macdonald family operated the local post office until the 1940s; in Pomquet, the DeYoung family managed the post office for over sixty years.

**HORSE-DRAWN
CARRIAGE
WITH DRIVER
IN TOP HAT ON
MAIN STREET,
ANTIGONISH,
C.1900**

The horse was a familiar feature of life in nineteenth-century Antigonish. The stagecoach service, the buggy ride to the country, and the races on the ice all relied on horse power. Before the arrival of the telephone and train, election results were delivered by horse. Cheers and hoots greeted the messengers, riding froth-covered horses, who galloped in from the polls at the cape, Ohio, Tracadie and other communities. In addition to the buggy, the horse was used to draw a variety of wheeled vehicles including the wagon, the brougham and two-wheeled shay. Horse-drawn vehicles could move at a fair clip, hence the 1888 speed regulation in Antigonish that no driver should "drive his horse faster than a slow or easy trot in or through any part of the Town." Local merchants accommodated this traffic by providing their customers with stabling space. These stables were lively spots where politicking and matrimonial bargaining occurred. By 1900, Antigonish had three local livery stables: Randall's, Sears's and Whidden's. Randall's advertised carriage horses for hire including a team of "beautiful white steeds," popular with newlyweds on their wedding day. As the *Christmas Greetings* for 1898 proclaimed, Randall's also catered to other special occasions: "When you go driving with 'her' on Christmas, get one of F. H. Randall's dandy rigs." Whidden's specialized drafthorses were contracted out to lumber camps. Some of the carriage horses at this stable became household names: The Flying Frenchman, Black Minister, and Red Lightning. Sears's livery stable also rented out horses and buggies for commercial and recreational purposes.

SLEIGH RIDE AT
PITCHERS FARM
WITH ELIZABETH
CAMERON
(LEFT) AND
UNIDENTIFIED
COMPANION,
C.1917

In the winter, travel, especially into town to shop or attend church, was invariably by sleigh or sleds; the latter also proved useful hauling puncheons of molasses or a load of cordwood. The procession of sleighs and horses with their jingling harness along Antigonish's Main Street on New Year's Day was a delightful scene. Here seated in a two-passenger open sleigh is Elizabeth Cameron wrapped in her sleigh robe. The popular cutter was regarded as light, stylish, and comfortable. It was the most effective form of transportation when maneuvering snow-blocked roads.

**BAYFIELD
STATION,
BAYFIELD ROAD,
C.1910**

According to local lore, David Floyd, an Irish immigrant who eventually settled in Springfield, Antigonish County, participated in the historic opening of Nova Scotia's first steam railway in the late 1830s at Albion Mines, Pictou County. He was the fireman on the first run, an occasion attended by several thousand onlookers who cheered the train as well as the parade of horses, bands, and miners. In the 1870s, railway fever swept Antigonish County. The Eastern Extension (later called the Intercolonial Railway) connection between New Glasgow and Antigonish was formally opened on 18 September 1879. It was marked by a gala affair attended by provincial dignitaries and newspaper reporters. An excursion train from New Glasgow included a locomotive, *Antigonish*, decked out in flags, evergreens and flowers. Crowds of Antigonishers greeted the first passenger train with cheers, and then an assemblage of stagecoaches and carriages proceeded to McDonald's Hall for speeches, feasting, and band music. William S. Archibald, then a boy, was a passenger on the first train to pull into Antigonish. Until the completion of a trestle bridge, the railway stopped at Murphy's Mills (Sylvan Valley), about a mile from town. There were no sheds, engine house, or station building, so wagons and carts were required to transport the mail and passengers on the final leg of the journey. By the early 1880s, there were daily express trains as well as freight trains three times a week through Antigonish. No fewer than fifteen stations dotted the line between Marshy Hope and the Strait of Canso. Most of these small stations were wooden structures equipped with a baggage room and a waiting room heated by a coal stove; the Linwood station was little more than a platform and shed.

LINWOOD
RAILWAY
STATION
(TRACADIE),
C.1920

RAILWAY
STATION
AT BRIERLY
BROOK,
C.1920S

Simon Landry, born in 1902, recalled a time when a train trip from Pomquet to Antigonish was ten cents one way. On market days, Tuesday, Thursday, and Saturday, the fare was cheaper; a return ticket was fifteen cents. Local train stations were also busy spots at election time, as enthusiastic voters gathered there to await results communicated by telegraph. In Heatherton, political rivalries ran so deep that Conservatives gravitated to the telephone office while Liberals converged at the railway station to learn about the election's outcome. During the depression, transients gravitated towards the small stations for shelter both day and night. They were also a popular hangout for the sectionmen on the line who stopped there to eat lunch or make some tea or cocoa.

ANTIGONISH RAILWAY STATION UNDER CONSTRUCTION, 1904

At the turn of the century, along with demands for a new railway station in Antigonish came pressure for a railway line from Antigonish to Country Harbour, and from Merigomish to Antigonish via Malignant Cove. These latter proposals never came to fruition. However, in 1908, the original wooden Antigonish Railway station at the East End was replaced by a more substantial brick building. The construction contract was awarded to Rhodes, Curry and Company of Amherst, one of the leading building contractors in Maritime Canada between 1880 and 1920. The station's most distinctive feature was its flared awning-like roof, which offered protective cover for waiting passengers. The station provided more comforts than its predecessor; there was a washroom as well as a men's and ladies' waiting room. In the latter location, women could wait for the train without being offended by tobacco smoke. In addition to these amenities, there was W. G. Cunningham's shuttle service, a tallyho coach, made by Campbell Brothers of Antigonish and pulled by four horses, which offered service on the route from the station.

SECTIONMEN AT JAMES RIVER, (RORY MACDONALD'S HOUSE IN BACKGROUND) C.1902

These sectionmen are, from left to right: Colin MacDonald, Billy Henry Williams, Bob Gordon, Archie "Coll" MacLean, Dan Chisholm and Hector Grant. The Intercolonial Railway provided essential employment to local men. They filled such positions as sectionman (track repair man), agent, lineman, and telegraph operator. The sectionmen were essential to the smooth and safe operation of the railway. They fulfilled myriad tasks, most importantly monitoring the condition of the track and roadbed. They replaced rotten ties, cleaned and filled switch stand lamps, cleared away brush, and erected snow fences. During the winter months, they shovelled snow from station platforms and switches. The men took immense pride in the condition of their assigned section, which they routinely inspected while riding a handcar loaded down with tools. In February 1905, the sectionmen were no match for severe snowdrifts that halted railway traffic at James River for almost fourteen hours.

Dr. Huntley MacDonald and wife with first car in Antigonish, c.1909

In the early twentieth century, the automobile revolution arrived in Antigonish. The first car in Antigonish was allegedly owned by Dr. Huntley MacDonald, grandson of the well-known pioneer physician, Dr. Alexander MacDonald. The four-cylinder vehicle, which boasted a top speed of fifty miles an hour, had a buggy top for the front seat passengers and a bucket seat in the rear. It cost about a thousand dollars. In 1911, MacDonald's car, while responding to a sick call, had an unfortunate encounter with a stonepile at Black Avon. It was salvaged with some makeshift repairs and was used by a local family to transport "many a group of young folk out to country picnics and ball games." (*Casket*, 1 May 1947) Another early car owner was Fred Randall, who operated the Main Street Livery Stables. His new Ford, sporting side curtains and lots of shiny brass, often literally stopped pedestrian and equestrian traffic. C. M. Henry, the local druggist, also purchased a Ford touring car, hoping to use it during the summer months to travel between Antigonish and Jimtown. He eventually disposed of the splendid car, frustrated by local regulations that closed the roads to vehicular traffic three days a week; physicians were exempted from this regulation. This meant that Henry's jaunts to Jimtown were less than efficient; on Friday he would leave for Jimtown, where he was stranded until Tuesday when he could legally return to town. Dr. J. J. Cameron, a prominent local physician, and J. H. Stewart, the egg merchant and tea importer, introduced the town to the Hupmobile built by the Detroit-based company, the Hupp Motor Company. It was hailed as the working man's car, reasonably priced and dependable. Few people mastered the early mysteries of the car as well as Nicholas Landry, who worked initially for Randall's stable. In 1913, A. J. (Phonse) Sears, born in Lochaber, urged his father, T. J., to branch into horseless carriages. This notion blossomed into The Antigonish Garage Company, better known as the Eastern Automobile Company. In February 1916, the company advertised the imminent arrival of five carloads of touring cars and roadsters. The price tag on the touring car was $530; for the roadster, $480. Described in a 1916 Antigonish Board of Trade brochure as "as one of the finest and best equipped garages in Nova Scotia," the company featured Ford cars, but eventually sold such models as Hudson-Essex, DeSoto, and Studebaker. In 1915, they opened an agency in New Glasgow and later added Mabou to their sphere of operations. The demand for cars quickly caught on. In 1913, the company sold five automobiles, while eighteen years later, five hundred cars were sold to customers. Cars made slower inroads into the rural areas. In 1921, Pomquet boasted only one car, which belonged to Howard DeYoung, also employed at Eastern Auto. The arrival of the car signaled the emergence of new traditions and the eclipse of old ones. Car dealerships proliferated, as did pavement. By 1916, Antigonish boasted a macadamized Main Street and fifteen miles (twenty-four kilometres) of well-graded streets. The street sweeper, who had followed the horse-drawn carriages with brooms and handcart, soon became a distant memory. The car's growing popularity also spelled the decline of the pack-carrying peddler who traveled mostly on foot.

STOPPING FOR
REFRESHMENT,
MARY MILLS
BEATON,
ANTIGONISH
COUNTY, 1928

The car had irresistible appeal to people in both urban and rural areas. It epitomized glamour and freedom. Here, proudly positioned in front of Angus MacInnis' house, are two Fords. The happy group, dressed in their finery, look almost as sporty as the vehicles. For Mary Mills Beaton, wife of Angus Beaton, one-time caretaker of the Antigonish Post Office, the car's running board was a convenient spot to sit while sipping a refreshment. Horses and cars did not always mix. In the early days of the so-called "devil machines," it was deemed courteous to stop to allow the buggy driver to dismount and lead his horse past the noisy vehicle. Sometimes sharing the road proved contentious, as one Antigonish physician discovered as he navigated his car along the narrow, winding road to Cape George. He found himself trailing behind a slow wagon and horse which paid no heed to his honking. "We own the road as much as ye do," was the defiant retort of the wagon's driver. There were legislated speeds on the country roads of fifteen miles (forty kilometres) per hour and half that in towns, and travel was restricted on country roads to Monday, Wednesday, and Friday. Penalties for breaking these laws included fines or jail terms. In 1922, Nova Scotia drivers converted from left- to right-side driving; this was largely a concession to American motor-driving tourists.

ROAD ALONG
EAST SIDE
LOCHABER,
MAE CAMERON
INGLIS AT ALEX
CAMERON
AND CHRISTIE
(MCNAUGHTON)
CAMERON'S
FARM,
C.1912–1913

Early cars had their limitations, especially during the winter months. At that time, they were usually raised on blocks and stored until the so-called mud season had passed. Born in 1906, Mary Falt recalled the early motoring days in Antigonish County: "The roads in those days were dirt roads and the motor guides were very specific: 'When you reach the crossroads in Merigomish where there is a big apple tree, take the road to your left,' or 'When you get to James River there is a fork in the road by McKenzie's red barn. Keep straight ahead.'" These photographs show typical road conditions in early twentieth century Lochaber. The muddy road, stencilled with wheel ruts, skirted the lake, meandered along pasture fences and even passed through barnyards.

D. McISAAC AND PETER MacDONALD, ANTIGONISH, C.1916

Even after the introduction of the car, interest in traditional forms of transportation continued. For example, in 1916 the Eastern Automobile Company offered garage services for auto painting and repairing, but also served as a distributor for carriages, wagons, sleighs, harness, robes, and general horse supplies. D. MacIsaac became the regional agent for Chevrolet and operated a modern garage with up-to-date engines and auto supplies. His carriage shop, however, continued to cater to the demand for harness and farm wagons. Similarly, Peter MacDonald at the East End also held an important niche in the market as a dealer in buggies, carriages, team wagons, cart wheels, driving harness, and sleighs. He specialized in Tudhope carriages, which were manufactured in Orillia, Ontario.

SPRINKLING CART, ANTIGONISH, C.1920S

For adults and children alike, the sprinkling cart was one of the more novel vehicles to appear on the streets of Antigonish. The cart was horse-drawn and carried a large, wooden, barrel-like tank filled with water from the West End fire hydrant. It was operated by Rod McLean, a robust six-foot, 200-pound (183 centimetre, 90 kilogram) Cape Bretoner, who perched on a spring-iron seat, regulating the rotating disc of water. The vehicle made the rounds of the town twice a day. Although Main Street had more than adequate width, travellers frequently complained that it was too low and level.

Consequently, it was muddy in wet weather and dusty during dry times. The sprinkling cart therefore served a practical purpose—it dampened the dusty streets during the summer months. Many young boys sprang to life on a hot day when they heard the familiar putt-putt sounds of the sprinkling cart and poised to jump into its cool shower of water. As the number of paved streets increased, Antigonish's early method of dust control quickly fell into disuse.

JOHN O'LEARY'S GAS STATION, LOCHABER LAKE, C.1920S — Gas stations dotted the landscape, catering to the needs of an ever-growing motoring public. At Lochaber Lake, John O'Leary installed a gas pump near his general store. It was typical at this time to erect a gas pump near a busy location. At O'Leary's in the 1920s, there was no service station, only a pump island equipped with a glass cylinder pump crowned by an illuminated globe. By 1934, Antigonish had four filling stations and garages, one of which employed approximately fifteen people.

**TRUCK AND
SLED ON
MAIN STREET,
ANTIGONISH,
C.1940**

Automobiles and horse-drawn vehicles continued to co-exist on the streets
of Antigonish, especially during the winter months, well into the 1940s.
Here in this juxtaposition of the modern and the traditional can be seen A.
E. Whidden's truck and a sled used for hauling barrels of carrots brought
in from Kings County. At this time, the town of Antigonish still retained
its rural appearance. Many houses had barns on their back lots and there
were cow pastures on the outskirts of town. By the Second World War,
there were no fewer than fifty cows housed in stables on eight streets.

Chapter 9

Recreational Pastimes

COSTUME PARTY, ANTIGONISH, C.1890S

Alexander McDougall, who settled in Antigonish in the late 1820s, found the village social scene dreary in the extreme. He complained of the scarcity of balls "or other evening amusements," noting that the women entertained themselves with "lapping tea and scattering scandal, and the men swallowing grog and masticating tobacco." Lord Dalhousie's recollections of his visit to Antigonish in 1817 tell a different story. He recounts an evening of dance, fiddle music, and piping: "our reels were kept up with great Glee, snapping of fingers & all the wildest, rudest & joyous expression of Highland fling; our ladies were neither formal nor shy with us, nor the Gentlemen too sober for the occasion." Among the early pioneers, music, verse, song, dance, and storytelling provided welcome relief to unrelenting daily routines.

Dances in the Keppoch during the early part of the nineteenth century were also lively affairs. Guests, clad in their homespun, anxiously awaited Red Ranald, the parish fiddler, with his fiddle wrapped in Peggie Bheag's red shawl. Soon the floorboards were thudding, the men shed their collars, and there was lots of "pushing and pulling and hauling." (Chisholm scrapbook, 177)

In the mid-nineteenth century there was a flurry of organizations established that embodied the middle class ideals of self-improvement and progress. In 1840, Antigonish had its own Mechanics Institute. Literary clubs or debating societies sprang up in rural communities such as Addington Forks, Marydale, St. Andrews, Dunmore, and Fraser's Mills. By 1853, the Antigonish Literary and Scientific Library had two hundred volumes in its collection. Unfortunately, the history of these literary clubs, societies and institutes remains obscure.

In the second half of the nineteenth century, leisure tastes diversified and entertainment came in many forms, from kitchen parties in local farmhouses to tea meetings to oyster suppers. The Antigonish Highland Society, established in 1861, played a key role in the social life of the town. According to early bylaws, members could "procure and wear on anniversary meetings and other occasions such plaids and bonnets" as they preferred. Their parties were often strenuous affairs such as the Highland Ball in 1877 that started at 7:30 p.m. with a highland reel and continued on to 5:00 a.m., with a brief interruption at midnight for a luncheon. There were other less socially exclusive diversions such as the grand concert at the Antigonish Court House; admission was fifty cents for adults and twenty-five cents for children in 1873. There was also a selection of activities aimed at an audience with loftier ideas of culture. In the 1890s, the Antigonish Amateur Dramatic Club entertained audiences, as did the Phoenix Orchestra, established around 1892. In the early twentieth century, Mount St. Bernard hosted visiting lecturers and vocalists as well as Professor Southwick of Emerson College, a perennial favorite with his Shakespearean readings.

Well into the twentieth century, the traditional frolic retained its appeal in rural areas. When Edmund Purcell of Pleasant Valley built his new barn in 1908, the Purcells hosted an evening house dance attended by 110 people; house dances were almost a weekly occurrence. Dougald Gillis of Pleasant Valley played the bagpipes while George and Davy Jackson of Antigonish performed as fiddlers. The party ended around 4 a.m.

In the Mi'kmaw communities, playing cards and waltes (a traditional game), and attending house dances were standard forms of social interaction. In Acadian communities, card playing ranked among the most popular forms of amusement, especially for raising money for needy local families. There was an admission fee as well as prizes such as mitts, socks, chickens, turkeys, or rabbits.

ROYAL SWINGSTERS, CRYSTAL CLIFFS, 1940

By the late nineteenth century, the parish picnic came into social prominence. This two-day event, consisting of suppers, athletic contests, games of chance, fiddling, and dancing was a crucial and highly popular vehicle for church fund-raising. Among the Mi'kmaq, the pie social was also an important fund-raiser, with the proceeds going towards the costs of the annual Feast of St. Anne.

In Antigonish town and county, one of the most anticipated events of the year was the Fall Fair. Starting in 1863, the Highland Games in Antigonish were also an annual social highlight. Spectators were thrilled by the parade of banners and pipers, athletic competitions and ball. (It is a little known fact that Arisaig also had its own Highland Games during the mid to late 1880s).

During this era, the temperance movement made inroads into the leisure culture of Antigonish. Temperance advocates loudly condemned the pervasive use of alcohol at social gatherings, especially the rural picnics where "black beer sold for five cents a glass and there was a fight every ten yards." (MacGillvray, 4) They called for more carefully planned alcohol-free activities such as strawberry socials and teas. In Antigonish, the local branch of the Women's Christian Temperance Union assembled in coffee

rooms at St. James Church, where they indulged in a respectable programme of readings, duets, recitations and selections of cornet and violin
music. The Band of Hope established in 1889, had weekly meetings for
girls and boys who were rewarded with handsome prizes of books for their
essays on the evils of liquor and tobacco. The Sons of Temperance often
organized picnics such as the one on 1 July 1898 at Dewar's Mills that
was attended by nearly seventy people from Antigonish, who came via the
freight train. The movement spilled into the early twentieth century, with
the League of the Cross, a Catholic organization (nicknamed the League of
the Cork) at the forefront of the cause. As late as the 1930s, its members
advocated more sober forms of recreation, entertaining themselves with
instrumentals and vocal music and playing 45s in their club rooms.

From the late nineteenth century onwards, children enjoyed an increasingly wide range of entertainments. They eagerly awaited the arrival of
the Ryan and Robinson's circus with its menagerie of animals and ring
performances. One of these circus acts was actually Buffalo Bill and His
Wild West Show. The pageant of entertainments in the 1920s included the
arrival of the hurdy-gurdy man with his organ grinder and monkey who
collected pennies in a hat. There was also the annual visit of the Gypsies
travelling in their covered wagons who camped under the willows near the
fall fair grounds on St. Andrew's Street. For local children, it was quite an
adventure to go to their camping site. Of course, there were lots of other
simple summer pleasures such as jumping rope, playing statues, rolling
hoops, going on hay rides, or visiting favourite trout-fishing and swimming
holes. Horseback racing on Hawthorne Street, from MacNaughton's to
MacDougall's, was also great sport. In the 1940s, teenagers at Jimtown and
Mahoney's Beach hung out at a popular haunt called the Old Pine Tree, a
canteen at the junction of the Harbour, Jimtown, and Fairmont roads.

For rural children, the popular social event was the school fair, which
featured competitions in plant collections, sewing, writing, cooking,
growing vegetables, livestock presentations, and public speaking. The
Heatherton school fair in 1926 was the first held in Antigonish County.
By the 1920s, the school was increasingly an important social centre, the
venue for dances, card parties, and socials. At Fraser's Grant school dances,
"The dancers would stir up so much dust that you could not see across the
room." (Fraser's Grant, n.p.)

The introduction of the school dance pointed the way to more pro-
found changes that would transform recreational activities throughout
Antigonish town and county. They became less home-based and more
consumer-oriented, especially as entertainment would be increasingly
focused on the dance hall and the movie theatre.

JOHN ANGUS "SOLOMON" MACDONALD, C.1900

Antigonish County has long been noted for its pipers. Here John Angus stands as a proud embodiment of his Celtic heritage. Born at North Lakevale in October 1871, his family had roots in Eastern Nova Scotia dating back to 1790. The nickname "Solomon" was bestowed on his grandfather, Sandy MacDonald, for his wise pronouncements, and has remained with that family. John Angus passed on his fondness for playing pipes to his son, Danny, "the Piper," or "Saskie." Pipers enjoyed considerable prestige as a beloved entertainers. Like fiddlers, they were honoured guests at weddings, frolics, kitchen parties, and country picnics. No funeral, procession, or parade was considered complete without a piper. They were part of a venerable tradition of performance. Their marches, reels, and jigs captured a wide range of moods and evoked powerful emotions. Even farm animals were not immune to the piper's charms. More than one piper led his cows home by playing the bagpipes. The story of Peter MacDonald of Doctor's Brook epitomizes the deep-seated passion that pipers had for their instruments. Shortly after his mother's death in 1927, MacDonald vowed to abstain from playing his pipes for one whole year. Shortly after, his resolve weakened. Local lumbermen overheard the faint sounds of MacDonald's pipes emanating from the depths of the forest. The promise had proved too hard to keep—no doubt his fellow pipers would have commiserated.

Antigonish, Friday August 8

POSITIVELY THE ONLY SHOW THAT WILL VISIT ANTIGONISH THIS YEAR

FRANK ROBBINS'

New Railroad Circus

ADVERTISEMENT FOR THE FRANK ROBBINS' NEW RAILROAD CIRCUS, 1884

The arrival of circus performers in town always generated great excitement. For children it was a dream come true. In 1862, Antigonishers were mesmerized by the daring aerial feats of Alfred Elson who navigated blindfolded a tightrope extended between the upper window of Cunningham's Hotel and the Harrington's house. Frank Robbins's Circus promised more breathtaking marvels including Queen Sarbro, the Royal Japanese Juggler; Mlle McDonald, the Female Somersault Rider; Andrew Caffney, the Modern Hercules; The Decoma Brothers, Wonderful Aerial Bicycle Performers; and The Irksovich Brothers, the Russian Skeleton Wonders. This troupe included an even more bizarre panoply of entertainers, including The Tatooed Lady, the Three-Headed Vocalist and The Hindoo Snake Charmer.

"Riding High,"
Bayfield,
c.1910

Left to right are an unidentified woman, Lucy Cunningham and John Lynwood Randall.

BICYCLE ENTHUSIASTS AT LOCHABER, C.1895

Left to right, the enthusiasts in the front row are: Milton Manson, unidentified man, Roberta (Sinclair) Kirk, Mr. and Mrs. George Manson, Mr. and Mrs. Alex Manson, and Mary Lee Manson; in the back row: an unidentified woman and Charlie Manson. Nova Scotians' infatuation with the bicycle began with the high wheel bicycle, which was introduced to the province in the early 1880s. Despite crude road conditions, clubs, race meets and tours proliferated and wheel men explored the countryside on their gleaming new playthings. The high wheel's most distinctive features were the large front wheel and the small back wheel, above which was positioned a small step by which the rider mounted the tricky machine. When American tourist Lyman H. Bagg visited Cape Breton around 1887, his high wheel was "greeted as a wonder-compelling novelty." (Watts, 19) His travels took him through Antigonish, where he estimated forty to fifty bicycles in existence. By the mid 1890s, the high wheel was increasingly regarded as old-fashioned. It was eclipsed by the popular safety bicycle and soon vanished from Nova Scotia's roads. John Lynwood Randall, the son of a tanner and currier in Bayfield, enjoyed cavorting on this high wheel, but it was clearly an outdated curiosity by 1910. Young women became enthusiastic fans of the safety bicycle; it became an important liberating force offering independence and freedom. Clearly, Lochaber's Manson family, men, women, and children enjoyed this entertaining craze and look poised to go on an outing.

As early as the 1840s, Antigonish boasted its own amateur band. It consisted of at least seventeen performers playing a range of instruments from French horn to trombone. One of their concerts in May 1846 attracted an audience of around 250 people; several carriages even came from Guysborough for the performance. By the 1870s, the Antigonish Brass Band came on the scene. It provided monthly entertainments at McDonald's Hall and occasional musical interludes at functions of the Antigonish Highland Society. The Post Office Square was also enlivened by their public performances. In May 1896, the Citizen's Band, composed largely of new members, made its first public appearance in front of the courthouse. On special occasions, the Antigonish Band looked resplendent in their uniforms, which consisted of dark blue coats adorned with gold braid, along with matching black pants with a gold stripe and a hussar helmet crowned with a white plume. They appeared frequently at the local band stand, originally situated on the corner of Main and College streets. The octagonal structure, reminiscent of a summerhouse, was a picturesque venue for evening and holiday concerts. It was built by Duncan Chisholm and his son in 1892 and could accommodate around twenty bandsmen. The Antigonish Band was also a popular addition at summer picnics and skating carnivals, and their free summer concerts on the circular porch of the Royal George Hotel always attracted an appreciative audience. The band strove for professionalism and by 1898 practiced regularly in the town's engine house. Its reputation reached beyond Antigonish. In 1882, they traveled to Baddeck to play at a grand picnic in aid of St. Michael's Church. One of the band's early members was William Turnbull, later superintendent of the fish hatchery at Fraser's Mills. He started playing as a young boy and later served as its bandmaster.

In the black community of Antigonish County, much music was to be found at home and church. Here the human spirit usually sprang forth in song. Entertainment was often practical and simple, and wood-chopping parties, quilting bees, and barn raisings were all part of life in places such as Rear Monastery and Upper Big Tracadie. For these communities, the Baptist church was the social centre. Church socials were well attended and few residents missed the annual church picnic at Tracadie United Baptist Church, which reunited friends and relatives alike. At this social highlight of the year, the women did much of the cooking outdoors and served substantial meals. On the church field there was an ice cream booth, fashioned from boards and boughs. A covered platform, erected a respectable distance from the church, served as a stage for square dancing and fiddle music. The church as a matter of principle did not accept monies raised from the dance; the money went instead to pay the fiddlers and other expenses. The merriment continued into the early hours, illuminated by the glow of kerosene lamps; the children were usually banished to bed shortly before dusk.

Recreations also included card games and house dances, the latter animated by the lively strains of fiddle music. The Jackson brothers of Antigonish, George and Davy, delighted dance hall audiences in both Antigonish town and county with their fiddle playing. During the Christmas season of 1898, George participated in a presentation of magic, light vaudeville, and dance given by the Back Diamond Variety Company at McDonald's Hall. He also performed on CJFX radio during its early years. The fiddling technique of these two sons of a one-time labourer and "General servant" was regarded as highly original. With nimble fingers, they played such popular tunes as "The Mockingbird," to dance halls of tapping and flying feet. Their rendition of this song bore an uncanny resemblance to the twittering sounds of birds. From boyhood, the two brothers were inseparable in both work and play and lived on the outskirts of Antigonish, near Highway 7.

GEORGE JACKSON AND FRIEND BECKY, C.1890

PICNIC AT LOCHABER, C.1890S

Summer was the season of picnics, strawberry festivals, and bazaars. Rural picnics were an especially favourite summertime event during the late nineteenth and early twentieth centuries. They were popular methods for fund-raising. For example, the 1883 picnic at Malignant Cove in aid of St. Margaret's Church drew over 1,200 people. In the summer of 1910, St. Vincent de Paul Society members drove by carriage to a picnic in Pomquet with a piper leading the way. Some of the more organized affairs featured bough-covered booths for refreshments and games and even a dance platform. Children eagerly looked forward to sampling such treats as strawberry and chocolate ice cream, penny candies, ginger ale, root beer, and sarsaparilla pop. The young men, some of whom had rented a horse and carriage from an Antigonish livery stable to attend the event, had other things on their minds—namely courtship. They anxiously awaited a glimpse of the young women who were home from Boston, and looked forward to the eight-hand reels and the fiddle tunes of George Jackson and Lauchie Gillis.

LAWN TENNIS AT CRYSTAL CLIFFS, c.1900

A visit to the Crerar Farm (known locally as Crystal Cliffs) at the turn of the century was a social highlight. The Crerar establishment was an impressive one, with a large residence, farmer's cottage, barn, outbuildings, and apple orchard. A row of linden trees lined the road to the house. By Antigonish standards, the Crerars, from Pictou, enjoyed a life of almost aristocratic affluence and pleasure. Their leisure time was consumed by boating, playing tennis and socializing with friends, relatives, and famous visitors. One of their most prominent guests was Lord Beaverbrook. The Crerars' circle of friends also included Antigonish's elite who travelled from town in their carriages to attend the exclusive soirées. There was also a steady traffic of visitors between The Manor and Jimtown with its budding colony of cottages. Idyllic summer days were spent yachting and attending tennis and lawn parties hosted by the Crerars. The summer resort at Jimtown, set in the midst of rolling meadowland, was the creation of Captain James MacDonald (Denoon). It started as a modest operation with a small number of cottages fashioned from a derelict lobster factory. By the twentieth century, there were seven cottages, all quaintly named, the most colourful of which was called Skunk's Rest. They were rented out on a seasonal basis with requests for reservations coming from as far away as Montreal and Boston. Many of the summer residents were local families who moved some of their furniture, and even their cows, down to the seaside for the summer season. By the late 1920s, most of the cottages were owned outright by some of Antigonish's elite: R. R. Griffin, P. M. Cunningham, A. L. Kerr, G. R. Brine, Dr. J. J. Cameron, C. M. Henry and A. J. Sears. Changes were also in store for Crystal Cliffs. Financial reverses along with the personal toll of the First World War eroded the opulent lifestyle of the Crerars. In 1918, they sold Crystal Cliffs to John Kennedy, a well-known railway contractor. From 1935 to 1949, the property was owned by the Sweets and run as a summer inn. Despite changes in ownership, Crystal Cliffs retained its charm. In 1947, the Department of Mines acquired Crystal Cliffs as the perfect location for a school of geology and surveying. The facility, with its added new features of a cookhouse and six residential cabins, was utilized by the Massachusetts Institute of Technology for ten years.

"NEWEL
AND WIFE,"
MI'KMAW
COUPLE AT THE
ANTIGONISH
LANDING, 1913

HEADING FOR
THE LANDING
WITH BROWNIE
CAMERAS, BIG
HATS, AND
LOLLIPOPS,
C.1910

A trip to The Landing was a popular outing for courting couples, children, and families. The area teemed with wildlife, everything from heron to osprey, from muskrat to deer. There was always the novelty of catching a glimpse of the trains. At the Landing, visitors could always entertain themselves birdwatching, hunting for clams, picnicking, and punting in a flat-bottomed boat. An excursion over to Falt's Island, situated in the harbour, was an exciting side jaunt. Navigating through the eel grass and shoals along the shoreline required some skill, but passage was facilitated by small spruce trees that marked the meandering channel.

UNIDENTIFIED
PHOTOGRAPHER
AT GASPEREAUX
LAKE, 1901

Photography was an all-consuming passion for Victorians. Almost every aspect of life, such as sporting events, economic activities, and royal visits came under the eye of the camera. Antigonishers readily embraced the camera in its infancy. John Boyd, founder of the *Casket*, familiarized himself with pioneering photographic techniques. His Antigonish office included an upstairs ambrotype room equipped with skylights. Angus McIsaac, Sr., of Caledonia Mills, learned the mechanics of early photography while employed by Boyd. Nicknamed "the Artist," he became proficient in the ambrotype process, which was a less expensive alternative to the daguerreotype and broadened photography's reach to a middle class clientele during the mid-nineteenth century. W. P. Simpson, who opened a photography studio over Charles Harrington's store, and Colin "The Chief" Chisholm joined the ranks of professional local photographers in the 1860s and 1870s. The Big Painter, Alexander MacDonald of Antigonish (1829–1910), who belonged to a family renowned for their musical and poetic talents, also distinguished himself as a photographer. Although he lacked any formal training, this one-time blacksmith, house painter, and mason enjoyed a reputation for portraiture. The 1871 census lists Alexander as well as two other brothers as photographers in the MacDonald household. As late as 1894, MacDonald advertised group pictures for families and operated a professional portrait studio on West Street, Antigonish.

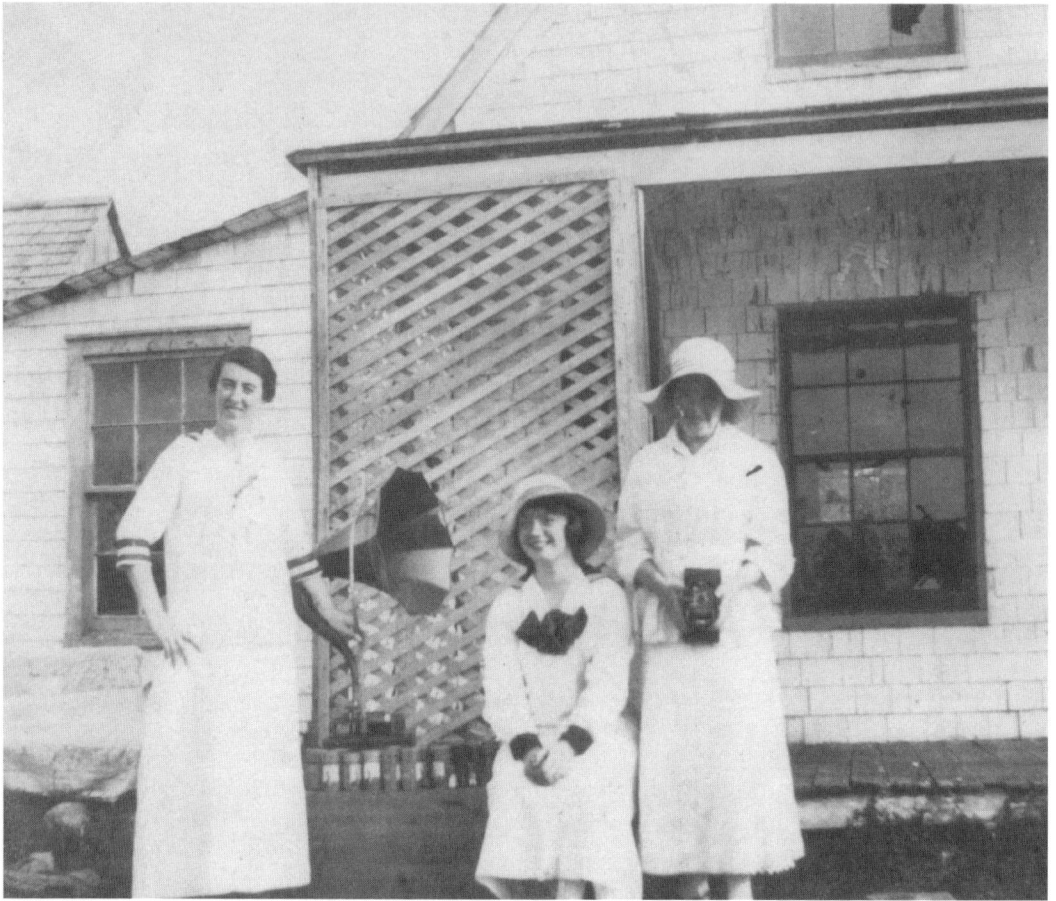

Lewis Rice of Montreal, who opened a studio in New Glasgow in the 1870s, also recognized the potential of the growing photography market in Antigonish. He established Rice's Photo Room in Gregory's building and catered to children and family groups as a specialty. At one point, he even operated out of a railway car which he called Rice's Railroad Photo Studio. George Waldren, who came to Nova Scotia from Kingston around 1890, followed in Rice's footsteps. He bought out the latter's New Glasgow business and opened a branch studio in Antigonish around 1900. Waldren was no dilettante. For almost five decades, he documented the human side of life in eastern Nova Scotia. In the 1890s, the nucleus of professional photographers in Antigonish also included Charles McIntosh and his brother-in-law, Charles Reid. By the 1880s, mass-produced cameras became increasingly accessible to the public. As early as 1900, the famous Brownie became a popular plaything for amateurs who enjoyed its speed and mobility. Here a trio of young Antigonish women are shown with two fashionable forms of entertainment, the phonograph (along with a row of cylinders) and a Brownie camera.

ALEX "LE LOUP" DEWOLFE AND UNKNOWN FRIEND FROM POMQUET, C.1910

Most Acadians grew up with music, and their households had at least one instrument. In Pomquet, the premier fiddling family was the DeWolfes. This family tradition started in the 1870s, with John "Le Loup" DeWolfe, a farmer and cobbler at Pomquet Head. Like most nineteenth-century Maritime cobblers who itinerated from home to home making shoes for local families, Le Loup travelled to William's store in Bayfield where he made shoes for the fishermen. John's family produced at least five fiddle players: William, Alex, Remi, Timothy (Timme), and Mary Elizabeth; the latter daughter was actually a Sister of Mercy. This photograph shows a broadly-smiling Alex tuning up his fiddle, which is adorned with ribbons. The next generation of DeWolfes who became popular musicians starting in the 1910s consisted of at least five fiddle players and one stepdancer. In the 1950s, Leo DeWolfe and his twin brother, Theo DeWolfe, were keepers of this family's fiddle tradition as members of Antigonish's popular Happy Go Luckys.

UNIDENTIFIED
MOUNT ST.
BERNARD
STUDENTS WITH
SNOWSHOES ON
MAIN STREET,
C.1910

At Mount St. Bernard College, regulations were stringent. Evening outings were strictly monitored and late arrivals were penalized. The sisters strove to balance the elements of work, play, and instruction. Although they admonished their students to be "temperate in recreation," they did not deny them the opportunity for jollity, and the female boarders at Mount St. Bernard College forged lifelong friendships through their recreational activities. Diversions came in the form of guest lectures, dramatic perform-ances, recitations and concerts at Immaculata Hall, autumn picnics at the Landing, excursions to the top of Sugar Loaf, afternoon visits to Brine's Ice Cream Parlor, at-homes with music, dancing, games and "dainty" colla-tions, sports activities such as tennis and basketball, and society organiza-tions. In the 1920s the tradition of the annual junior prom began. The graduation teas and the Bishop's Feast Day were favourite annual tradi-tions, the latter usually marked by a stroll to St. Ninian's Cemetery to gather mayflowers. The winter months brought merriment in the form of sleigh drives, tobogganing, and skating. By 1921, there was an open-air rink on the college grounds: "What a chance for stargazing!" exclaimed one student. "Mount girls" were even more thrilled by skating parties at the St. Francis Xavier rink: "A happy group of girls was soon assembled and off to the rink we fairly flew. What a delightful time we had." (*Memorare*, May 1918, 34) The black-and-white silent movies in Immaculata Hall were a popular treat. In June 1920, students watched the landmark epic film *Birth of a Nation* five years after its American premiere. Games at St. Francis Xavier University always drew a crowd of cheering young female students from the Mount. In the 1930s, they attended X-Men hockey games once or twice a week and were known to "holler their heads off up to the last whistle" at the X-Men's rugby games (Cote, 30).

CLARA SEAMAN'S GARDEN, ANTIGONISH, C.1910S

Gardening occupied the leisure time of some of Antigonish's middle and upper class women. This pastime mirrored the late nineteenth century surge of interest in nature and landscape gardening. Gardening clubs, horticultural societies, seed companies, and gardening guides proliferated as North America found itself in the grip of urbanization and industrialization. Clara Cunningham Seaman was one of Antigonish's premier gardeners. Her garden was a lush paradise of roses, peonies, and hollyhocks and served as a decorative stage for family gatherings and tea parties. In 1914, Clara swept the categories for flowers and vegetables at the fall fair. One of her greatest honours was the fact that the bouquet presented to Lady Byng during her Antigonish visit came from the Seaman's Court Street garden. Clara's interest in gardening took on crusading fervour. She was a driving force as one of the members of the managing committee overseeing the "domestic department" of the annual fall fair. As one of the founders of the Ladies' Civic League, she made landscape improvements one of its main platforms and even offered Antigonish boys and girls prizes for the best window flower boxes. In August 1915, William D. Cameron remarked on the cultivation of flowering plants throughout the town and the decorative floral displays on the balcony of the Merrimac Hotel and the Royal George. He attributed this beautification to the impact of the Ladies' Civic League. Two years later, he noted favourably the activities of the School Children's Union, who were planting and cultivating vegetable gardens. In both the county and town, the travelling peddler was often the source of flowering plants and seedlings.

FUND-RAISER AT THE HARRIS HOUSE, ST. MARTHA'S HOSPITAL, C.1918

In late-nineteenth-century Antigonish, there was always a flurry of teas, musicals, dances, card parties, and bazaars as fund-raisers. Few social events rivaled the appeal of the grand bazaars or great picnics that helped generate funds for the cathedral. The grand bazaar staged in 1871 was a fund-raising event of unparalleled proportions. Crowds streamed in from the county, and even Cape Breton; one contemporary newspaper reported that no fewer than 375 boats were drawn up on the beach near Gillis Cove during the bazaar. One Gillis family recollected feeding thirty strangers. Fund-raisers were sometimes elaborate affairs. In August 1897, the Gregorys at Fernwood hosted a garden party to aid St. Paul's Anglican Church. Guests were treated to the musical entertainment of the Citizen's Band, croquet, lawn tennis, games, refreshments, and an evening illumination display. The local hospital also relied on fund-raisers as a source of revenue. In the early twentieth century, the medical needs of Antigonishers were served nobly by the Sisters of St. Martha. In 1906 they opened a cottage hospital at the Campbell House on St. Ninian Street. It was a humble improvisation that accommodated no more than six patients. The location of the second hospital was far more propitious. The Harris House, owned by C. E. Harris, a bank agent, became the site of a twenty-bed, three-storey hospital in 1907. The congregation purchased and converted this spacious family dwelling—one of the most handsome residences in Antigonish—into "a house of mercy on a rock." (*Souvenir* n.p.) Overcrowding became a serious problem. The sisters' hospital expanded at a rapid rate, with the addition of a new three-storey wing in 1912. The private rooms and wards in the fifty-bed facility were pushed beyond capacity, often admitting as many as seventy-five patients. Six years later, the roof of the Harris house was raised to accommodate six more beds. Operating with limited means, the sisters endured considerable financial strain, alleviated somewhat by donations, hospital picnics, patients' fees, and government subsidies.

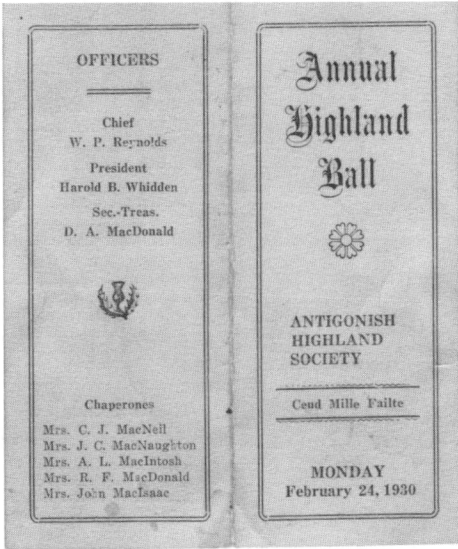

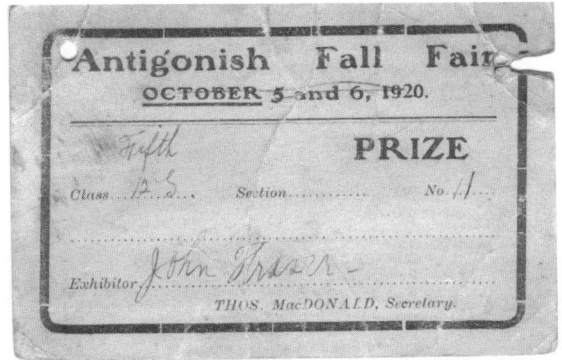

OFFICERS

Chief
W. P. Reynolds

President
Harold B. Whidden

Sec.-Treas.
D. A. MacDonald

Chaperones
Mrs. C. J. MacNeil
Mrs. J. C. MacNaughton
Mrs. A. L. MacIntosh
Mrs. R. F. MacDonald
Mrs. John MacIsaac

Annual
Highland
Ball

ANTIGONISH
HIGHLAND
SOCIETY

Ceud Mille Failte

MONDAY
February 24, 1930

Antigonish Fall Fair
OCTOBER 5 and 6, 1920.

PRIZE

Class .... Section .... No. ....

Exhibitor John Fraser

THOS. MacDONALD, Secretary.

PROGRAMME FOR ANNUAL HIGHLAND BALL, 1930

PRIZE CARD FOR ANTIGONISH FALL FAIR, 1920

The Annual Highland Ball was a social highlight for many Antigonishers. In February 1930, attendees were treated to orchestral music and the culinary creations of the Royal George chef. Back in 1884, the Highland Ball was a far less grand affair. It was held in St. Andrew's Hall, which was adorned with bunting, flags, and Chinese lanterns. The guests, fortified by Scotch scones, oat cakes, and country cheese, enjoyed a lively mixture of Scotch reels, quadrilles, and lancers into the "wee sma' hours." Agriculture exhibitions have had a long tradition in Antigonish County. In 1863, the village hosted the Eastern Counties Exhibition of Agricultural Products and Domestic Industry. Over 510 animals, the principal portion from Antigonish County, were exhibited in the fields of the Hon. W. A. Henry, at the far end of College Street. St. Andrew's Hall accommodated the display of root crops, cereals, and domestic manufactures, including hearth rugs, balmoral skirts, bed quilts, shawls, and plaids. By the 1880s, the Antigonish County Exhibition was a large-scale demonstration of agricultural and domestic prowess. The offshoot of this tradition was the annual fall fair, starting around 1906, which drew large crowds. This event was originally held in late September or early October on the Elm Grounds and provided farmers and gardeners alike with an opportunity to showcase their vegetables, fruit, flowers, and prize livestock. While the men showed off their purebreds, women were encouraged to exhibit homespun textiles, decorative handiwork, plant varieties and culinary specialties. Children under sixteen were also welcomed as contributors of initialed handkerchiefs, crocheted lace, dressed dolls and samples of mending or patching. The Fall Fair also featured sideshows, games of chance and dance platforms that reverberated with the impact of square-dancing and and step-dancing.

HALLOWEEN PLAY AT MOUNT ST. BERNARD, 1922

An account of the Halloween party at Mount St. Bernard in 1922 reads as follows: "An air of mystery in keeping with the traditions of Spookland prevailed all afternoon. That the Seniors and Juniors were concocting "Something" was evident. But what could it be? We wondered—waited— and were finally rewarded at eight o'clock by a most original and novel entertainment." In the 1920s, Halloween was celebrated at the Mount by all sorts of amusements including lantern slides, music, ghost stories, and bobbing for apples. Students delighted in the pumpkin lanterns and the costumed witches and elfin sprites. The traditional furag that involved searching for the ring and button in the mixture of oatmeal and whipped cream always generated great excitement.

OFF TO THE SPOOK HOUSE, CALEDONIA MILLS, FEBRUARY 1922

The male students at St. Francis Xavier University found recreational outlets in such sports as hockey, rugby, and boxing. They also escaped the academic grind by joining the debating society, *Xaverian*, dramatic club, athletic association, and college orchestra. Walks to the summit of Sugar Loaf, the annual junior prom, movies at Immaculata Hall, and later the chaperoned dances at the Celtic Hall were welcome breaks from the monotonous routine of schedules and regulations. The tough disciplinary regimen that policed the interaction of male and female students drew fire from some undergraduates. One frustrated suitor lamented: "A Mount girl is something like a mirage. A thing seen only under unusual conditions and only for a short time. If a dance is arranged the boys must beg for the girls' release. Once obtained the girl like a rented costume must be returned under a time limit, even before the dance is ended." (Cameron 2000, 255–56) In the winter of 1922, the poltergeistic-like happenings at Alexander "Black John" MacDonald's homestead at Caledonia Mills captured international headlines. There was a steady stream of curiosity seekers who travelled by sleigh to the lonely farm. Students from StFX, some wrapped in their buffalo robes, joined the procession. Their interest was piqued by the bizarre stories about Spook's Farm and the handsome reward of two hundred dollars offered to anyone who solved the ghostly mystery of the small farming community of Caledonia Mills.

CELTIC HALL, MAY 1919

The first hall in Antigonish was probably St. Andrew's Hall, on the corner of Sydney and Main Streets. It served as the venue for the annual Antigonish Highland Society balls and doubled as a military drill hall. It was later eclipsed by McDonald's Hall, located on the upper floor of Allan (Denoon) MacDonald's general store. During the late nineteenth and early twentieth centuries, this popular locale accommodated dances, bachelor's balls, Christmas celebrations, and political rallies; it served as Liberal headquarters at election time. For one brief interlude, it also housed James Kelso's shooting gallery. The hall also welcomed interesting guests, including the famous saloon smasher, Carrie Nation, who descanted on the evils of tobacco and liquor. In 1905, the Catholic Mutual Benefit Association constructed the Celtic Hall. This memorable landmark on The Main became a focal point of the social, political, and cultural life in Antigonish. The Celtic Hall, boasting a theatre with a stage and balcony as well as a seating capacity for five hundred patrons, served as the forum for social gatherings, elections, political gatherings, recruitment meetings, and graduations. On 15 May 1917, the students processed from Mockler Hall to Celtic Hall, with graduating caps and gowns on their arms, to receive their degrees. Shortly after the hall opened, the newly formed women's basketball team used the facility for their practices. The Celtic Hall boasted ample room for the performances of such popular stage troupes as the Mae Edward Players and H. Price Webber Company. It also showcased Shakespearean readings, local plays and musicals, housed one of the best known dance halls in the area and operated as the town's movie theatre. Many Antigonish children reveled in their blissful Saturday afternoons, watching black-and-white movies at the Celtic Hall; admission was only five cents. There was the occasional opera singer as well as travelling shows like *Ten Nights in a Bar Room* and *Over the Hill to the Poor House*. In 1939, the hall was purchased by R. K. MacDonald and W. E. Landry, who remodelled the basement and added three bowling lanes and a billiard room with three tables. In the late 1940s, the Celtic Hall held Saturday afternoon dances for StFX students and nursing students who swung to the band tunes of the Happy Go Luckys. The Hall was lost in a fire in 1962.

OLD CAPITOL THEATRE, ANTIGONISH, 1939

Pictured here are Olaf Fraser (left), projectionist, and Reggie Leadbeater. Moving pictures debuted in Antigonish at the College Hall in December 1900. The Biograph Exhibition, produced by the Biograph Company, treated Antigonish audiences to a selection of footage of Pope Leo XIII and the Boer War: admission was twenty-five cents and reserved seats were thirty-five cents. Edison's Waragraph arrived at McDonald's Hall in January 1901 and stirred viewers with its footage of the Boer War. As the fledgling film industry captured the popular imagination, movie houses proliferated throughout North America. The old Capitol Theatre was built in the late 1930s by W. E. Landry. It was a pale reflection of the elaborate big city movie palaces of the previous decade. Still, the theatre, which was operated by the Saint John firm of Bernstein and Lieberman, captivated audiences who were more than willing to spend their leisure dollars watching the latest Hollywood releases. The movie theatre consisted of a centre box office, a lobby trimmed in gold paint, a candy shop, a projection room, stage, proscenium arch, and plush covered seats for around 540 people. In the 1940s, there were shows every day (except Sunday) and matinees each Wednesday and Saturday. Lacking a marquee, the Capitol Theatre used the poster board near the theatre for advertising. It was plastered with large posters promoting the movies that changed every two days. The old Capitol Theatre sometimes showcased live acts like Hank Snow, the Singing Ranger, who toured throughout Canada in the 1940s. The old Capitol Theatre burned down in 1965 while the movie *Mary Poppins* was in town. Changing public tastes in Antigonish did not go unremarked. The Church, which closely monitored local cultural standards, adopted a high moral tone in 1910, expressing the need to censor harmful movies. The lurid posters on the poster board often elicited critical comment.

HAPPY GO LUCKYS, C.1947–49

These Happy Go Luckys are, from left to right, Theo DeWolfe, Henry Snook, Leo DeWolfe, Tommy Grant, and Frank "Fanny" Pelly. The Happy Go Luckys charmed audiences with their polkas and round dances into the early 1950s. They appeared primarily in Antigonish, but their gigs also took them to Shebrooke, Mulgrave, Pomquet, Heatherton, Port Hawkesbury, Williams Point, and Tracadie. The composition of the group changed from time to time. Benny Leadbeater, the local barber, joined later as a saxophonist; he also distinguished himself as a member of such groups as X-Men of Note, The Flamingos, and the Peerless Orchestra in New Glasgow. Heatherton-born Leo DeWolfe made his first public appearance around fifteen years of age as a performer at the Heatherton Hall; he gave a rendition of "Old Black Joe" accompanied by Aubrey Carmel playing the ukelele. During the war, the popular Wednesday night barn dances at Crystal Cliffs were legendary. The crowds, eager to hear the big band rhythms of Gib Whitney and the Antigonish Orchestra, sometimes numbered as many as three hundred people.

MISS SADIE
FRANCIS AND
RICHARD
JOHNSON,
HEATHERTON,
C.1938

Richard Johnson, along with his brother, Charlie, were highly regarded as good hunters in their community. They also had a flair for music and performed in a band. They sometimes played alongside Joe Marble of Heatherton, a gifted Mi'kmaw fiddler, who started entertaining at dances at the tender age of ten years. Joe's father, Peter J. Marble, made him his first fiddle, created from a cigar box and twine; the bow was made of ash and black thread. On this homemade instrument, the eight-year-old Joe managed to pick out The Irish Washerwoman by ear. After that, his love for fiddle music as well as the traditional songs of his people became insatiable. In 1939, he performed for several CBC radio broadcasts in Halifax. Throughout the 1940s and 1950s, Marble was a favourite performer at house dances. He died in 1960; a picture of a fiddle is etched on his tombstone.

ROBBY
ROBERTSON
AND CLYDE
NUNN AT CJFX,
1943

The radio station CJFX went on the air at 6 p.m., 25 March 1943. It had been approved in principle by the StFX Board of Governors and Atlantic Broadcasters Limited, a company formed in 1941. Many of its shareholders were StFX alumni. Dr. Dan McCormack of StFX was president of the board of directors and Clyde Nunn, a StFX graduate, who had previous commercial radio experience in Sydney, was appointed general manager. Gordon MacDougall and Rev. Ernest Clarke of the StFX physics department provided innovative technical expertise. One of the station's primary objectives was to promote the Antigonish Movement's blueprint for adult education. Another principle of operation was that general entertainment programs should foster local talent and promote regional culture. On that opening night there were violin performances by John Y. Gillis of MacKinnon's Harbour and Angus Allan Gillis of Upper Margaree accompanied by Mrs. W. J. MacDonald, a popular organist at St. Ninian's Cathedral. Michael MacDonald of Antigonish rendered piano selections. Dan Joe MacEachern, president of the Antigonish Highland Society, gave some remarks in Gaelic; thus, the celtic connection was there from the beginning. Time slots were later set aside for local artists. One program, which attracted some local performers, was "Fun at Five," hosted by Clyde Nunn. It proved to be popular for many years. So too did the traditional fiddle tunes of The Highland Four, a group consisting of Wilfred Gillis, Angus Macquarrie, Jay MacDonald, fiddlers, and John (Roddie Angus) MacDonald on the piano.

In 1945, a group of StFX faculty produced a program called "University of the Air," through which information was provided on social and economic problems, science, nature, health and home economics. Rev. Joe A. MacDonald of StFX started a weekly series in 1943 called "Labor School of the Air" and later Rev. George Kane, a faculty member, offered a course called "Radio Workshop" that enabled his students to familiarize themselves with broadcasting techniques. Both students and faculty worked as radio announcers, the best known being Danny Gallivan and Ann Terry MacLellan. In those initial years, under the direction of Clyde Nunn and some university faculty, CJFX promoted the ideas of social conscience and greater cultural awareness.

From left to right, these local children are Adelaide Adams, Eileen Adams, Marguerite Roberts, and Charlotte Roberts. For young people in Antigonish, a trip to Ballantyne's Cove Wharf, especially on a Sunday afternoon, was always a welcome diversion. Childhood pleasures still possessed a simple innocence in the 1940s. Entertainment included games like 45s, donkey, and checkers and activities like school concerts, coasting and skating on The Pond. Picking blueberries at Rear Georgeville, enjoying Don Messer and His Islanders on the battery radio, or listening to the old phonograph crank out Yankee Doodle—these were all memorable experiences for the Adams children at the Cape. Few events generated as much excitement as locating a pen pal through the *Family Herald.* For many children at the cape, the greatest novelty was the infrequent visit to town with the mail car, to attend such annual highlights as the Fall Fair and Highland Games.

Fiddle music enlivened many formal and informal entertainments in Antigonish County. According to George Murphy's recollections, the master fiddlers were highly esteemed and the best chair in the household was reserved for them as honoured guests. They received only a nominal payment for their services, a dollar or a bottle of liquor or both. In Arisaig, for example, musicians like Angus Macquarrie, fiddler and piper, Jay MacDonald, fiddler, Joe "Miller" MacDonald, accordion player, John Macquarrie, mandolin player, and Wilfred Gillis, fiddler, played for countless kitchen parties, schoolhouse dances, picnics, and weddings during the 1930s and 40s. The musicians were not exclusively men. For example, Annie Jane Kennedy (later Chisholm), who worked at the Cribbons Wharf lobster plant around 1915, played the fiddle for extra money. Even in her early twenties, she was regarded as a gifted player. One of the county's most memorable musicians was Hughie A. MacDonald (1889–1976), known variously as Hughie Number Eleven, Hughie the Fiddler, and The Polka King. His nickname of Hughie Number Eleven harked back to his pioneering ancestors who had settled at lot number eleven. Born in Lanark into a musical family, Hughie was a popular guest at barn raisings and ploughing frolics. He enjoyed the status of a local celebrity, for his music reached a wide audience through the Highland Ball, Highland Games, CJFX radio, and Bernie MacIsaac's Celtic Music store. Hughie was a versatile fiddler, but he favoured the polka with its sprightly rhythm. Some of his most requested tunes were "The Honeymoon Polka," "The Crooked Stovepipe," and "The Starlight Waltz." During the mid-1930s, he traveled to Montreal, accompanied by Bess Siddall MacDonald and Colin J. Boyd of Lakevale, to record his first 78 rpm's, including a selection of jigs and polka melodies. They were released under the Celtic label. Hughie has been called "one of the first fiddlers to record Scottish fiddle music" in Canada (Thirteenth Annual, 5). The MacDonald fiddling legacy lives on in Hughie Number Eleven's grandchildren, present-day fiddlers Kendra and Troy MacGillvray.

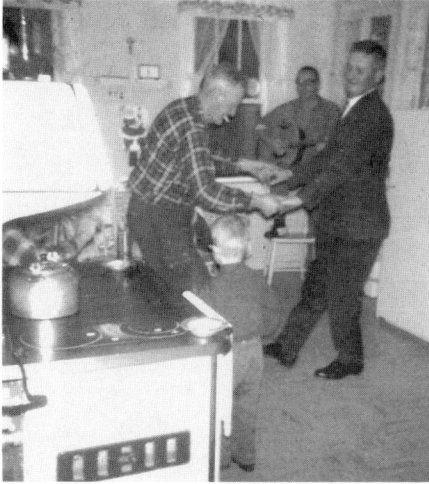

DANCE STAGE AT BRIERLY BROOK, 1927

KITCHEN
PARTY, OHIO,
C.1967–1969

Revellers, from left to right, are Billie Duncan MacDonald, Ronnie Mac Lean, and Hughie Chisholm.

[2nd picture] Dance stage outside the MacDonald home at Brierly Brook, Mary Isabella MacDonald and her mother, Katie MacDonald, c. August/September 1927.

Few social events are more popular than the kitchen party, known as the ceilidh in Gaelic folk culture. During the early settlement period, this form of household entertainment unfolded around the main source of heat, the kitchen fireplace (later the stove), and helped pass the long nights. These informal gatherings, where friends met to socialize and trade songs, tunes, jokes, and stories, lasted into the early morning hours before running out of steam. Storytelling, singing, fiddling, and stepdancing were (and continue to be) the mainstays of the kitchen party. Although the fiddle was in high demand, others contributed to the entertainment by playing the spoons or mouth organ. The merrymaking was festive, relaxed, and spontaneous and participants were well fortified with biscuits and tea; rum, however, was the favourite refreshment. Children were not excluded from this time-honoured festivity and usually sat listening at the top of the stairs or crowded around the stovepipe. Not all parties were limited to the confines of a house. Oftentimes, a stage or dance platform was erected outdoors to accommodate larger numbers of guests. In this instance, the MacDonald family held a dance to celebrate Anna MacDonald's upcoming nuptials to Arthur McKenna of Brierly Brook. The family prepared all the food—cookies, cake, and sandwiches for over a hundred guests, who danced to the musical accompaniment of fiddler Billy Kell and organist Florence MacLean.

Chapter 10

Sports

SETTING UP THE NETS, REV. H. J. MACDONALD, HEATHERTON, 1928

Organized sports became an integral part of life in late nineteenth century Antigonish. Sports competitions helped reinforce community spirit and provided an outlet for local rivalries, as teams mirrored such dichotomies as town-gown or the feuds between the West End, College Streeters, and Milltown. There were sports activities to suit all tastes. As early as the 1870s, Antigonish boasted the Heather Cricket Club. The fate of this organization is not known, but cricket matches were reported as late as the 1890s. Around the same time, there were two juvenile cricket teams called the Peanuts and Chestnuts. Although cycling was the chief infatuation of the day, there were other forms of so-called moral and healthful pastimes, such as lawn tennis. By 1894, StFX was equipped with tennis courts and croquet grounds, and sponsored activities such as baseball, handball, football, and gymnastic exercises. One of the principal forces behind local sports was the Antigonish Amateur Athletic Association. Its members lent significant support to the promotion of baseball, track and field, and bicycling. In July 1899, at one of their meets, spectators were thrilled to witness four Maritime province records broken at the track in a single afternoon. In the early 1900s, sports, particularly baseball, track and field, and hockey, also played a significant role in the recreational lives of county residents. Tug-of-war was an especially popular form of entertainment at rural picnics and competitive gatherings where male contestants vied to demonstrate their superior brawn over rival communities.

The town and county of Antigonish have produced some impressive sports heros. Several names stand out, most notably Ronald MacDonald, who won the second Boston Marathon in 1898 in 2 hours 42 minutes; the first Canadian to win this race. There was also the track star, James Grant, son of Duncan Grant of Fraser's Grant, who competed extensively in track meets throughout the United States during the 1880s. In 1884, he ran a three mile race in Cleveland and even though he came in second, his performance still beat "the best time on record in America." (*Aurora*, 26 November 1884) Then there were the less-heralded sports feats of speed-walker Joseph Abraham of Glassburn who claimed in March 1921 that he could "reel off fifty miles daily with ease under ordinary conditions." (*Casket*, 31 March 1921)

ANTIGONISH BICYCLE CLUB, 1893

In the 1890s, Nova Scotians fell in love with the bicycle. C. B. Whidden & Son stocked a wide selection of bicycles ranging in price from fifty dollars to a hundred dollars. The Antigonish Amateur Athletic Association, which consisted of forty members in 1890, became the leading proponent of cycling as well as track and field. In 1897, they leased the Elm Grounds and made ambitious plans for a fence and bicycle track; this objective was realized the following year with an oval-shaped track that met regulation requirements. The mass-produced safety bicycle made bicycling accessible to both genders, but racing was restricted to men. Antigonish claimed to possess "the speediest track that can be vaunted by any club in the province." (*Casket*, 27 July 1899) Local athletes did not disappoint their thrilled audiences. W. S. Archibald ranked among the best in Nova Scotia. He won first place in a one-mile (one-and-a-half kilometre) race in Truro in September 1894. The next day he broke a Maritime record, cycling three miles (five kilometres) in eight minutes seventeen seconds. Another local champion was Willard Borden, who broke the two-mile Maritime record in July 1899. In the early 1900s, Middle South River's Hugh McMillan capped his cycling career at Patterson, New Jersey, by setting a world record for a twenty mile (thirty-two kilometre) bicycle race. Alexander and Hugh McLean also belonged to this local pantheon of cyclists. A Fraser's Mills native, Hugh participated successfully in racing matches in both the United States and Europe. The sport required skill and was often dangerous as evidenced by Hugh's premature death. In December 1906, he fractured his skull during a fall from his bicycle while participating in a six-day bicycle race in Madison Square Garden, New York.

THE HIGHLAND GAMES, ANTIGONISH, C.1890S

Apple Tree Island, on the "beautiful grounds of W. C. Hierlihy, Esquire," was the site of Antigonish's first Highland Games in 1863 (*Casket*, 22 October 1863). Located just northeast of St. Andrew's Street, it was considered to be a "fitting and beautiful place" for the games and the weather on that day was perfect. Members of the Highland Society formed in procession and, headed by banners and pipers, marched from D. C. Chisholm's store towards the grounds. There were large crowds on both sides of the river ready to cheer on their favourites. The games began with a number of ladies and gentlemen performing in some Scotch reels. Following this musical exhibition, the games began and featured traditional Highland sports along with wheelbarrow and sack races. Some of the performances fell short of athletic perfection. The Casket's editor later reported that a few contestants in the footrace "ran like moose." However, the games quickly gained popularity. In 1866, the grounds were decorated with flags and evergreen arches and spectators were accommodated in two tiers of seats as well as a grandstand, about eighty feet (twenty-four metres) long, consisting of eight tiers of seats; in this latter location sat the bishop, his fellow clergy and "the other respectable men of the County." (Donald Og Chisholm MS., 186) Throughout the 1860s and 1870s, the games were staged at various locations such as W. A. Henry's grounds, Cathedral Hill, Cunningham's Field, and C. C. Gregory's Fernwood estate. Audiences numbering as many as two thousand were reported in September 1865; six years later, the attendance figures were even more striking at three thousand persons. By 1875, admission cost twenty-five cents while the entrance fee to the grandstand was fifty cents. In the closing decades of the century, special train excursion rates drew visitors from as far away as Halifax and

Sydney. As a showplace for local athletic talent, the games tested strength, speed and training, and promoted intense rivalries. In July 1883, John McDonald (Painter), threw down the gauntlet to all his adversaries by publishing his challenge: "I hereby challenge any man in America to dance a Scotch Reel for $20 a side and the championship of America, match to take place on the day of the Scotch Games at Antigonish 20th inst." (John A. Chisholm Scrapbook, 55)

Curiously, the games lost some steam between 1909 and 1919, but they were reinvigorated in the 1920s with the addition of a fiddle competition, boxing exhibition, ladies' and girls' track and field events, and a Gaelic concert of dance, songs, and readings. By the 1950s, Antigonish's Highland Games became a major tourist attraction as well as a popular cultural event. The once traditional showcase of athletic, dance, and bagpiping talent was now embellished by a pre-games parade with floats and a pervasive mood of commercialism. This picture is believed to be one of the earliest photographs of the Highland Games.

HORSE RACING ON LOCHABER LAKE IN WINTER, C.1890S

Few sports stirred as much passion as Sunday-afternoon horse racing on the harbour ice, Gaspereaux Lake, and Lochaber Lake. The frozen surfaces provided a ready-made track for running heats. There were two favourite types of contest: the free-for-all trot and the gentlemen's driving race. In March 1894, Lochaber Lake was the scene of an exciting competition between Downie Kirk's Snyder, H. McDougall's Pushie Tom and Milton Manson's Bashaw. As late as February 1916, Charles Manson won the "free-for-all-trot" with his prize horse, Nellie Bangs, on Lochaber Lake. Horse racing on the ice enjoyed a long history in the area from the 1890s to the 1950s. In 1901, Herbert Smith's prize horse, Nettie Wilkes, qualified for the Dominion Day races in Sydney, after a winning performance on the harbour ice. In 1884, an estimated five hundred spectators gathered, shivering in the wind, to witness the sport. There was always some betting on the side and purses to be won. Some horses were pushed to near exhaustion and throwing a shoe was a common occurrence. In the early twentieth century, competitive feelings ran high and rivalries among horses from the stables of Ed Haley, Jack MacPherson, and John Kirk were well known. From time to time, a small minority of fans, their fervour heightened by alcohol, got out of hand. Such behaviour did not escape the attention of the *Casket*, which wrote chidingly in its March 14, 1895 edition: "If the promoters of the these races can't hold them out of Lent hereafter, they ought to drop them, and avoid giving occasions for such scenes of drunkenness as were witnessed on the streets last evening." There was often playful banter between the contestants. On one occasion, Vincent J. MacDonald called out to Ed Haley as their teams raced across Gaspereaux Lake: "You'd better keep going Haley because the ducks are coming in."

MRS. H. K. BRINE AND UNIDENTIFIED MALE FRIEND IN SKATING COSTUMES, C.1897

WILLIAM SNOW ARCHIBALD HOLDING HIS SKATES AND WEARING HIS MEDALS, C.1946

During the late nineneenth century, fancy dress skating carnivals, with the accompaniment of the Antigonish Brass Band, attracted large audiences at the local town rink. In March 1883, the participants were colourfully decorated in costumes representing the Keppoch Fisherman, Tracadie Dandie, Scotch Lassie Jane and Gypsy Countess. In this photograph, Elizabeth Brine, wife of a local businessman, is dressed in a graduation cap and gown; her friend shows more sartorial splendour in his large feathered hat, cloak decorated with hearts and a shirt with ruffled sleeves. Regarded as the dean of Antigonish sportsmen, W. S. Archibald was one of Antigonish's celebrated figureskaters. Son of the town's first mayor, Archibald worked alongside his father in the condensed milk and cheese manufacturing business. It was his performances as a bicycle racer, yachtsman, and skater that sealed his reputation as a versatile athlete. He also enjoyed the distinction of refereeing the town's first known hockey match. Archibald continued his lifelong love of sports into his early eighties. He actually treated spectators to an exhibition of figure skating at StFX's Memorial Rink in 1946 when he was 71.

Antigonish Ice Sickles 1919–20

**ANTIGONISH
ICE SICKLES,
1919–1920**

Hockey was not exclusively a male game in Antigonish. There was a female team as early as 1900. By 1920, discussion about women's hockey generated considerable interest and enthusiasm. At that time, two women's teams were organized: the Ice Sickles and the Fleetfoot. Initially local experts were scornful of the whole idea, but they quickly conceded that the teams demonstrated skill and grace, and promised fans a superior brand of hockey. Antigonishers packed the rink to witness the Ice Sickles's first game against a women's team from New Glasgow. There was nothing effete about their playing which the *Casket* characterized as "fast and rough, with both teams working hard." Zina Cameron, Theresa Sears, and Mary Hanrahan proved themselves worthy adversaries on the ice. The newspaper noted with ill-disguised partiality that Cameron was "a neat stick handler and a wicked shot" while Cassie Cullen, a player on the opposing team, was "somewhat weak as a shot and given to loafing offside."

ANTIGONISH VICTORIAS, 1910

From left to right, the hockey players in the back row are: James Fraser, Joseph Sears, and Ranald McGillivray; in the front: Gladstone MacDonald, William Wilmot, Charles Whidden (captain), Vincent McIsaac, and Harold Whidden (manager). Hockey was first played in Antigonish on a semi-regular basis on the salt ponds, the harbour ice, Mooney's Lake and the Flats. The county was also dotted with outdoor ponds that served as skating rinks for local youth such as Priest's Pond at St. Andrews. Many young children improvised with alder branches, a rubber ball and baseball mitts to play their favourite game. By the early 1930s, both S. Andrews and Heatherton had outdoor skating rinks fitted with electric lights that permitted skating and hockey almost every evening.

There were some local hockey scrimmages in Antigonish during the 1880s, but it appears that the earliest organized competitions with outside teams took place against New Glasgow, Pictou, and Truro in 1897. Antigonish's first hockey club, consisting of "Judge" Henry (captain), Dan McLean, Ralph McDonald, Colin McKinnon, Willie Borden, Willie McKinnon, and Archy Chisholm, also played that year against StFX's first hockey team. On their first encounter, the town hockey team trounced their adversaries with a victory of 8 to 1. Town residents soon developed a fierce loyalty for their team, nicknamed the Fighting Seven, and the heated rivalry between town and college players attracted a wide following. By

1899, the admission fee to local games was twenty cents.

Throughout the 1920s, Antigonish's League of the Cross hockey team, wearing white and maroon wool jerseys, was a commanding presence on the ice. In 1922, they won the amateur championship of the Maritimes, the Morton and Thompson trophy. Even sweeter was the victory over the Halifax Wanderers' team, 2 to 1 in overtime. Four thousand fans attended the game and Halifax newspapers deemed it "the most spectacular exhibition of hockey ever seen in Halifax." This victory was due in no small part to the effective leadership of the team's captain, Jack Chisholm. This native of Caledonia had learned the subtleties of the game while working as a young man in British Columbia. He was known to pack a wallop of a bodycheck. One one occasion he checked an opponent on the ice with such force that he landed among the spectators.

The construction of Antigonish's Memorial Rink in 1922 gave considerable impetus to the development of Antigonish's hockey tradition, as did the establishment of the Antigonish-Pictou-Colchester League that same year. Throughout the 1920s, the Antigonish Vics attracted widespread support with their winning reputation, while good fortune smiled on the university hockey team that captured four successive Maritime intercollegiate titles during that same decade. Hockey in the county also enjoyed significant success. By the mid 1920s, The *Casket* regularly reported details of games at the Memorial Rink featuring teams from St. Andrews, Williams Point, and Heatherton. In 1932, the Antigonish Juniors, coached by Jack Chisholm, swept onto the scene and garnered some impressive victories such as the Nova Scotia Junior championship and Maritime championship; they were the first team from the Maritimes to play in the Memorial Cup playdowns. The team consisted of players whose names took on a legendary aura: Frank McGibbon, Neil McKenna, Donald Victor MacDonald, Pat Purcell, Irvin McGibbon, Jack MacDonald, Cyril Munroe, Alan MacMillan, Ed Perry, and Curly MacIsaac. The following year, the more senior members of this team reinvented themselves as the Antigonish Bulldogs. To this day, hockey is a subject not taken lightly in Antigonish and inspires an almost messianic fervour among its fans.

EAST END GIRLS BASKETBALL TEAM, C.1905 Around 1905, a group of young women in the east end of town formed their own basketball team and competed against other teams in the area. They had a simple uniform, including a vest decorated with the bold letters EE. The woman in the front row (left) is Elizabeth (Kirk) MacDonald, later Mrs. W. J. Ross of Hillcrest Street. Alongside Miss MacDonald was Rebecca MacLean, long-time secretary to Dr. P. J. Nicholson of StFX. The other team members have not been identified.

THE ROYALS, ANTIGONISH, C.1912

Baseball was first played in an organized way around 1889 when a StFX student, J. C. Weldon of Pittsburgh, Pennsylvania, taught the fundamentals of the game to interested youth of the town. By 1890, the Antigonish Base-Ball Club was established, and the game quickly spread to the county.

Local teams played against each other over the next few decades and the occasional game was held against outside competition. In September 1897, two baseball teams from Trenton arrived in town; the local juniors defeated their Trenton counterparts 27 to 12, in what must have been a pitcher's nightmare. The seniors also won a 12 to 10 victory. This was the first baseball title claimed by the town.

Exhibition games were held irregularly and schedules were drawn up for regular games from time to time against teams from Truro, New Glasgow, Pictou, Ohio, Mulgrave, Canso, Sherbrooke, and StFX. Antigonish fared well in these competitions. Throughout the 1920s and 1930s, games with the same communities were held on a fairly regular basis. In the 1930s softball gained in popularity partly because neither as much field space or equipment was needed. Baseball revived after the Second World War and a town league in Antigonish in the 1950s provided entertainment for the fans and experience for those picked to represent the town in intermediate playoffs. The local Bulldogs baseball team did quite well in provincial playdowns and in 1959 and 1961 won the provincial intermediate championship.

ANTIGONISH CURLING TEAM, C.1925–1930

Curling came to Canada during the late eighteenth century with Scottish immigrants. By the end of the century, this sport enjoyed widespread currency throughout Canada. Dubbed the roaring game, curling was one of the more popular activities in Antigonish. Little is known about the first curling club, established in 1850; however, one of its original members, John Bishop, helped found the Antigonish Curling Club in 1883. Within the year, the club sponsored an annual bonspiel in their covered rink. Antigonishers were passionate fans of the sport and players travelled to New Glasgow, Truro, Halifax, and Sydney for matches. Long remembered was the time the team trounced their Sydney adversaries in 1892 when the latter's stones were impeded by the soft ice. In 1907, Tupper Foster, president of the local club, despatched a team to the Maritime bonspiel held in Amherst. Team members H. H. Crerar and Dr. Agnew both distinguished themselves at this tournament. In January 1910, local curlers cheered the opening of a new rink equipped with modern tungsten lamps. One wonders if they paid much heed to the strict prohibition against "rough skating" in the newly built facility.

In 1910, E. F. MacNeill, manager of the local Bank of Nova Scotia, donated a trophy for an annual curling competition in Antigonish. It became a much-coveted honour for local curlers. Seated alongside the silver cup are, from left to right, Dr. A. O. Phillips, Allan Cameron, Elwyn Smith and Dan A. MacDonald. They were an interesting mix of people: a physician, a fox breeder, a schoolteacher and a contractor. Displayed at their feet are shiny new hipwaders, one of the awards for the winning team.

View at - Riverside Trotting Park
Antigonish Co- Opening day
Aug 5 / 25 - ☐

RIVERSIDE TRACK AT WEST RIVER, 1925

Horse racing was once one of the most popular leisure pursuits in Antigonish. Even before the establishment of Riverside Trotting Park, Main Street sometimes doubled as a race track. The street was cleared and spectators gathered to cheer the contenders. There were always disputes over those races that ended in a dead heat. The so-called sport of kings tended to be reserved for the town's wealthier residents like the Kirks, Kennedys, and Sweets. After all, feeding, stabling, grooming, and breeding horses for racing were expensive propositions. Such horses as Minnehaha, Snider, Highland General, and Pushie Tom became local sports heros. In August 1925, the Riverside Track opened at West River, launched with an impressive roster of competitors billed as "the finest line-up of fast horses to be seen on any track in the Maritime Provinces." (*Casket*, 30 July 1925) A crowd of 2,500 attended the event, completely undeterred by traffic jams and billowing clouds of dust from the track. By 1930 the track advertised handsome $750 purses. The history of horse racing in Maritime Canada is synonymous with the name of Ed Haley, nicknamed Father Haley because of his thick white hair. His skill as a driver, trainer, and breeder was widely recognized and over four decades, his horses garnered reputations at tracks in North Sydney, New Glasgow, Truro, and Halifax; in later years, he participated in races at Toronto's Dufferin Park and Montreal's Blue Bonnets. His West River Stock Farms, founded in 1959, enjoys the distinction of being the first registered standardbred stock farm in Nova Scotia; it has produced impressive bloodlines for stakes champions.

Father "Dempsey" Chisholm, the son of Alexander and Mary C. Gillis Chisholm, was born in Ohio in 1899. During his childhood, he was diagnosed with pulmonary disease and seemed fated to a life of poor health. But a philosophy of self-discipline and a rigorous daily regimen of sprinting, distance running, weightlifting, and weightputting turned him into a fine athlete instead. Chisholm was an imposing, big-framed man, almost six feet five inches in height. During his early days as a local sports hero, his athletic feats at the Antigonish Highland Games and on the Ohio Tug-of-war team attracted widespread admiration throughout the county. He was nicknamed Dempsey after William Harrison "Jack" Dempsey, who reigned as the heavyweight boxing champion during part of the 1920s. During this same decade, Chisholm capped his athletic career as Canadian champion in the hammer throw and the 440-yard (400-metre) dash. Although invited to join the Canadian Olympic team in the late 1920s, the serious-minded Chisholm could not accept the invitation because of seminary studies. He even declined the overtures of the Toronto police force who wanted to recruit the "muscular giant." (Antigonish Board of Trade, n.p.) In order to further his education he worked as a telegrapher and lumberman in the woods of Antigonish and Guysborough counties. It is said that he used to walk from the lumber camp to Mass each Sunday and back, a distance of forty miles (sixty-four kilometres). Dempsey was ordained by Bishop James Morrison in May 1931. That same year, he was appointed curate at St. John the Baptist Church in New Glasgow; he became parish priest in 1941 and remained there until his death in 1964.

HARNESS RACING ON GASPEREAUX LAKE, HARRY MACDONALD, HIS SON, GERRY AND "PAL MOON," C.1945

During the 1930s to mid 1940s, Harry MacDonald was a well-known figure at horse races on Gaspereaux Lake and St. Joseph's Lake. His love of racing originated with his father, Allan C. MacDonald, who raced horses on these two lakes during the 1920s. Allan C's horses, Don and Paddy, enjoyed a winning reputation. In 1928, he won the Chevrolet Sales Company Cup under the auspices of the Antigonish Horse Trotting Association on St. Joseph's Lake. Starting in January, crowds gathered on the ice on Sunday afternoons to urge on the racers like Peter MacLean of Ohio, Phonse Kennedy of Purl Brook, Ed Haley of West River, Collie MacDonald of Beaver Meadow and Charlie "the 20" MacLean of Cross Roads Ohio. For Harry, horse racing was his hobby, but shoeing horses was his business. This St. Joseph's blacksmith operated a forge near his home from 1932 to 1945. He manufactured horseshoes, mended harness and buckles, made and repaired racing sulkies. The MacDonald home also housed the St. Joseph's post office from 1932 to 1954 and the telephone central office from 1938 to 1954. Harry MacDonald's wife, Mary, ran these two operations, which served around fifteen families.

The MacIsaacs standing are, from left to right, are: Clemmie, Gussie, Altie, Greg, Francis, Huntley, John L., Daniel and Alex MacIsaac. As early as the 1920s, the farming community of Ohio and Cross Roads Ohio had its own baseball team. Its well-established sports tradition also included track and field, tug-of-war, hockey, and softball. Ohio's tug-of-war team during the 1930s was legendary for its strength. It is said that they used to train by pulling on a rope tied to a willow tree near John D. MacDonald's country store in Ohio. The "strong men from Ohio" frequently walked off with championships at the Antigonish County fall fair spurred on by their fans chanting "Heave Ohio." In the late 1940s this region boasted another sports phenomenon, a baseball team of nine brothers, the MacIsaacs of Crossroads Ohio. The *Casket* remarked on this singular situation: "We doubt very much if there is any baseball team in Canada can boast of nine brothers on its rosters." Francis and Greg played in the town baseball league in the early 1950s, while Greg and Gussie played on the St. Joseph's soft-ball team, which competed for the provincial intermediate title in 1952. The MacIsaacs played against the Ohio team in friendly competition, and some played for Ohio when outside teams were involved. The brothers were athletically inclined and highly competitive. In addition to baseball and hockey, tug-of-war teams from Ohio sometimes had one of the MacIsaac brothers pulling and tugging for Ohio's bragging rights. The MacIsaac brothers provided their share of athletic enjoyment for their many fans throughout the "High-Oes." The battle cry of the Ohio sporting interests was "Ohio Rough, Ohio Tough, We're from Ohio, That's Enough!"

Chapter 11

Events

VICE-REGAL VISIT OF GOVERNOR GENERAL AND LADY ABERDEEN, ANTIGONISH, OCTOBER 1897

Antigonish was all decked out for the arrival of the Aberdeens. Post Office Square was transformed into "a bower of beauty," its entrance adorned with an arch of evergreen and a sign proclaiming "Welcome." (*Casket*, 7 October 1897) Most of the stores and other buildings on Main Street were decorated for the occasion. The pealing of bells across town heralded the arrival of the Aberdeens at the train station. Two barouches, each drawn by four grey horses, headed to the post office with the vice-regal party, accompanied by the Citizens' Band and a number of carriages from town and county. The governor general addressed the throng of spectators from a specially erected platform and his message generated enthusiastic applause. The couple then proceeded to visit the college, Mount St. Bernard, and the Bishop's residence. For Lady Aberdeen there was a special treat—she was formally introduced to Alex W. MacDonald of Glen Alpine, who had worked as a boy for her father, Lord Tweedmouth, on his estate in Strathglass. The Aberdeens continued the next stage of the journey to Guysborough and Arichat on board the *HMS Partridge*.

OBSERVING THE DEATH OF QUEEN VICTORIA, ANTIGONISH POST HOUSE, JANUARY 1901

The death of Queen Victoria was solemnly observed by Antigonishers in January 1901. The Bishop decreed that on the day of the Queen's funeral all church bells in the diocese should be tolled for a least a half hour "in token of loving respect for Her Majesty's memory." The whole front of the town's post office was draped in black banners to mark the occasion. Throughout the empire, there were elaborate manifestations of public mourning for a queen who was regarded with an affection bordering on veneration.

John Cameron died as Bishop of Antigonish on 6 April 1910 and his funeral mass was held at St. Ninian's Cathedral one week later. The *Halifax Herald* acknowledged his demise with this accolade: "...the Catholic Church in Canada is robbed of its ablest and most distinguished prelate, and the country at large loses one of its most high minded and patriotic citizens..." It is estimated that five thousand people attended Cameron's funeral, the majority having to stand outside the cathedral. Approximately 160 priests, all holding lighted candles, filled the front pews of the cathedral. Hundreds of laity arrived by train. In fact, there were three specially scheduled trains the day before the funeral. Shops and banks were closed and the town itself seemed to take on an abnormal hush. Pontifical High Mass was celebrated by Archbishop McCarthy of Halifax, assisted by the president of StFX, Dr. H. P. MacPherson, and the late bishop's nephew, Rev. Colin MacKinnon of Sydney Mines. Following the funeral mass, the huge crowd, led by surpliced clerics, wended its way to the cemetery in what was the largest funeral procession ever seen in the town. The theologian, scholar, administrator, and political mover and shaker was buried in St. Ninian's Cemetery, only miles from his birthplace.

FUNERAL OF KENNETH CHISHOLM AND HIS DAUGHTER, ANNIE JANE, MAIN STREET, ANTIGONISH, APRIL 1926

Death had a central place in everyday life. The double funeral for Kenneth Chisholm and his daughter, Annie Jane, both of whom died of pneumonia, was a sombre occasion. Annie was only sixteen and her father, a native of Caledonia Mills, left behind a wife and four children. In an earlier period, death tended to be a brief, private occasion. However, by the late nineteenth century, it became a more formalized public ritual. Patrick S. Floyd, one-time mayor and carriage marker, started operating as an undertaker on St. Mary's Street in the 1890s. He introduced the new technology of embalming to Antigonish. He also operated a carriage hearse, adorned with lanterns, fringed curtains and oval plate glass windows; this vehicle was last used in 1943. Mourning was also signified by other practices such as fastening a black wreath to the front door of the grieving household. It was not uncommon for a team of white horses to draw the hearse especially in the case of a young person.

FIRE AT MOUNT ST. BERNARD, ANTIGONISH, 5 JULY 1898

This photograph is a rare shot of the fire that devastated Mount St. Bernard in the early morning hours of 5 July 1898. Starting in the furnace room, the blaze spread quickly, destroying the original building and the recently completed east wing of the extension. The convent bell sounded the alarm, followed by the cathedral bell. Soon, there was a deafening peal of bells throughout town. The cries of the servant boy at the Mount awakened the sisters and the senior boarders sleeping in west-wing dormitory. The other sisters and junior boarders in the main building's dormitory awakened to almost suffocating smoke. Some of the residents, most of them in their night clothes, took to the windows and the roof as their only routes of escape. They were escorted down ladders to the ground. The townspeople and the fire department responded quickly to the crisis. They worked feverishly to rescue furniture and the musical instruments; the former sustained heavy losses, but the instruments were only slightly damaged. The fire, however, got quickly out of control, especially after one of the branch pipes burst. Even the old hand engine, drawing its water supply from the river directly below the convent, malfunctioned at a critical point. The sisters' misfortune inspired an outpouring of generosity from the CND Motherhouse and other religious communities. The town's residents quickly organized a mass meeting and started collecting donations. H. H. McCurdy magnanimously offered to wire the new building at his expense and to cover the costs of electrical service for six months. Bishop Cameron reassured the CNDs, students, and townspeople that Mount St. Bernard "shall rise again," and like the proverbial phoenix, the Mount was virtually rebuilt by December. During the early phase of construction, the sisters found temporary accommodation initially at the bishop's residence and later in a house on St. Ninian's Street; the student boarders stayed with local residents. By August, the sisters were determined to return to some measure of normality and resumed classes for the advanced students despite the continuing hubbub of hammers and saws.

Church of St. Margaret of Scotland, Arisaig, after the fire, c.1928

The majestic Arisaig Church, designed by the prominent architect Sylvester Donoghue in the 1870s, was almost lost in a fire in the fall of 1928. On a hot September day, the steeple was struck by lightning. Mrs. MacKenzie, the housekeeper for the parish priest, Father Dougall MacEachern, was one of the first to notice the smoke. The church seemed doomed to destruction until John (Charleston) MacDonald of Doctor's Brook, a well-known carpenter, took the initiative. While a crowd of people gathered below, he climbed inside the tower where, balancing perilously on the rafters, he used an axe to cut away the flaming section of the steeple. It was then pulled down onto the road with a rope and the rest of the church was miraculously saved. MacDonald's heroism will long be remembered, for the church was a central force in the lives of the people of Arisaig. Later that November, construction on a new steeple began. In this photograph, the cow grazes in what was known as the priest's pasture, quite oblivious to the group of men surveying the debris on the ground in front of the church.

The devastating West End fire of April 1939, which caused more than $40,000 in damage, is believed to have started in the harness room of Sweet's hardware store. It spread quickly even though the fire truck arrived on the scene before the warning bell had stopped ringing. One line was quickly hooked up to a nearby hydrant and another was placed in the Brierly Brook, to the rear of the building. Despite these efforts, the fire completely destroyed the Sweet store, built by McCurdy and MacMillan in 1882, before heading eastward, engulfing the building occupied by A. E. Whidden, coal and vegetable dealer, and C. G. Whidden, raw fur dealer, as well as the home of Mrs. Colin A. Chisholm. Mrs. Chisholm's chief regret was that she had just finished papering three rooms in her house; otherwise, she took her misfortune very philosophically. Firemen managed to save an adjoining house belonging to the Barley Beers MacDonalds but a barn to the rear of the house was a total loss. J. A. Chisholm's shoe store, located directly across the street from Sweet's hardware store, was largely destroyed, including an upstairs apartment over the store. On the opposite side of Chisholm's was the liquor store; its windows were broken by the extreme heat but otherwise it survived. Offers to salvage the stock were rejected. Burning shingles carried by wind currents across town ignited a rash of other fires including one at MacLellan's Mill, Frank MacLean's barn, Sears and MacIntosh livery stable, William Vinten's house, C. G. Whidden's house and barn, and a warehouse located to the rear of the Antigonish Wholesalers which was a quarter of a mile (two-fifths of a kilometre) away. The fire changed the west end section of Antigonish but much of the area was rebuilt and the Whiddens and J. A. Chisholm lost little time in starting over again. Earlier in the decade the town had endured a succession of mysterious fires. One night the fire brigade responded to thirteen calls. Townspeople had many sleepless nights until the perpetrator, a pyromaniac called "Felix the Cat," was finally caught.

July and August 1947 were dangerously dry months in Antigonish County. With so little snow during the previous winter, the slash lying around from earlier lumbering operations heightened the threat of fire. On 11 August, the worst fears were realized when residents saw heavy smoke arising in the vicinity of the Glebe Road. Flames were soon seen sweeping towards Cape George; tragically, there was little water available in the small brooks. On 12 August, people began to remove furniture from their homes to the west of Cape George; hundreds of feet of hose were brought in, along with a bulldozer in an effort to set up barriers to stall the advancing flames. A plane monitored the increasingly dangerous situation while pumpers were set up in any brook where there was sufficient water. MacInnis's Brook and the Big Spring on Hardin's Mountain enabled the firefighters to contain the worst outbreaks. Still the fire hung on stubbornly, leaping from one section to another. Finally, on 3 September, after three weeks of battling the blaze, there was a heavy rainfall for about an hour. It brought temporary relief but did not extinguish the flames. The day-long rain on 15 September, over a month after the fire's initial outbreak, was far more effective and helped bring the inferno under control. Just three days earlier, the sisters and student nurses at St. Martha's School of Nursing had watched with horror as the fire raged towards the Sugar Loaf. Fearing that the safety of both the hospital and convent were threatened, they had their bags packed and were on alert to evacuate at a moment's notice. Over one hundred volunteers, many of them fortified by regular lunches supplied by the Antigonish Red Cross, fought the cape George fire of 1947. It is estimated that more than 15,000 acres (6,000 hectares)were destroyed in what is now regarded as the worst fire in the county's history.

For the early settlers, weather was more often foe than friend. The gale of October 1811 levelled extensive tracts of forest "like hay before the mower's scythe" while the big storm of October 1839 devastated woodlands throughout Antigonish County (Rankin, 29). During the latter storm, the MacGillivrays in Knoydart took refuge from the storm's fury in the milk house dug in the ground. The summer of 1847 brought the county a different kind of disaster—drought, grain shortages, and threatened starvation. The black families in Rear Tracadie suffered two years from failed potato and grain crops. One resident of Cape George recalled that some of his neighbours came to his door begging "a piece of bread before they could have the strength to raise their nets in the morning." (Rankin, 32) Other weather-related disasters also stand out in local memory such as the Big Sleet of 1881 that crushed old buildings and ruined wood lots in Ohio and Lochaber or the fierce wind and rain storm of October 1900 that left widespread devastation in St. Andrews, Heatherton, Tracadie, and Havre Boucher; some sixty barns were toppled along the road from Antigonish to Isaac's Harbour.

In Antigonish town, residents used to brace themselves annually for the spring flood. As the ice thawed, the swollen Brierly Brook and Wrights River usually overflowed their banks. The December 1906 freshet was particularly destructive. The combination of warm temperatures, melting snow, and torrential rains left the low-lying areas of Antigonish submerged. Some residents reported two feet (three-fifths of a metre) of water in their houses. Fences, outhouses, and other structures were swept away by rushing floodwaters and several streets were jammed with ice cakes piled as high as four feet (over a metre). Local men worked all day dismantling an ice jam on Main Street. Some distance up the West River, the Sherbrooke mail was transferred to a boat and transported to town. All travel via the South River Road into town was also halted.

W. P. C. CUNNINGHAM STANDING BESIDE SNOWBANK IN FRONT OF ST. JAMES CHURCH, 4 JANUARY 1922

The winter months also presented challenges for local residents. The winter of 1904 was particularly arduous. As early as mid-December, roads and railroads were snowbound, and farmers, some of whom suffered irreparable damage, despaired of finding adequate hay to feed their starving livestock. In the early twentieth century, the town had a horse-drawn plough operated by the Whiddens, but severe snowstorms usually reduced the Main to a one-way street. It was heavy slogging for the storeowners to clear the sidewalks in front of their premises. The piles of shoveled snow near Wilkie and Cunningham's store sometimes loomed as high as two storeys. For traffic, the snow-covered Main Street was an obstacle course, often rising three feet (a metre) above the sidewalks and deeply rutted by tracks left by the horses and the sleigh runners. There were always snarls when two teams met head on, and one had to pull over.

**WRECK OF THE
*EMPEROR OF
SAINT JOHN*,
6 DECEMBER
1926**

The coastline of Antigonish County has had more than its fair share of shipping disasters. One of the most tragic was the loss of the Graham ship, The *Commissioner*, a victim of the infamous August Gale in August 1873, a devastating hurricane that littered the shores of Maritime Canada with wreckage. The *Commissioner*, while on its maiden voyage, sank off Cape George, losing its captain and crew; part of the cabin, main hatch, and two life buoys bearing the vessel's name drifted ashore. Another poignant tragedy was the shipwreck of Captain James Forestall's schooner, the *Kitty*, bound for Gloucester, Massachusetts from Mulgrave. Sixty-three passengers and crew members perished in a fierce storm on 2 April 1876. Included among the fatalities was the captain, married for just one day to the widow of Captain Dan MacDonald of Cape George. Cape George was also the setting of another, far less dramatic, mishap at sea. In early December 1926, the *Emperor of Saint John*, a 1400-ton steamer built in 1919, was heading to Sonora, Guysborough to pick up a load of pulpwood. On 6 December, a blinding snowstorm and high seas forced the vessel to take shelter in Ballantyne's Cove. During the night, the vessel's anchors dragged and the ship went aground on MacPhee's Beach. The skipper was optimistic that the next high tide would help dislodge the vessel with its cargo of bunker coal, but local fishermen knew better. The crew rigged up a chair and cable to serve as a connection between the stranded steamer and the shore. At least nineteen men headed for New York to sign on with a sister ship, while a skeleton crew stayed behind to supervise The Emperor of Saint John until spring. Some of the ship's contents were eventually salvaged and sold off, and the captain's desk and chair were bought for the local school. In the summer of 1937, a portion of the vessel was transported by scow as scrap to the Sydney Steel Plant. Remnants of the ill-starred *Emperor of Saint John* can still be seen today in the waters off Cape George.

TROOPS
MARCHING
ACROSS THE
BRIDGE AT THE
EAST END OF
MAIN STREET EN
ROUTE TO THE
ANTIGONISH
RAILWAY
STATION, 1916

From fall 1914 onwards, the town of Antigonish periodically witnessed the departure of young men and women heading off to war. They were given an emotional send-off as the townspeople and brass band escorted them to the train station. Khaki-clad men became a conspicuous presence on the streets of Antigonish. There were even pickets or guards who patrolled the town each night to make sure that the military billets were ensconced in their quarters by 10 p.m. There was a collective shudder throughout Antigonish County when news arrived about the first local fatality, John Angus McNeil, of Malignant Cove, in September 1915. Antigonishers were galvanized to meet the hardships of war head-on. Young men enlisted to fight for king and country and joined the stream heading off to training camps and in due time to the front. During 1915–1916, recruitment drives were a fact of life in Antigonish. In March 1916, the recruitment meeting at the Celtic Hall attracted such a large crowd that a second meeting was held at the courthouse. Immediately after this stirring appeal for recruits, twenty-nine local men, many of them mere boys from 17 to 20 years, signed up. Local organizations launched fundraising collections, and children were asked to economize, knit, and cultivate garden plots. The war also helped erase denominational divisions throughout the area, as Catholics and Protestants united to campaign for local donations. During the winter of 1915–16 there were two hundred soldiers boarding in town and there was a special mass held for them every Sunday morning at 9:30 a.m. In 1916, around sixty-five Acadian men, primarily from Richmond and Inverness Counties, were billeted in Antigonish for three months, where they awaited their orders to head for Moncton to join the 163rd Regiment. They were given a rousing send-off with a splendid banquet at the Royal George.

St. Francis Xavier University was not insulated from this extensive militarization of life. The editor of the student newspaper, the *Xaverian*, noted: "Today the College is a veritable Valcartier." As early as the summer of 1915, a company of the Canadian Officers' Training Corps was established at the university. By 1916, there was also a recruiting office on site and drilling and khaki uniforms were commonplace sights on campus. In June of that year, it was reported that two hundred students or alumni and four faculty had enlisted for active service. The institution struggled to cope with the war's eroding impact on its finances, student enrolments, and faculty numbers. However, StFX officials rallied to make a significant contribution to the war effort and threw their support behind the formation of the StFX Hospital unit No. 9 Stationary Hospital in 1916. It was hoped that this unit, consisting of 160 officers, nursing sisters and men, would proudly bear the university's name overseas and ensure a strong Catholic presence at the front.

TWO CARS IN FRONT OF J. A. WALL'S HOUSE, ANTIGONISH, DECORATED FOR ARMISTICE DAY CELEBRATIONS, 11 NOVEMBER 1918

The end of the war was the occasion for widespread celebration. There followed a giddy display of parades, flags, and processions. On 7 November, bells rang all over Antigonish. At the Mount, some of the students leapt to their feet at the joyful noise and a breathless maid rushed around bearing the good news. On 11 November, the university announced a holiday and the peal of church bells could be heard all over the Antigonish diocese. That evening, Bishop Morrison officiated at a thanksgiving service at St. Ninian's Cathedral. Two more days of holidays were proclaimed, the first by the federal government, the second by Mayor Kirk to commemorate the lieutenant-governor's visit to Antigonish. On 27 November, the freshmen students at the Mount organized a victory sale. The colours of the Allied nations were prominently displayed. Costumed Miss Americas served ice cream from a star-spangled booth, Miss Canadas offered both coffee and delicious cake, while France and Belgium were represented by a selection of homemade candy. After the sense of relief and euphoria passed, Antigonish town and county now faced the sobering realities of tallying its human losses and mourning its dead. The following year, on the first anniversary of Armistice Day, the town observed the two minutes of silence at eleven o'clock. The cathedral, college, convent, school, and fire bells then rang out vigorously. The male students at the university organized impromptu parades with bands. Later that evening, the Ladies' Auxiliary of the Great War Veteran's Association hosted a dance at the Celtic Hall.

PARADE DRILL, ANTIGONISH, SEPTEMBER 1939

With the outbreak of the Second World War, Antigonish town and county braced themselves for the upheavals of war. Like other Maritimers, Antigonishers rallied to the cause with intense patriotism. Both town and county suffered fatalities. The first to make the sacrifice was Lloyd MacDonald, son of Len MacDonald, East End, Main Street. The signs of militarization throughout town were quickly apparent. Guards were stationed at times around the Sylvan Valley Bridge, the Pleasant Valley Water Tank, and on various trestles and bridges throughout the district, all designed to protect railway property and to ensure the safe movement of people and goods. StFX students mobilized themselves with fundraising, selling war savings stamps, donating blood and dispatching gifts to StFX soldiers overseas. The campus bustled once again with the gun drills, leadership training lectures and parades of the Canadian Officers' Training Corps (COTC), which had been an organized presence on campus during the First World War. The university offered courses in radio and navigation, both directly relevant to military service, and threw its support behind the activities of the University Air Training Plan (UATP) and University Naval Training Division (UNTD). Coastal communities also felt the intrusions of war. In East Havre Boucher, soldiers were posted to the North Canso lighthouse to monitor the activities of vessels and drill practices were conducted on the village road. Along with a magazine, barracks were also hastily constructed in the small community; it was all part of a strategy to strengthen the line of coastal defences guarding the Strait of Canso, especially the movement of coal and steel from Cape Breton to the mainland.

RESERVE ARMY TRAINING IN ARISAIG, C.1940

Shown in this photograph is a group of men undergoing Reserve Army training on the Arisaig school grounds. Numbered among their ranks were Hugh MacPherson, Jay MacDonald, C. D. Gillis, Danny MacEachern, Angus Dan MacDonald, Joe Johnnie Joe MacDonald, John Andrew MacDonald, Wilfred Gillis, Joe (Donald Alex) MacDonald, Danny MacDonald and Angus MacGillivray. Their instructor was Willy Dougald MacKinnon of Maryvale, a veteran of the First World War. Instructors were often veterans of the First World War or men who had served in the militia prior to the outbreak of war. Although far from the killing fields, the Reserve Army recruits provided some measure of internal security at vulnerable locations and allayed the insecurities of local residents, especially after German U-boats started to invade the waters of the Gulf of St. Lawrence and the river itself. The military equipment the men used was sometimes makeshift; after all, priority was given to the active army in the distribution of armaments.

HMCS ANTIGONISH HEADING INTO MULGRAVE, OCTOBER 1944

In 1944, residents of town and county were thrilled to read about the plans to name one of Canada's new frigates, HMCS *Antigonish*. The vessel was commissioned at Victoria, BC on 4 July 1944. Town officials quickly organized to establish the Antigonish Frigate Fund and to canvass local donations and gifts for the crew of the HMCS *Antigonish*. The local branch of the Canadian Legion offered to supply fifty decks of cards. Pupils in local rural schools launched a campaign to order two hundred books for the ship's library. The local Knights of Columbus promised to contribute a gramophone and records, while the town's mayor announced that the town would subsidize the purchase of a washing machine for the vessel. HMCS *Antigonish* arrived at Halifax on 22 August and headed for Bermuda in early October. Local residents regretted that the harbour's navigational limitations would not permit a visit from the frigate and had to content themselves with travelling to Mulgrave to visit the vessel during its brief stopover. Town officials, however, were keen to provide the officers and ratings with a rousing send-off. Plans were made to transport some of the frigate's personnel by train to Antigonish where they would be treated to a civic greeting at the Celtic Hall, a theatre party, a softball game, dinner receptions in local homes, and an evening dance at the Celtic Hall. The vessel's wartime career consisted largely of patrol and support duty, including two trips to Gibraltar. After the war, the HMCS *Antigonish* was used extensively for training purposes.

MEMBERS
OF THE
ANTIGONISH
RED CROSS
FOLDING
BANDAGES
AT BETHANY,
C.1941

The Antigonish Red Cross, which had contributed generously during the First World War, was energized by the Second World War. Once again, they were knitting and sewing at top speed. The county auxiliaries also responded wholeheartedly to the call for "Warm clothing for every British bombed civilian." (*Casket*, 3 July 1941) Women of all backgrounds became willing volunteers in this cause. For Antigonish resident Alice Bigelow, age was no excuse for sitting idle. Even in her late eighties, she contributed frequently to the shipments of mitts overseas. The Red Cross rooms in town provided female volunteers with ready-cut garments to sew. They also kept on hand a supply of fine yarn and soft flannelette. Mitts and socks were the standard donations, but quilts, dresses, sweaters, pyjamas, and nightgowns were also contributed by the local women. During the summer of 1941, there was stepped-up production of items for layettes such as bonnets, bootees, diapers, baby shirts, and gowns. In September 1941, the Antigonish Red Cross launched a two-day aluminium drive; the window of Wong's Café, the use of which was donated for the cause, was piled high with pots and pans for several days. The organization netted 130 pounds (60 kilograms) of metal and Norm Fee provided carting services. Auxiliary branches in South Lochaber and Goshen held their own scrap drive. The bustle of volunteer activity also included rolling bandages, collecting relief monies, and preparing packages for military forces and prisoners of war.

Chapter 12

The Many Faces of Antigonish

ALEX MACLEAN, MARSHY HOPE, C.1930S

In this photograph, Alex MacLean poses with the horn of his famous grandfather, Bard John MacLean. The horn, a gift from Col. William Forbes of Pictou Landing, measured sixteen inches (forty centimetres) in length and could hold three and a half pints (over one and a half litres). For MacLean, it was a source of liquid refreshment but also literary inspiration. In fact, the horn was featured prominently in one of his Gaelic poems.

Born on Tiree, Inner Hebrides, in 1787, Bard MacLean came to Nova Scotia in 1819, in the second large wave of Highland emigration. The son of Margaret MacFayden and Allan MacLean, a whiskey distiller, he was a well-known poet before leaving Scotland. In 1818, he published a book of poetry dedicated to the Laird of Coll, Alexander MacLean, his personal patron. Landing at Pictou, the Bard MacLean soon after bought a farm at Barney's River and settled there with his wife and three children. Being inclined to follow literary pursuits, he was not really suited to the backbreaking challenges of homesteading. His time in Barney's River was a difficult period for him and spurred him on to write his best-known poem "A Choille Gruamach" (The Gloomy Forest), which describes the hardships of pioneering. The poem, it is said, gained a wide audience and proved a powerful deterrent to subsequent emigration from the Highlands. MacLean did, however, continue to write, and eventually publish, about other aspects of life in old and new Scotland. In 1830, he moved to Marshy Hope, a few miles eastward. Pangs of homesickness lessened with time and the burdens of farming were greatly eased by his children, now old enough to be helpful, and his capable wife who could handle a sickle, hoe, and rake with great proficiency. A sociable man, MacLean liked to visit and converse about Scottish history and literature with fellow settlers. It was on one such visit to a friend in Addington Forks on 26 January 1848 that he suffered a fatal stroke. MacLean has been described as one of the best Gaelic bards ever to leave Scotland and his flowing verse became well known in eastern Nova Scotia and Scotland.

DR. ALEXANDER MACDONALD, C.1860S

Born in Armadale, Isle of Skye, on 17 January 1782, Dr. MacDonald began his education in Armadale and later registered at the University of Edinburgh where he graduated at the top of his class as a physician and surgeon. In 1806 he agreed to assist in taking a shipload of emigrants to Prince Edward Island but conditions aboard the ship were intolerable and he refused to return on the same vessel. The young Presbyterian doctor ended up in Pictou, and eventually headed to Arisaig, hoping to encounter a young priest, Rev. Alexander MacDonald (*Alasdair Mor Chlianaig*), who at one time had worked on his father's estate in Skye. The two men quickly forged a strong friendship that transcended religious differences. Dr. MacDonald stayed in Arisaig for about a year, but he could barely eke out a living. Such bleak career prospects prompted him to set out for Jamaica where he stayed for three years and enjoyed a successful medical practice. A severe attack of yellow fever left MacDonald's health greatly impaired. Some friends returned him to Halifax, where he eventually recovered. From there he went again to Arisaig and Father MacDonald persuaded him to stay in the area. The settlement of Doctor's Brook is allegedly named after him, although he did not remain there but settled permanently in Antigonish in 1810. At that time, this medical pioneer was one of only two qualified physicians and surgeons in the entire province. His practice was fraught with numerous hardships, especially hair-raising experiences as he navigated the bridle paths, harbour ice, and cliff tops during the winter months.

Highly respected and well liked, and also notoriously absent-minded, he became heavily involved in village affairs. In 1812 he married Charlotte, daughter of Daniel Harrington, and built a dwelling on Doctor's Hill, known today as Mount Cameron. MacDonald and his wife raised a large family. One daughter, Sophia Caroline, married a Father of Confederation. Another, Charlotte, laboured as a missionary with her husband the Rev. John Geddie in the New Hebrides for more than twenty years. Dr. MacDonald passed away in 1871.

This is allegedly a photograph of John Boyd (Printer), born in 1823 at South River, the son of John Boyd (Bard) and Mary (MacDonald) Boyd of Lakevale. His grandfather was Hugh Boyd (Pioneer) who had come to Nova Scotia in 1801. John Boyd (Printer) attended school at South River and later at the St. Andrew's Grammar School, following which he taught school for a few years at Bailey's Brook and Malignant Cove.

Fluent in Gaelic, he prepared an English-Gaelic vocabulary which he had printed at the *Eastern Chronicle* in New Glasgow. It was this venture that got him interested in printing and there he acquired some type which he used in his own printing efforts. With the help of a carpenter, Angus MacGillivray, he built a crude press; they experimented until letters came out clearly on a page. This was in December of 1849; on 24 June 1852 he published the first edition of the *Casket*, the oldest continuing weekly in Canada. From the beginning the paper carried articles in Gaelic and a large volume of community and Catholic news items. Material from other parts of the world was also copied and published.

His early years as publisher were lean ones and between January and June of 1861 he published the paper from Halifax. However, a disastrous fire gutted the Halifax office and he returned to Antigonish, putting the paper under the management of his half brother Angus Boyd, who remained at the helm until 1888. John Boyd resided some time in Halifax but most of his remaining years were spent in the United States. He died in Boston on 28 December 1880 at the age of fifty-seven. A visionary, his major accomplishment, the *Casket*, has survived and his memory is therein preserved.

JOHN BOYD,
C.1860S

W. J. Landry,
c.1890

The Pomquet-born William J. Landry enjoys the distinction of being Antigonish's first policeman. In the early 1870s, he opted for a career as a blacksmith and served his apprenticeship with John Cunnningham. In 1889, Landry realized that the town's incorporation offered another career opportunity. At that time, the first town fathers were considering possible candidates for such appointments as fire wardens, superintendent of streets and keeper of the lockup. Landry applied for the posts of policeman and license inspector. With the mayor casting a tie-breaking vote, he managed to secure these positions over his competition, James O'Brien. Landry was promised an annual salary of $225 and was provided $25 to purchase a uniform; in his new attire, he sported a pair of handcuffs, fastened to his belt, as well as a badge. The following year, O'Brien made the town councillors a tempting offer; he would perform the duties of policeman as well as lamplighter for $300. Landry's appointment was renewed; however, the position was dogged with conflict and uncertainty. Landry also served the town in several other capacities as fireman and superintendent of the water works. This latter appointment enabled the Antigonish blacksmith to familiarize himself with many of the basic rudiments of engineering. By the turn of the century, his career branched into contracting. He secured some lucrative water pipeline contracts with the Intercolonial Railway in Cape Breton and Quebec and several commisions during the early 1900s related to wharf construction. One of his most significant public works projects was the installation of a sewer system in Fredericton in 1906. Landry died in June 1912, aged sixty-one. His son, William (Billy) E. Landry, was also a prominent contractor. He was involved in the construction of wharves and breakwaters in eastern Nova Scotia and Cape Breton. In 1916, he built the new church in Havre Boucher, and obtained the contracts to build Morrison School and the university gym the following year. He was also general contractor of the building of the Capitol Theatre in 1936. Billy Landry was mayor of Antigonish 1940–41 and was re-elected but died in 1944 before completing his second term.

Francis Cunningham was the son of Maj. John Cunningham, one-time assemblyman for Sydney County and registrar of deeds. In the nineteenth century, Francis became one of Antigonish's leading house-builders and carpenters. He is credited with the construction of Main Street's Cunningham Hotel (latter the Merrimac) in 1859, which he leased to his brother, John Day Cunningham. This imposing twenty-five-room two-storey structure catered to discriminating clientele and served as a major stop on the stagecoach run. Cunningham's buildings, some of which survive today, testify to his high level of craftsmanship and his ability to blend vernacular tradition and the popular architectural idioms of the day. House construction was a generational tradition for the Cunninghams: the 1891 census also lists John G. Cunningham and John McLean Cunningham as house carpenters. Francis Cunningham married well, for his wife was the daughter of Captain David Graham, a leading shipbuilder, who operated two shipyards at Graham's Cove, on the northwest side of Antigonish Harbour. Cunningham also enjoyed a high degree of material prosperity. According to the 1871 census, he owned six village building lots, four dwellings, four barns, and two warehouses. At that time, he also operated a joiner's shop which employed six men year-round.

Sylvester O'Donoghue ranked among the elite of Antigonish's nine-teenth-century master builders. This native of County Wicklow, Ireland set out for Boston with his two other brothers around 1854. They were waylaid in Halifax because of engine problems and decided to put down roots in Nova Scotia instead. In Halifax, O'Donoghue learned about architecture, masonry, and carpentry. One of his most significant commissions was the construction of St. Ninian's Cathedral. His involvement in this project was immortalized in the poetry of Alexander MacDonald of Keppoch who praised his "great skill" and "commanding voice." Shortly after O'Donoghue won this career-making contract he relocated to Antigonish where he raised a large family and continued to flourish as a master builder. Arisaig's Church of St. Margaret of Scotland, Canso's Stella Maris Church (1891), both fine specimens of Gothic architecture, and the Church of the Immaculate Conception (1897) at Mabou are also his handiwork. O'Donoghue was equally adept in wood and stone construction and demonstrated remarkable technical and mechanical ability. He was also responsible for the addition of a new tower, spire and belfry to St. Patrick's in Merland (1891), a three-wing extension to the Tracadie Monastery (1894), and a one-and-a-quarter mile (two-and-a-half kilometre) span of the Inverness Railway (1899), constructed with stone quarried near Cribbons Point. O'Donoghue died of pneumonia in Antigonish in March 1903. On his death, the *Casket* lamented the loss of one of its outstanding citizens and summed up his life in these words: "He was a most competent workman, being a skilled draughtsman and carpenter, and an artist in carving either in wood or stone."

THOMAS GARVIE, ANTIGONISH COUNTY, C.1890S

Thomas Garvie is the sort of person often relegated to the limbo of the forgotten. This Irish immigrant had little in the way of wordly goods. A single man, he moved about, surviving on the odd jobs he was able to find. For a while, he farmed in the Upper Ohio and then moved to Pictou County. By the early 1890s, he was a common labourer, living as a lodger with William D. MacDonald in Lochaber. According to community lore, he headed to Halifax not long before the Halifax Explosion and disappeared shortly thereafter. This coincidence gave rise to the rumour that he had died in the blast.

Born in 1852 in the small farming community of Ashdale, "Big Alex" MacDonald, son of "Black Bill" MacDonald and Kate Chisholm, attended the local school and worked briefly with local construction companies. Around 1880, he headed off to Montana and Colorado, where he accumulated invaluable experience as a miner. He then followed the news of gold strikes northward, first to the Alaskan Panhandle and then to the Yukon. MacDonald is credited with perfecting the lay system, that is, the business practice of buying and leasing out his claims. By the end of 1897, the land-hungry MacDonald owned twenty-eight claims and was heralded by the Dawson *Daily News* as the "largest mine owner in the Klondike and Indian River districts." The following year his wealth was reckoned by some observers to be close to $3 million; by the end of the century, estimates of his fortune were as high as $12 million. Journalists of the day noted with admiration that the Klondike King did not smoke, drink, frequent saloons, or flaunt his wealth with ostentatious goldnugget watch chains or scarf pins. This gruff, humble man was far more at home in the bush wearing the plain clothes of a workman. His massive size and physical stamina were almost as legendary as his fabulous wealth. Big Alex's fame spread quickly. In 1900, the governor general, the Earl of Minto and his wife, paid a special visit to Big Alex MacDonald's claims on Bonanza during an official visit to Dawson.

In addition to his mining interests, MacDonald invested extensively in Dawson real estate. At one time, he reputedly owned half the city of Dawson. Among his properties was the Chisholm block, Bank of British North America building, and the MacDonald Hotel, which was deemed at the time the finest hotel north of Vancouver. The Klondike King was also a big-hearted philanthropist and contributed generously toward the rebuilding of St. Mary's Church after it was destroyed by fire in 1898, and towards the construction of St. Mary's Hospital.

MacDonald married Margaret Chisholm, twenty-year-old daughter of the superintendant of the Thames Water Police in London, England, but they spent much of their time apart. MacDonald's life was filled with other regrets and reverses. He endured losses to fire, expensive lawsuits, and dishonest partners. Being overly trustworthy and susceptible to too many hard-luck stories, he died with little wealth to show or leave behind. In February 1909, he suffered a fatal heart attack while splitting wood by the side of his cabin at Clear Lake. MacDonald is buried outside Dawson City. A small picket fence surrounds his grave, hardly a fitting site for a king.

**WILLIAM
CHISHOLM
AND HIS WIFE,
ELIZABETH
MACLEAN AT
BEECHHILL,
C.1900**

**BIG JOHN
STEWART
AND ANN
MACDONALD,
LOCHABER,
C.1867–69**

In the faces of these couples, weathered by time, can be seen the resting place for the memories of early Antigonish County. William Chisholm, born in Strathglass, migrated to Nova Scotia as a child in 1832. The family settled in Monk's Head and then moved on to Brierly Brook. The twice-married Chisholm earned his living as a joiner and later as a farmer. He and his wife, fourteen years his junior, raised ten children. Here he stands, with pipe in hand and outfitted in his Sunday best, alongside his wife in front of their Beechhill farm. His face is about to crinkle into a faint smile. The photograph of Big John Stewart of Perthshire and his wife, Ann Mac-Donald of Invernessshire, both early settlers of Middle Point, Lochaber, projects a grim pioneering determination. Big John immigrated to Nova Scotia in 1818 at the age of thirty years, a native of Blair Athol, Perthshire, Scotland. He and his wife, Ann MacDonald of Gaspereau Lake, raised nine children. Their photograph displays a sense of gruffness. They were people of strong character with a learned respect for work. Both couples were linked by the mutual bond of shared hardship in a lifetime of struggle to carve out homes and farms.

Winner of the Boston Marathon in 1898, Ronald J. MacDonald was born in Fraser's Grant on 13 June 1876, the son of Lauchlin (Drover) and Elizabeth (Chisholm) MacDonald. Lauchlin, his father, drowned aboard the vessel *Mary Ellen* on its return trip to Nova Scotia after delivering a shipment of cattle to Newfoundland. A terrible storm caused the loss of the ship and all hands on board.

A few years later, MacDonald's mother moved to Massachusetts with her six children and at the age of sixteen, Ronald began to work for the New England Telephone and Telegraph Company as a lineman. He entered a track meet in Newton in 1896 and defeated an American runner who held the United States mile record. Following that victory, MacDonald began to train seriously, both on the track and at the gym. In 1898 the twenty-two-year-old runner entered and won the Boston Marathon, cutting more than thirteen minutes off the previous year's time and setting a new world record. He was proclaimed by the *Boston Globe* to be "the champion Marathon road racer of the world." Local Antigonishers were thrilled with the athletic triumph of the young man known as one of the Betsy MacDonalds and he was billed by organizers of the 1898 Antigonish Highland Games as the "World's Strongest and Fleetest Runner." MacDonald entered Boston College in 1899 in order to study medicine; he was also attracted by the college's popular track programme. In 1900 he was chosen for the American Olympic Team to compete in a marathon in Paris. The race proved disappointing, for many of the runners were overcome by the blistering heat of the day and the refreshments, which consisted of champagne and wine; MacDonald reported temperatures as high as ninety-nine degrees Farenheit (thirty-seven degrees Celsius). He was even more bitter about what he considered "French trickery." (*Casket*, 4 October 1900) There were no officials posted along the route and some of the French contestants covered part of the course on bicycles. MacDonald claimed that he and one other American competitor were the only two to cover the full twenty-five miles (forty-kilometres) on foot. MacDonald's experience at the Boston Marathon in 1901 was even more distressing. The "pride of Boston College" (Sullivan, 45) collapsed during the race, allegedly drugged with a chloroform-soaked sponge handed to him by a mysterious man dressed in an American military uniform. The incident, probably one of Canada's earliest doping scandals, was quickly swept under the rug by Boston Marathon officials.

MacDonald transferred to St. Francis Xavier University in 1901 to continue his pre-medical studies. He also continued his strict training regimen of running ten to twelve miles (sixteen to nineteen kilometres) a day, often in the Lower South River and Saltsprings areas. Local residents, who watched him outrun horse-drawn wagons and carriages on the dusty back roads of Antigonish County, noted with bemusement: "What a grand doctor he'll make. When he gets a sick call, he'll not have to go to the stable. He'll just grab up his bag and set off on the run, and be half way there before a horse could be hitched up." (*Casket*, 24 April 1947) Despite his athletic exploits, MacDonald did not lose sight of his career plans to become a doctor. He registered at Tufts Medical School in 1907 and did some post graduate work at Harvard. In 1908, he began his rural medical practice in Aguathuna, Newfoundland, remaining there for twenty-seven years. In 1938, he relocated his practice and returned with his family to Antigonish. Dr. MacDonald made his last appearance at a track meet as a starter at the Highland Games in 1942. Later that year, he suffered a stroke but remained semi-active until his death in 1947. In his long athletic career, MacDonald garnered 135 trophies.

Affectionately known as "Little Doc Hughie," Rev. Dr. Hugh MacPherson was born in Fraser's Mills, Antigonish County in 1872. After attending St. Andrew's Grammar School, he entered StFX University, graduating in 1893. He then attended Urban College in Rome and was ordained in 1898. He later studied engineering and geology at the University of Lille in France. From 1900 to 1950, MacPherson was professor of engineering and geology at St. Francis Xavier University; he enjoys the distinction of being one of the first scientists at the university. He even provided instruction in languages and music and for a time coached the varsity hockey team.

Dr. MacPherson's greatest loves were the study of agriculture and teaching scientific methods to the local farmers. From 1914 to 1920, he served as Antigonish's first government agricultural representative. This appointment highlighted for him the urgent need for improved farm production and marketing techniques. As manager of Mount Cameron farm from 1915–1919, MacPherson studied the science and technology of farming and promoted the advantages of raising purebred hogs and Ayrshire cattle; he even built up an impressive Ayrshire herd at the university farm. This facility became a laboratory showcasing superior methods of crop rotation, soil testing, and livestock breeding. MacPherson, who regarded agriculture as the backbone of Antigonish town and county, refused to turn a blind eye to rural depopulation and decline. He became a leading exponent of the co-operative ideal and helped disseminate this progressive vision to local farmers. In 1912, he pioneered what is regarded as the first co-op dairy in Nova Scotia. He was also instrumental in the organization in 1922 of the first Boys and Girls Club in Nova Scotia, a forerunner of the 4-H Club. This club was designed to kindle the interest of younger generations in the farming way of life.

Little Doc Hughie died in 1960. His life exemplified the power of ideas and the agricultural community is indebted to this learned and versatile man.

REVEREND HUGH MACPHERSON, C.1900

CAROLINE
PROSPER WITH
HER CHILDREN,
MICHAEL
AND MARY
ELIZABETH,
C.1910

SADIE
(MACPHEE)
ELMS,
TRACADIE,
C.1910

Caroline Prosper was the only daughter of Thomas and Elizabeth Kennedy, residents of the Summerside area. Around the age of nineteen years, this daughter of a farmer/cooper and a Mi'kmaw woman, became the wife of John Prosper of Afton. They had eight children, several of whom died prematurely, including Mary Elizabeth. As parents, Caroline and John were ambitious for their children, especially Michael, their first-born son, who aspired to be a teacher. Although rendered lame by a childhood accident, Michael projected a dignified sense of pride, especially in his native heritage. John Prosper, who made hockey sticks, butter tubs and axe handles at a camp in nearby Brierly Brook, worked diligently to raise enough money to finance his son's education at the Normal School. Michael's objective was to return to serve as a teacher to his own people. This dream was thwarted by government officials and he accepted a position at the Avonside school in Monastery where he was well respected in the black community. Regrettably, Prosper's career was cut short in his twenties; he died around 1934. At least three of his siblings went to the United States to find employment. His brother Wilfred served three terms as Chief at the Afton Reserve (now Paq'tnkek) from 1961 to 1967. Caroline Prosper, who was highly esteemed for her leadership as an elder, died in 1974, at the age of eighty-seven.

For New Glasgow–born Sadie (MacPhee) Elms, the church and her family of eleven children were the mainstays of her life. She played the organ at the Tracadie United Baptist Church until her death in 1941, and never accepted any financial compensation for this work. Music provided a vital outlet for her strong faith. She even matched the rhythms of her household chores with a song; "Mother's Prayers Have Followed Me" was one of her favourites. An active member of the Lend-a-Hand Club, during the late 1930s and early 1940s Sadie helped local women such as Hattie Ash and Ann Day to organize the annual church fundraiser, the Tracadie United Baptist Church picnic, held in July. It was a much-anticipated event. Food donations were solicited door to door throughout Antigonish and Guysborough counties and a large crowd poured in to attend the event. Some of the visitors "from away" were accommodated in tents.

JOHN "THE TWENTY" MACLEAN IN FRONT OF ST. JOSEPH'S GLEBE HOUSE, C.1912

A Cross Roads Ohio farmer, John "The Twenty" MacLean used to drive the mail, normally passing St. Joseph's glebe house on his mail rounds. He customarily headed over to James River Station to pick up the mail, which then was delivered five times a week to St. Joseph's. Here he dropped off letters and parcels at Harry MacDonald's before proceeding to John D. MacDonald's store in Pinkietown and Christina MacLean's at Cross Roads Ohio. John "The Twenty" prided himself on his fine black horse, which could make the trip to James River in jig time. As a sideline, he also drove a long wagon to transport caskets to the cemetery. MacLean had deep roots in the region, dating back to his great-grandfather, Angus MacLean, (Pioneer), who settled in the area around 1813.

FLORA
MACDOUGALL
(ON FAR
RIGHT) WITH
UNIDENTIFIED
NURSING
SISTERS, C.1916

Approximately three thousand Canadian women served as army nurses during the Great War. Flora MacDougall of Maryvale joined their ranks as a nursing sister in both England and France. The daughter of Captain Archibald and Annie MacDougall, she was the only girl in a family with seven brothers. She was born on her father's vessel during its stopover in New York harbour in January 1880. MacDougall received her nursing education in Massachusetts and later served as a public health nurse in Boston. The outbreak of war brought her back to Canada. She signed on with the Canadian Army Medical Corps, who served heroically in such settings as dressing stations, casualty clearing stations, stationary and general hospitals, ambulance trains, and hospital ships. At least thirty-five young women from Antigonish Diocese went overseas as nursing sisters. In April 1916, Flora shipped out from Halifax with the StFX Stationary Hospital Unit. She was a stern, no-nonsense personality, but these traits provided her with emotional protective armour against the bloody horrors of war. After the war, she returned to a more routine field of activity as a public health nurse in Antigonish and Guysborough Counties, where she monitored children's health in the schools and visited tuberculosis patients in their homes. Schoolchildren often dreaded the visits of this tall woman with the wiry grey hair and forbidding manner. She died in 1957 and was buried with military honours; some of the nurses who had served with her overseas acted as honorary pallbearers.

SADIE AND ALEX J. GILLIS, MORAR, C.1918

Sadie MacKinnon Gillis, born in Lismore, was a well-known midwife in the Georgeville area. She also frequently prepared bodies for local burial and lined the coffins made by her husband, a farmer and postmaster. Their house served as the Morar post office for several years. In rural areas, the store-bought casket made slow inroads during the twentieth century. Preparing the corpse, constructing the coffin, making the linings, and digging the grave continued to be community responsibilities as relatives and neighbours alike extended a helping hand in the rituals of death. Traditionally, a woman reputed to be a good hand at laying out was entrusted with washing and preparing the body before the wake.

R. Cedric Griffin, c.1920

Mrs. H. H. McCurdy and daughter on West Main, c.1890

Cedric Griffin, posing on his rocking horse, was born into luxury. He was the only child of prominent lawyer R. R. Griffin, mayor of Antigonish from 1913 to 1914. He lived on Church Street, which enjoyed considerable social cachet with such prestigious residents as doctors, lawyers, and shopowners. No expense was spared on the Griffin house, described as the "last grand house of its period"; it was equipped with servants' quarters, smoking veranda, and servants' buzzers (Inventory of Pre-1914, vol. I). H. H. McCurdy's daughter also travelled in the exclusive circle of Antigonish's monied and elegant elite. She epitomized her father's social status in her Persian wool muff and feathered hat, no less fashionable than her stylishly dressed mother.

GROUP OF BOYS AT EAST END, C.1910

GROUP OF MI'KMAW CHILDREN, PROBABLY AT THE LANDING, C.1910

In striking contrast to such privileged upbringings, many children in rural areas were drawn into farm work and household chores such as caring for domestic animals, gardening, spinning, and food preparation. In their lives and play, they endured economic deprivation, settling for necessities rather than luxuries. Still, even lower class childhoods held the promise of simple pleasures. There were such delights as picking wild flowers, skipping, hop-scotch and playing "hoist the green sail." Summertimes offered outings at local swimming holes; Alex McAdam's Swimming Hole was a magnet for children in Malignant Cove. For more daring boys in the West River area, there was always the big iron bridge to be scaled. At Doctor's Brook, berry picking expeditions by wagon to Eigg and Brown's mountains offered children a welcome source of amusement. Pomquet Beach always attracted a cluster of women and children, who arrived in the morning and left mid-afternoon with their baskets brimming with berries. There was also the annual pilgrimage of pickers from Bayfield who crossed over to Pomquet Beach on September 15, so-called Cranberry Day. Wintertime meant skating on ponds like Brennan's Pond at Springfield, or coasting down the Bishop's Bowl in Antigonish. As seen in two of these photographs, childhood diversions could include a sparring match with one's buddy or posing in one's best clothes for a local photographer.

One of Maritime Canada's leading railway builders was John Kennedy. Like M. J. O'Brien and the Klondike King, he won his laurels through hard work. Kennedy was born in 1843 at Ohio, the son of Alexander Kennedy and Catherine Chisholm. He left home at thirteen years and got a job with a railway construction gang near Windsor Junction. This experience marked the beginning of an illustrious career as a railroad contractor. In 1903, he formed a partnership with one of his nephews, Alexander Kennedy MacDonald of Copper Lake. Kennedy and MacDonald Contracting Company enjoyed financial success, winning contracts to lay track in Nova Scotia, New Brunswick, Quebec, and Ontario. Their work crews were frequently composed of young men from Ohio, Lochaber, James River, St. Andrews, and other parts of Antigonish County. According to one local historian, they were probably the only railway contractors in North America to use Gaelic almost exclusively in their day-to-day operations. As railway contracts in the post-war period dwindled, Kennedy and MacDonald branched out into highway construction work, especially in Cape Breton. In 1915, the firm purchased the Antigonish dry goods business formerly owned by A. Kirk and Company. Kennedy's other local investments included such properties as Crystal Cliffs at Ogden's Pond and the Royal George Hotel. In 1927, Kennedy died at the age of eighty-seven. During his lifetime, he had participated first hand in the greatest period of railway building in Canada. The tribute which appeared in the *Halifax Chronicle* was laudatory: "He was one of Nova Scotia's captains of industry and one of the greatest sons of Antigonish."

JOHN KENNEDY AND HIS WIFE CHRISTINE CHISHOLM, C.1900

JOHN
CHISHOLM
AND MARY
ANN POWER,
LANARK,
C.1920S

Long-time Antigonish County blacksmith John Chisholm was born in North River, a short distance north of Lanark, in 1833. His parents were Donald Chisholm (Miller) and Catherine Chisholm, both born in Scotland. At twenty-two, John Chisholm began a three-year apprenticeship at a Tracadie blacksmith shop, working "sweatshop" hours, from 7 a.m. to 9 p.m. for three cents a day, plus board. Following his apprenticeship, Chisholm returned to Lanark where he manufactured ironwork for the Graham shipyard in Antigonish Harbour. When the shipbuilding industry declined, he continued with general blacksmithing, spending much of his time shoeing horses and oxen. Chisholm boasted another skill—he was a self-trained veterinarian with an innate knowledge of how to cure sick or injured farm animals. His reputation for this natural gift spread throughout the region. Consequently, the "horse doctor" was in high demand, and he travelled by sleigh or wagon to reach the far corners of the county where his medical and surgical services were often rendered without fee.

Chisholm married Mary Ann Power, the daughter of Patrick Power and Fannie (Sutton) Power of Antigonish Landing, on November 25, 1875. He died in February 1933, one month shy of his one hundredth birthday.

M. J. O'BRIEN
AND HIS
DAUGHTER,
MARY GRACE,
RENFREW,
ONTARIO, 21
SEPTEMBER
1921

A native of Lochaber, Michael J. O'Brien started his career around the age of fourteen by working as a water boy, for 10¢ a pail, on a railway construction site. By the time he was nineteen, this rawboned, six-foot-two (one-and-a-ninth metres) young man, bursting with self-confidence, was subcontracting railway jobs himself. He bought and sold mine claims and engaged in railway construction, mainly in Ontario. He made a fortune in these ventures, primarily in the O'Brien Mine at Cobalt, one of the world's richest silver mines. The vast business empire of this financier, manufacturer, mine and smelter owner, stockbreeder, merchant, and landowner was centred on Renfrew, Ontario, which served as O'Brien's main base of operations. It included literally dozens of companies. During the 1920s and 1930s, a number of young men from Antigonish County sought employment working for O'Brien's holdings in Cobalt; one James River family got the nickname "Cobalt" MacDonalds from having worked there and talking so much about it when they came home. During the First World World War, O'Brien's business interests prospered, especially with the establishment of O'Brien's Munitions and Energite, which made shell casings, munitions and explosives; at the height of the war, his munitions plants in Renfrew employed as many as three thousand people.

The multimillionaire O'Brien was a towering figure, both financially and physically. With his full beard, long stride and intense blue eyes, he projected what his biographers, Scott and Astrid Young, call an "electrifying presence." Today, O'Brien is also regarded as a legendary figure in the history of Canadian hockey. Originally, he financed the Renfrew Creamery Kings (later called the Renfrew Millionaires), a small town hockey team described as "arguably the best amateur hockeyteam ever fielded." (The Patricks [website]) But his dream mushroomed into something much grander. By 1910, Michael O'Brien and his son, Ambrose, were instrumental in the creation of the National Hockey Association, a forerunner of the National Hockey League. Initially, the family financed four of the five teams in the league: the Renfrew Millionnaires, Cobalt, Haileybury, and Les Canadiens of Montreal. O'Brien died in Renfrew in 1940 at the age of eighty-nine. The business mogul with the Midas touch left an estate valued at just over $5 million.

MARY ANN MOSEY (LEFT), HER DAUGHTER, MAGGIE SALOME, AND DAN PROSPER (IN THE BACKGROUND), ANTIGONISH LANDING, C.1920S

Mary Ann Mosey was widely regarded as a skilled basketmaker and kind-hearted woman. Most mornings of the week, she travelled with an armload of baskets from the Mi'kmaw reserve east of Heatherton to Antigonish. She was welcomed into the kitchens of many local residents, eager to learn the news she had gathered on her trip into town. She was especially famous for her teacup readings. For H. M. MacDonald, later county inspector of schools, early memories of her visits were unforgettable. As a child, he watched spellbound as she huddled beside the wooden stove, rotating the inverted teacup three times before studying its contents of brewed tea leaves. Mary Ann Mosey, a venerable member of the Mi'kmaw community, died in 1932, at the home of her grandson, Noel Poulette of Indian Chapel Cove, Heatherton.

L-R, FRONT
ROW: KEN,
GREG, JANET,
MAUREEN
AND PATRICIA
MACKINNON;
BACK ROW:
DR. W. F.
MACKINNON,
BILL AND JOHN
MACKINNON,
1934

Dr. W. F. MacKinnon, a highly respected Antigonish physician, was born in West Merigomish, Pictou County, the son of William MacKinnon and Janet (Boyd) MacKinnon of Fraser's Mills. Educated in Antigonish, he received his BA from StFX in 1897 at the age of nineteen. He taught for one year at St. Ann's College in Church Point and then registered at Dalhousie Medical School from which he received his MD in 1902. Dr. MacKinnon began his medical career in Antigonish and often carried out surgical operations under makeshift conditions, prior to the opening of a small hospital unit in 1906. For MacKinnon, his working knowledge of French, a proficiency acquired during his brief employment at St. Ann's, proved a real asset. His clientele included a sizeable number of French-speaking patients from Pomquet. Active in community affairs, MacKinnon served the town as mayor, president of the Antigonish Highland Society, member of the Board of Governors of StFX, and a charter member of the Antigonish Golf Club. Provincially, he was named president of the Nova Scotia Health Officers Association and in 1920 he was elected a fellow of the American College of Surgeons. As a doctor he was noted for his care and compassion in the treatment of his patients and for his high standards of medical practice. He passed away in 1952 after having suffered a stroke in 1947. The MacKinnons have been prominent in Antigonish for almost two centuries in the fields of education, religion, and politics.

Even as far away as Antigonish, the impact of the Halifax Explosion was felt. Local residents noticed the dishes rattling on the shelves and the windows of Morrison School shook. Food supplies, clothing, building materials, and skilled labourers poured into Halifax from across North America. The town of Antigonish mobilized its own relief effort. The local Victory Loan Committee, chaired by Rev. J. J. Tompkins, agreed to reconstitute itself as a Relief Committee. It was quickly decided that StFX University, the Knights of Columbus, Celtic Hall, the hospital and House of Providence could accommodate some of Halifax's wounded and homeless. There was a generous response to the appeal for several days' supplies of bread and clothes. The college students helped package these donations. By 20 December, canvassers had collected over two thousand dollars from a sympathetic public. Some Antigonishers opened their homes to relatives and others left homeless by the explosion. Drs. J. J. Cameron, W. F. MacKinnon and R. F. MacDonald promptly headed to Halifax to volunteer medical assistance. There were also Antigonishers like stone cutter and contractor John R. MacDonald, a native of Brown's Mountain, who were involved in the rebuilding of the devastated city. The town itself mourned the loss of Isabelle Pratt, whose body was brought home for burial when she died from injuries five months after the explosion. The disaster left other consequences in its wake. Laura Stuart, left orphaned by the explosion, was adopted by Willie Webb and his wife, a childless couple in Havre Boucher. The five-year-old Laura was on her way to school with her older sister when the explosion struck. The sister was fatally injured and her mother died within nine days, leaving behind seven children. Three of the little girls, Laura, Helen, and Evelyn, were placed in the temporary care of St. Joseph's Orphanage in Halifax. With great reluctance, their father permitted them to be put up for adoption. This was arranged by Sister Ambrosine McKeough, formerly of Linwood; she was closely related to the three couples who eventually adopted the Stuart sisters. The children headed separately to homes in Linwood, Bayfield, and Havre Boucher where they eventually reclaimed their shattered lives as members of these tightly knit communities. In Pomquet, Stella Steele and her sister, Irene, also left orphaned by the Halifax Explosion, found a home with Father Daniel Chisholm.

The arrival of a relative from the States was always the occasion for excitement, especially when they came bearing gifts. On this occasion, the MacDonald brothers, sons of the farmer and fisherman Alex Dan, posed for a special photograph. They were dressed in the sailor suits brought from Boston by their oldest sister Zena. They revelled in the attention that set them apart from their numerous siblings. The outfits were a great novelty, so strikingly different from the usual boyhood attire of overalls. Far from practical, the sailor suits which were "store boughten" and "from away," symbolized the big city and an exotic world far from Doctor's Brook.

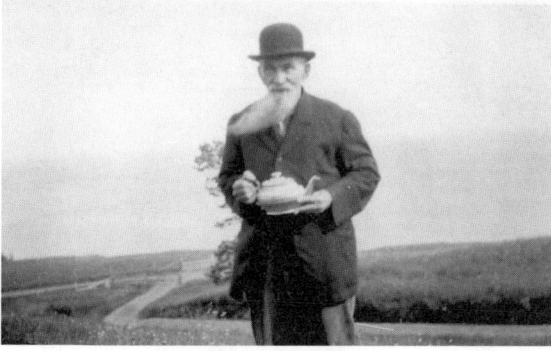

CAPTAIN ANGUS MACDONALD, BALLANTYNE'S COVE, C.1930

One of the most colourful figures born in Antigonish County was Captain Angus MacDonald of Ballantyne's Cove. He was born at Cape George in August 1839, the son of John MacDonald and Mary MacPherson of Georgeville. Angus MacDonald first went to sea as a boy. He studied navigation at Pictou and received his Master's "ticket" in 1860. It is alleged that he made fifty-two crossings of the Atlantic during his long career at sea.

During one ocean crossing in November 1881, a severe storm arose and he caught sight of the dismasted *Coronet* floundering in high seas. Initially there appeared to be no sign of life aboard, and the vessel was so heavily damaged that it was stripped of its spars, cabins, rigging, and deckload of lumber. It required enormous skill and daring for MacDonald and his crew to save the captain and his wife, along with seventeen crewmen, who were all suffering from acute hunger, thirst, and exposure. A wet barrel of flour, a small pig, and melted snow and hail had provided them with their only nourishment during their nineteen-day ordeal at sea. The captain's wife was unconscious when she was rescued; MacDonald fed her with a spoon for several days. Almost three weeks later, the Coronet's passengers were dropped off at Port Benzanges in Spain. For his great act of bravery, the British government awarded Captain Angus a handsome silver teapot with an ebony handle. The presentation took place at the Antigonish Court House. The inscription on the teapot reads: "Presented by Her Majesty's Government to Captain A. MacDonald of the brigantine 'Trust' of Maitland, N.S., in acknowledgement of his humanity and kindness to the shipwrecked crew of the ship 'Coronet' of Liverpool, which was abandoned in Nov. 1881."

Between 1893 and 1897 MacDonald captained the rail ferry between Mulgrave and Point Tupper and then retired to Ballantyne's Cove. Well into his nineties, Captain Angus remained remarkably agile and eagerly reminisced about his thrilling adventures at sea. One of his favourite tales related to a crewman who, before he died, extracted the promise that he would be returned to his beloved Antigonish County for burial. The body was transported back home in a barrel of rum. "And not a drop was wasted," quipped Captain Angus with a twinkle in his eye. The sea captain died in 1933 at the reported age of ninety-nine.

ANGUS MACQUARRIE, DOCTOR'S BROOK, C.1930S

In the 1930s, newspaper reporter and journalist Clara Dennis snapped this photograph of Angus MacQuarrie, a well-known farmer in Doctor's Brook. She was charmed by the agile old man who played the pipes with such vigour and vibrancy. Son of John and Sarah MacQuarrie, Angus was born at Rear Doctor's Brook in 1862. He spent most of his earlier life in the United States and Western Canada, before returning to Doctor's Brook to farm. Music was in his genes and the tradition of piping was passed down to him by his father and his uncle Archie. In 1889, he went to Scotland for about a year, primarily to broaden his expertise in piping. Widely regarded as an authority on pipe music and a dynamic strathspey and reel player, his services as a piper were frequently sought by the Antigonish Highland Society; he also served several years as a piping judge at the Antigonish Highland Games. He died in November 1944.

HUBERT PETIPAS, EAST TRACADIE, C.1930S

Hubert Petipas also caught the eye of Clara Denis during her travels throughout Antigonish County in the 1930s. This Acadian farmer was regarded as one of East Tracadie's oldest and most highly respected citizens. In this photograph, his weathered face projects a strong character shaped by struggles with the land. At this stage of life, there were few activities that he enjoyed more than sitting in his big rocking chair and playing cards. The great events of Petipas's life were his marriage to Mary DeCoste, the sister of his father's second wife, and the births of his ten children. For them, he was the patriarch of a family that in his old age had multiplied into forty-two grandchildren and six great-grandchildren. In 1891, Hubert and his wife, along with their growing family, shared a house with his seventy-four-year-old father, Désiré Petipas, and second wife. His father was also a commanding presence and is best known for having donated a parcel of land to be used as the school at East Tracadie.

LAUCHLIN
GILLIS OF
ARISAIG
DRESSED FOR
HIS ROLE IN
DONALD OF
THE TROUBLES,
C.1930S

Lauchlin Gillis was a versatile entertainer—a fiddler, piper, and also an actor. One of his favourite plays in which he played the main character was *Domhnull Nan Triablaid* (Donald of the Troubles). This Gaelic play was performed in Arisaig during the 1930s. His wife, Mary MacDonald, also participated by performing the role of Seonaid. The local acting troupe gathered at the Gillis home to prepare for their theatrical productions. The occasion was always marked by great hilarity. The group's repertoire also included *Reiteachadh Morag* (Sarah's Engagement). These dramas were taken on the road to places like New Glasgow. Despite the inroads of Anglicization, there was still much demand for Gaelic entertainment in those parts of Antigonish County where the Gaelic oral tradition was very much alive. At the banquet of the Lismore Council of the Scottish Catholic Society of Canada in August 1931, there was a hefty dose of Gaelic in everything from the opening address to readings to the closing song performed by local boys and girls. The district was long accustomed to using the language; Matthew MacLauglin conducted his school classes there in Gaelic in the late 1850s. According to John L. Campbell's *Unofficial Gaelic Census for 1932*, an estimated 325 people out of 374 in Arisaig spoke Gaelic, and despite its declining use, even children had a working knowledge of the language. For a period of time Lauchlin Gillis, along with Sandy MacDonald of Arisaig, operated a packet which transported passengers and goods from Pictou to smaller communities along the coast such as Arisaig, Livingstone Cove, and Ballantyne's Cove; one of the packets was called the *Helen and Hilda*, another the *Alvin S.*

During the nineteenth and early twentieth centuries, the lines between traditional men's work and women's work were sometimes blurred, particularly among rural women who shouldered tasks in the fields and the barn. There was a deep-seated taboo against men doing women's chores as some perceived threat to their masculinity. In most farming households, the men's role in the production of cloth consisted of raising the sheep, as well as shearing and washing the fleece. Home spinning, knitting, and weaving were usually left to the women. However, Alex DeWolfe defied the stereotypes of the day. This one-time farmer from Pomquet Point, who worked in the United States as a bridge riveter, enjoyed spinning as an old man. He also knitted undershirts, long johns, and mitts, which he sold to the fishermen in Bayfield.

ALEX TOM MACDONALD, CROFT, C.1930

This unmarried casual labourer lived in a small, two-room house in Springfield. He was reclusive in his manner; his back deformity and his illegitimate birth set him apart from other people. According to local tradition, he worked in a Quebec lumber camp during the First World War, where he skilfully managed to evade conscription. In the communities of Springfield, Beauly, and Croft he was best known for his midwinter visits. Wading through snowdrifts, he came bearing the latest gossip, which he gathered during his social circuit. He arrived at the door with a knock, unannounced but not unexpected. He was easily spotted in the distance, carrying his shining lantern during the dusky late afternoons. Once inside, he would brush off the snow and sit down, the water from his boots pooling on the floor. Throughout the community, MacDonald was admired for his special gift. He was considered a "sloinneadh," the self-appointed custodian of communal memory who could trace back the family pedigrees of everyone in the district. As such, he was part of a long-established Celtic tradition of folk historians whose minds became a virtual storehouse of tribal information.

CHILDREN OF GEORGE AND MOLLY WONG, AND GORDON AND DOROTHY WONG, ANTIGONISH, C.1938

These children are, from left to right: Edward Wong, Henry Wong, Helen Wong, Joyce Wong, William Wong, Richard Wong, Stanley Wong, and Jenny Wong. George Len Wong immigrated from Guangdong, Southern China to British Columbia around 1912. In his native village of Nam Toon, he had served briefly as a teacher. He even played the mandolin in performances of Chinese opera. For him, Canada held the promise of great opportunity despite its chilly reception towards Asian newcomers; starting in 1885, the Canadian government levied a hefty head tax on Chinese immigrants as a deterrent. During the post-war era of discrimination, many Chinese fanned out across Canada creating opportunities for self-employment and opening up restaurants and laundries. George Wong's life also followed this pattern. He travelled eastward across Canada, stopping with friends and relatives. London, Ontario restaurant owner Lem Wong, who operated the first Canadian Wong's Café, was a major influence: his establishment served as the training ground for many Wong family members who then went on to establish their own restaurant businesses in Bridgewater, New Glasgow, Glace Bay, Sydney, Liverpool, Yarmouth, North Sydney, and Antigonish. For a while, George worked as a cook at the Lingan Golf Club and at Wong's Café in Sydney. By 1928, he moved to Antigonish, convinced that the town was a promising location for a restaurant. At that time, the Chinese population in Antigonish County was negligible. As early as 1901, John Charlie Wong and his younger cousin, Kwoon Let Wong, both of whom emigrated to Canada in 1896, operated a laundry on Sydney Street. Before George Wong's entrepreneurial dream of a café could be fully realized, he and his cousin Gordon Wong of New Glasgow set off for Victoria, British Columbia, with matrimony on their minds. George married the nineteen-year-old Molly Lee in 1930. Molly, who arrived in Canada at the age of seven, endured great upheaval in her flight from her war-torn village in China to Hong Kong, later Singapore and finally to Canada. She was the first Chinese woman in Antigonish. Molly Wong took an active hand in the running of the café, but family was clearly her priority; she firmly believed that education was the passport to success. She excelled as a photographer with the encouragement of George Waldren of Waldren Studio. This photograph of George and Gordon Wong's families, with the Sydney Street firehall and laundry as its backdrop, is undoubtedly one of her photographs. The Wongs regarded the family business as a secure foundation on which to build the lives of their children and expand their opportunities as first-generation Canadians. They quickly won community respect for their work ethic and generosity.

LOTTIE MELANSON AT JACK ADAMS'S FARM AT BALLANTYNE'S COVE, C.1942

Lottie Melanson, champion sheep shearer, was one of Antigonish County's most memorable characters. An unconventional, salty-tongued woman who engaged in the occasional brawl, she tested notions about gender roles. Her appearance was decidedly mannish, rough and ready, an impression accentuated by her short hair, colourful vocabulary, and work clothes. In shearing competitions, she often bested the men; even when they used electric shears they were still no match for her proficiency with hand shears. She made the rounds shearing for farmers throughout the county. Melanson usually boarded with the family that engaged her services before heading to her next stop on the circuit. She always started her sheep-shearing sessions with a glass of milk to settle her stomach; some suspected that it was an antidote for the effects of the previous night's carousing. Many parents strived to keep their children out of earshot while Melanson was working for fear they overheard some of her more pungent expletives. There were few activities Lottie enjoyed as much as telling ghost stories after supper, especially to children who hung with horrified fascination on her every word. Lottie died in 1990, at the age of seventy-eight years.

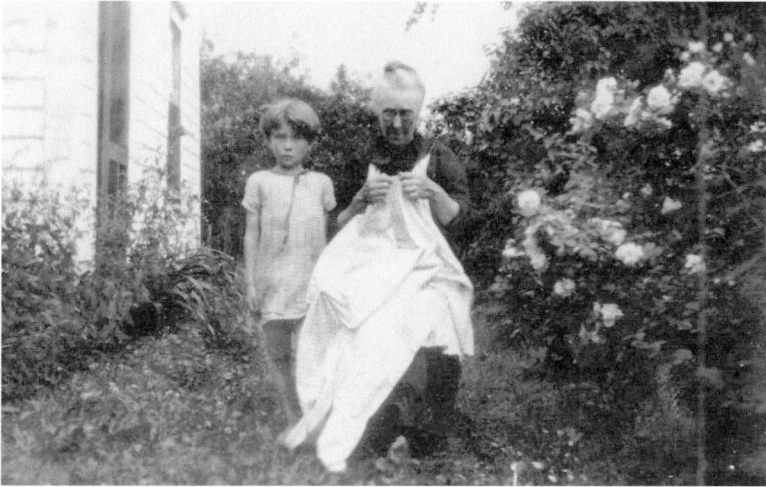

Born in July 1867, Catherine (Katie) MacEachern was a remarkable woman in her own right. She was married to John Colin MacDonald, a farmer and mailman at Brown's Mountain. A resourceful, hard-working woman, this diminutive powerhouse, who never weighed more than ninety-eight pounds (forty-four-and-a-half kilograms) and was barely five feet tall (one-and-a-half metres), could turn her hand to almost anything. She handled all the farm chores from milking to planting. Nothing went to waste in her household. Pothead, tripe, eastpan, haggis, and sausage were the products of her thrifty ways. Katie was renowned throughout the Brown's Mountain and New Strathglass areas as a midwife. She even went as far afield as Pictou Landing and Marshy Hope to tend to expectant mothers, travelling by horse and wagon, sleigh, or train. Usually she stayed with the new mother from ten to thirty days. Katie also ministered to other medical conditions, providing bottled tansy to women for their cramps and applying poultices of milk, bread, and onions to infections. She sought no monetary compensation for these services, satisfied with gifts of food or other household items from grateful families. Katie's expertise was also solicited when people died. In Brown's Mountain, she assumed the task of cleaning and preparing the corpse for the wake.

Her natural talent as a healer extended to animals. On one occasion, she operated on a choking hen, cutting it open, extracting the obstruction and sewing it up in scant time; the kitchen table doubled as an operating table. Despite her crippled condition, she once treated a calving cow with complications in her late seventies; she was transported to the barn in a chair. Katie supplemented her income by weaving blankets, shirts, and underwear for D. D. MacDonald's General Store at Bailey's Brook. She also sold her knitted socks, sweaters and mitts to lumber crews working in the camps. There was no time for idleness during daylight hours; her crowded days included the production of quilts, hooked mats, and spun and dyed wool. Katie died in August 1961 at the age of ninety-four years.

John "Red" Archie MacGillivray, a native of Brierly Brook, was another memorable Antigonish resident. He was chief of police in Antigonish between 1938 and 1952, having served in a similar capacity in Canso between 1932 and 1937. His earlier career was varied and took him from the mines in Montana to the wheatfields of Saskatchewan, the railroads of Quebec, Ontario, and British Columbia and the coalmines of Thorburn, Nova Scotia. The long-time Antigonish police chief, widely known for his geniality, earned the nickname "Red" Archie because of his red hair. He was especially popular with local children whom he guided daily across busy streets on their way to and from school. He regularly walked the beat, keeping a paternal eye over the town and tempering justice with compassion. Firm words rather than physical force were his preferred technique of law enforcement. Red Archie was outgoing with tourists, often greeting them with a handshake. One of his more interesting challenges was dealing with the so-called king of the hoboes who arrived in Antigonish aboard the fast freight. Red Archie offered the unwelcome visitor temporary lodgings at the Blue Bell Inn, where he boarded himself, but gently sent him packing via train the following morning. Red Archie died in May 1959 at the age of seventy-two. According to the *Casket*, his funeral was attended by council members, town employees, firemen, boy scouts, and scores of citizens.

Although relative newcomers to Antigonish County, the Dutch have played a pivotal role in its economic and cultural life. The largest influx of Dutch immigrants arrived between 1951 and 1956. They brought with them a vast heritage of agricultural knowledge. Their arrival was opportune and helped cushion the impact of Antigonish County's alarming rate of rural depopulation. Bishop John R. MacDonald and the StFX extension department, in collaboration with several Dutch priests and brothers, the Dutch Embassy in Ottawa and the Nova Scotia Land Settlement Board, helped facilitate their placement on available farms. Approximately 110 Dutch families participated in the resettlement scheme in the Diocese of Antigonish. Their story is one of triumph tinged with hardship. Among the earliest Dutch immigrants in Antigonish County were several war brides who married Canadian soldiers stationed in Holland during the Second World War, as well as the families of Anton and Feem Overmars and John and Wilhelmina Westenenk who settled on farms in the St. Andrews area. The Van de Wiel family, twelve in all, packed up their lives in suitcases and crates, and migrated from a war-ravaged Holland to Canada in April 1950. After a year in Rockland, Ontario, working for their sponsors, the family headed for Antigonish, eager to have a farm of their own. To many Dutch immigrants, the county seemed "a rough looking country" (MacLean 1981, n.p.) and the long cold winters were daunting. Some even contemplated retracing their steps to Holland, but this impulse was quickly checked by their lack of money. The Van De Weils, who boarded briefly with the Westenenks in Dunmore, acquired a farm in Beauly, along with some livestock. The day they moved in was a memorable one of mixed emotions. Still, they valued their new-found sense of security and the prospect of sleeping in their own beds. By the 1960s, there was a substantial Dutch population dispersed throughout Antigonish County.

Bibliography

Archival Sources

Antigonish Heritage Museum:

   MacPhee Collection

   Dellie Sweet Scrapbooks

   John A. Chisholm Scrapbook

   Donald Og Chisholm MS.

   Minutes of the Antigonish Highland Society 1861–1881

   School Registers, Main Street School 1889–1916,

   St. Ninian Street School 1933–1945, Mount St. Bernard 1884–1945

   Inventory of Pre-1914 Buildings and Homes: Antigonish & Nine Districts

Public Archives of Nova Scotia:

   White Collection MFM #14962

   Scrapbooks MFM #15087, #15099

Newspapers

Acadian Recorder (Halifax) 1857, 1871

The *Aurora* (Antigonish) 1881–1885

The *Casket* (Antigonish) 1852–1990

Christmas Greetings (Antigonish) Christmas 1898

Halifax Herald (Halifax) 1927

The *Memorare* (Mount St. Bernard, Antigonish) 1910, 1914–1942

Morning Herald (Halifax) 1883

The *Morrisonian* (Morrison School, Antigonish) 1948–1955

Novascotian (Halifax) 1840, 1846, 1867

Xaverian (St. Francis Xavier University, Antigonish) 1908–1945

Directories and Guides

Hutchinson's Nova Scotia Directory, 1864–65

McAlpine's Gazetteer and Guide, 1904

McAlpine's Maritime Provinces Directory, 1870–71

McAlpine's Nova Scotia Directory, 1890–97, 1914

Nova Scotia Blue Book and Encyclopedia, 1932

Government Records

Census for Antigonish County, 1817, 1827, 1838, 1861, 1871, 1881, 1891, 1901

Department of Indian Affairs Annual Reports, 1864–1952 (http://www.collectionscanada.ca/2/23/index-e.html)

Journals of the House of Assembly (Nova Scotia), 1843–1920

Other Sources

Antigonish County Genealogical Website. Antigonish Regional Development Authority. http://www.antigonishrda.ns.ca/genealogy/ (accessed 15 March 2004).

Antigonish Town and County. Antigonish Board of Trade, 1916.

Antigonish Board of Trade Magazine. Antigonish Board of Trade, 1964.

Bannon, R. V. *Eastland Echoes.* Toronto: Macmillan, 1937.

Bagg, Lyman H. *Ten Thousand Miles on a Bicycle.* New York: Kron, 1887.

Baxter, Jessie, ed. *St. James United Church, Antigonish, N.S.: The Story, 1804–1979.* Antigonish: *Casket* Printing & Publishing, 1980.

Bird, Will R. *This is Nova Scotia.* Toronto: Ryerson Press, 1950.

Boudreau, E. *Le Petit Clairvaux, Cent ans de vie cistercienne à Tracadie en Nouvelle-Ecosse.* Moncton: Editions d'acadie, 1980.

Braid, Angus, ed. *Hard at Work.* New Horizons Program, 1990.

Brewer, C.G. "The Diocese of Antigonish and World War I." Master's thesis, University of New Brunswick, 1975.

———. *St. Joseph's Parish, Antigonish County.* Antigonish, n.p., 1976.

Brow, Eileen. *Through the Years, A History of St. Paul's Parish, Havre Boucher, Nova Scotia*, N.p., n.d.

Brownspriggs Historical Committee. *The History of the Little Tracadie Black Loyalists.* N.p., 2000–2001.

Cameron, James. *'And Martha Served'; History of the Sisters of St. Martha, Antigonish, Nova Scotia.* Halifax: Nimbus Publishing, 2000.

———. *For the People, A History of St. Francis Xavier University.* Kingston/Montreal: McGill-Queen's University Press, 1991.

Cameron, James M. *American Pioneers in Antigonish, Pushee, Williams, Hulburt.* N.p., n.d., 1982.

Campbell, D. and R. A. MacLean. *Beyond the Atlantic Roar: A Study of Nova Scotia's Scots.* Toronto: McClelland & Stewart, 1974.

Carlson, Michelle D. "The Scottish Spinning and Weaving Traditions in Cape Breton and Eastern Nova Scotia." Bachelor's diss., St. Francis Xavier University, 1997.

Carter, Rose Sutherland. *Ripples from Copper Lake.* New Minas: Gaspereau Press, 2003.

Catholics of the Diocese of Antigonish, Nova Scotia and the War 1914–1919 with Nominal Enlistment Rolls by Parishes. Antigonish: St. Francis Xavier University Press, c.1930.

Cheska, Alyce T. "The Antigonish Highland Games: A Community's Involvement in the Scottish Festival of Eastern Canada." *Nova Scotia Historical Review*, 3, (1983):, 51–63.

Chisholm, Katherine Anne and Donna Kennedy. *St. Joseph's Parish & Community, 1848–1998.* Antigonish:, N.p., 1976.

Chisholm, Lewis B. *Limbs.* Victoria: Trafford Publishing, 2002.

Chisholm, Ronald R. "A Biographical Survey of the Members of Parliament for Antigonish 1867–1982." Bachelor's diss., St. Francis Xavier University, 1982.

Cochrane, William. *The Canadian Album: Men of Canada.* 4 vols. (Brantford: Bradley, Garretson & Co., 1895).

Cote, Laura. "A History of Mount Saint Bernard from 1883 to 1939: To 'Make and Mark the True Woman.' " Bachelor's thesis, St. Francis Xavier University, 1999.

DeCoste, Dennis. *Reminiscences.* N.p., 1992.

———. *History of Mattie Settlement.* N.p., n.d.

———. *The History of Mattie Settlement and Reminiscences.* N.p., n.d.

DeCoste, Evelyn. *West Havre Boucher, Linwood, Frankville, A Journey to the Past.* N.p., n.d.

———. *Cape Jack Road, A Journey to the Past.* N.p., c.1994.

———. *The Village and East Havre Boucher, A Journey to the Past.* N.p., n.d.

Dennis, Clara. *More Above Nova Scotia.* Toronto: Ryerson Press, 1937.

Evans, R. D. "Stage Coaches in Nova Scotia, 1815 to 1867." *Collections of the Nova Scotia Historical Society*, vol. 24. 107–134

Falt, Mary H. *A Star in the Apple, The Memoirs of Mary Helen Falt*. Almonte: Faltless Publishing, 2001.

Feltmate, Lori J. *A Brief History of Lochaber, Sydney's Sylvan Pride*. Lochaber Community Development Association, 1995.

Fraser's Grant School Section no. 35. N.p., n.d.

Fraser, Mary L. *Folklore of Nova Scotia*, Antigonish: Formac, c.1975

Gentilcore, R. Louis. "The Agricultural Background of Settlement in Eastern Nova Scotia." *Annals of the Association of American Geographers*, 46 (December 1956): 378–404.

Gillis, M.E. "Members of the Legislative Assembly representing Antigonish from 1785 to the Present." Bachelor's diss., St. Francis Xavier University, 1981.

Grant, Margaret A. "The History of Springfield" Typescript. 1973.

Halvorson, Clara E. B. comp. *A Heart for Healing*. Portland: Binford & Mort Publishing, 2003.

Heatherton 4-H. "History of Heatherton." Typescript. 1994.

Heatherton Heritage Group. "Reminiscences of Heatherton." Typescript. 1994.

Inglis, R. E. "Lochaber: A Typical Rural Community." *Collections of the Nova Scotia Historical Society* 39, (1977): 89–105.

Johnston, A. A. *A History of the Catholic Church Eastern Nova Scotia*. 2 vols, Antigonish: St. Francis Xavier University Press, 1960, 1972.

Johnston, A. A. *Antigonish Priests and Bishops, 1786-1925*. Edited by K. M. MacKenzie. Antigonish: *Casket* Printing & Publishing, 1994.

Joudrey, G. N. "The Public Life of A. S. Macmillan." Master's thesis, Dalhousie University, 1966.

Landry, Simon Louis, and Mary Ida Landry. *Simon Louis Landry Speaks of Pomquet*. Pomquet: Pomquet Press, 1990.

Lotz, Pat. "Scots in Groups: The Origin and History of Scottish Societies with Particular Reference to those established in Nova Scotia." Master's thesis, St. Francis Xavier University, 1975.

Maas, Yvonne and Bernie MacDonald. "MacDonald 'Charleston' 1797–2002." Typescript. 2002.

MacDonald, Gerard. "Stories and Notes pertaining to the communities of St. Joseph's and Ohio-based on recollections of Carmen Richard." Typescript. 2003.

MacDonald, H. Joe. *St. Andrews Then and Now*. Antigonish: Casket Printing & Publishing, 2000.

MacDonald, H. M. *Down Memory Lane*, 1972.

——. *The Builders, Biographical Sketches of the Architects of the Diocese of Antigonish*. Antigonish: Casket Printing & Publishing, 1968.

——. *Memorable Years, A Century of Education in the County of Antigonish*. Antigonish: Casket Printing & Publishing, 1964.

——. "The Story of St. Ninian's Cathedral in Antigonish, N.S." Typescript. 1963.

MacDonald, H. M. and Allan Gibson. "Diocese of Antigonish, Profiles on Parishes from Newspapers."

MacDonald, J. W. History of Antigonish County 1876, Antigonish: Formac, 1975.

MacDonald, Paul. "From Glengarry to Antigonish and Beyond (Beaver Meadow)." Typescript. 2003.

MacDonald, Ronald A. "The Squires of Antigonish." *Nova Scotia Historical Review*, 10, (1990):, 53–73.

——. "Early Merchants of Antigonish." Paper read at meeting, Antigonish Heritage Museum, 11 January 1993.

MacEachern, Cameron. "Cape George Forest Fire Diary." Typescript. 1947.

MacEachern, Joyce. *History of Holy Rosary Church, Ballantynes Cove: A Hundred Years, 1891–1991*. N.p., 1991.

MacEachern, Rosalie. "A Study of Selected Inspector of Schools Reports for the County of Antigonish," Bachelor's diss., St. Francis Xavier University, 1977.

MacFarlane, D., and R. A. MacLean, eds. *Drummer on Foot*. Antigonish: Casket Printing & Publishing, 1999.

MacFarland, John, *75 Years of Hockey*, Antigonish: St. Francis Xavier Press, 1971.

MacGillvray, C. J. *Timothy Hierlihy and His Times, The Story of the Founder of Antigonish, N.S.* Antigonish: Casket Printing, 1935.

MacGregor, John. "History of Upper South River." Typescript. c.1960s.

MacIntyre, N. Carroll. *The Fire-Spook of Caledonia Mills*. Antigonish: Sundown Publications, 1985.

MacKenzie, A. A. *Scottish Lights*. Wreck Cove: Breton Books, 2004.

———. "Sailors & Sailing Vessels of The Gulf Shore and Guysborough." Typescript. 2003.

Mackinnon, Clarence. *A Brief Sketch of the Life of the Reverend John Franklin Forbes*. Saint John: Saint John Globe Publishing, 1905.

Making History, A Record of the Stories and Lives of Seniors and Veterans in Antigonish Town & County. Antigonish Career Resource Centre and Human Resources Development Canada, 2001.

MacLean, A. Kennedy. *A Brief Historic Account of Angus and Rebecca (MacMillan) MacLean, Pioneers, Their Descendants and Married Relations The Kennedys of Glen Road and Ohio*. N.p., n.d.

MacLean, Joseph F. "From the Keppoch…to the end." Typescript. 1988.

MacLean, Juanita. "A Study of the Remnant Gaelic Culture along the North-Eastern Shore of Nova Scotia." Bachelor's diss., St. Francis Xavier University, 1992.

MacLean, R. A. *Bishop John Cameron, Piety and Politics*. Antigonish: Casket Printing & Publishing, 1991.

———. *The Casket: 1852–1992, From Gutenberg to Internet: The Story of a Small Town Weekly*. Antigonish: Casket Printing & Publishing, c.1966.

———. *Canadians from Holland—A Generation Later*. Atlantic Canada Studies Programme and the International Education Centre, Saint Mary's University, Ethnic Identity in Atlantic Canada Series. 1981.

MacLean, R. A., ed. *History of Antigonish*. 2 vols., Antigonish: Casket Printing & Publishing, 1976.

MacLean, R. A., ed. *Recollections* (Margaret "Peg" MacGillvray). Antigonish: Casket Printing & Publishing, 1976

MacLellan, Marie. "A History of Pleasant Valley" Bachelor's diss., St. Francis Xavier University, 1973.

MacNeil, Alan. "Cultural Stereotypes and highland farming in Eastern Nova Scotia, 1827–1861." *Histoire sociale/Social History,* 37 (May 1986): 39–56.

Moorsom, W. S. *Letters from Nova Scotia*. London: Henry Goulburn, 1830.

Murphy, G. H. *Wood, Hay and Stubble*. Antigonish: Casket Printing & Publishing, 1956.

Nash, Ronald L., and Frances L. Stewart. *Mi'kmaq: Economics and Evolution*. Nova Scotia Museum, 1986.

O'Reilly, Mary Lou. *In Profile*. Antigonish: Casket Printing & Publishing, 1986.

Ormond, Douglas Somers. *A Century Ago at Arichat and Antigonish*. Hantsport: Lancelot Press, 1985.

Parks, M.G., ed. *Western and Eastern Rambles: Travel Sketches of Nova Scotia*. Toronto: University of Toronto Press, 1973.

"The Patricks: Lester and Frank, Hockey's Royal Family." http://collections.ic.gc.ca/heirloom_series/volume5/182–185.htm

Patterson, George. *History of the County of Pictou, Nova Scotia*. Belleville: Mika Studio, 1972.

Penny, Wilena MacInnis. "Fishing Villages of Nova Scotia." Typescript. 1980.

———. "A Century Ago at Cape George." Typescript. 1980.

Pope, A. M., trans. *Memoirs of Father Vincent de Paul, Religious of La Trappe*. Charlottetown: John Coombs, 1886.

Randall, E., J. Randall and B. Mattie, "History of Bayfield." Typescript. 1971.

Rankin, D. J. *A History of the County of Antigonish, Nova Scotia*. Macmillan, 1929.

Robertson, Carmelita. *Black Loyalists of Nova Scotia: Tracing the History of Tracadie Loyalists 1776–1787*. Nova Scotia Museum, 2000.

Schrepfer, Luke. *Pioneer Monks in Nova Scotia*. Tracadie: St. Augustine's Monastery, 1947.

Sears, Anne-Marie. *Antigonish Town and County (A Collection of Facts and Stories about our Town and County Areas)*. N.p., n.d.

Souvenir, "Formal Opening of St. Martha's Hospital, Antigonish, Nova Scotia, May eleventh 1926".

Stanley-Blackwell, Laurie, ed. From Querns to Quilts: A Select View of the Material Culture of Antigonish, Nova Scotia. *http://www.stfx.ca/people/lstanley/material* (accessed 15 March 2004).

——. A Virtual Tour of the Architectural Heritage of Antigonish, Nova Scotia. *http//www.stfx.ca/people/lstanley/history/* (accessed 15 March 2004).

Stewart, J. B. "The Bayfield Randalls and their Connections" Typescript. 2003.

Sullivan, George. "The case of the champion who fell." *Boston College Magazine*, 1998: 41–45.

Taylor, Sister Ina. "Information concerning Bayfield (Little River)." Typescript. N.d.

"Thirteenth Annual Hank Snow Tribute." Official program. 2003.

Vander Vorst, Brian. "The History of Heatherton Parish." Bachelor's diss., St. Francis Xavier University, 1969.

Vossen, Rebecca E. (Cameron). "Warts and All." Typescript. 1983.

Wallace, Ann. *Monastery and its People*. Antigonish: Casket Printing & Publishing, 1990.

——. *Irish Village, Glimpses of South Merland and its People*. N.p.,1989.

——. *St. Peter's Parish Tracadie: A Parish History, 1803-2003*. N.p., 2003.

Walsh, Patrick. *The History of Antigonish, Antigonish*. Casket Printing & Publishing, 1989.

Warner, Charles D. *Baddeck, and that Sort of Thing*. Boston: Houghton, Mifflin, 1884.

Wasson, Terry. "The Development of the Homestead Property of 'Oakdell' at Lochaber Lake, Antigonish County." *Nova Scotia Historical Review* 16, (1996): 91–95.

Watts, Heather. *Silent Steeds: Cycling in Nova Scotia to 1900*. Halifax: Nova Scotia Museum, 1985.

Webber, Mary. "A History of St. James United Church, Antigonish." Bachelor's diss., St. Francis Xavier University, 1985.

Whidden, Charles Edgar. "The Whiddens of Antigonish, Nova Scotia, Canada." Typescript. 2002.

"The Alexander James Chisholm and Elizabeth MacDonald Crocket Family, West River, Antigonish County." Typescript. 2003.

Whidden, D. G. *The History of the Town of Antigonish*, Antigonish: Casket, 1934.

Williams, Scott. *Pipers of Nova Scotia, Biographical Sketches, 1773–2000*, Antigonish: Scott Williams Publishing, 2000.

Willson, Beckles. *Nova Scotia: The Province that has been Passed By*. New York: F. A. Stokes, 1911.

Young, Scott and Astrid Young. *O'Brien, From Water Boy to One Million a Year*. Toronto: Ryerson Press, 1967.

Photo Credits

Cover Photograph: AHM

Title Page: Francis DeWolfe and Claire Dickson

Introduction: 1. Association of American Geographers; 2. Margaret and Al Jennings; 3. AHM; 4. R.A. MacLean; 5. Bill MacKenzie

Communities: 1. Zoe Hayes; 2. Nova Scotia Museum; 3. AHM; 4. John Allan MacGillvray; 5. Clara Dennis Collection, NSARM; 6. AHM; 7. Mary MacDonald; 8.Geological Survey of Canada/National Archives/PA-038044; 9. J. Keele/National Archives of Canada/PA-045222; 10. John and Laurie Blackwell; 11. Hattie Farrell; 12. Don MacMillan 13. Collie MacIntosh; 14. Hugh Webb; 15. Rick Grace; 16. Gordon and Joan Randall; 17. Gordon and Joan Randall; 18. Joe and Veronica Delorey; 19. Robert Brown; 20. Joanne Decoste

House and Home: 1. AHM; 2. Thomas Kinney; 3. Ella MacVicar; 4. Roy Smith; 5. Arthur LeBrun; 6. Ronnie Gunn; 7. Rev. James E. O'Neal; 8. Roy Smith; 9. Rev. James E. O'Neal 10. Nancy Pitts; 11. Archibald Collection, AHM; 12. Dr. David McCurdy; 13. Isabel Whidden; 14. Isabel Whidden; 15. Isabel Whidden; 16. Gilbert Landry

Living off the Land and the Sea: 1. Rick Grace; 2. John Blackwell; 3. Gilbert Landry; 4. Nancy MacLean; 5. Michael Anderson; 6. Margie Bailey; 7. Peter and Angela DeGruchy; 8. Cape George Heritage School; 9. Ronnie Gunn; 10. AHM; 11. Arthur Arbuckle; 12. Francis Johnson; 13. Allan Francis MacDonnell; 14. Isabel Whidden; 15. Angus Grant; 16. Ronnie Gunn; 17. Hattie Farrell; 18. William Paulette; 19. Gordon and Joan Randall; 20. Gordon and Joan Randall; 21. Joyce MacEachern; 22. Eileen Adams; 23. Cape George Heritage School; 24. AHM; 25. Archibald Collection, AHM; 26. Ronald MacDonald

Trades, Businesses and Industries: 1. Waldren Collection, Dalhousie University Archives; 2. Hugh Webb; 3. Peter and Angela DeGruchy; 4. Archie Mills; 5. AHM; 6. Arthur LeBrun; 7. AHM; 8. Anne Sears; 9. AHM; 10. Hattie Farrell; 11. William Paulette; 12. AHM; 13. AHM; 14. AHM; 15. Richard and Betty Glencross; 16. C.J. MacGillivray Collection, AHM; 17. Hugh Webb; 18. Margaret Bowie; 19. AHM; 20. AHM; 21. Mary Falt; 22. AHM; 23. Margaret Bowie; 24. Isabel Whidden; 25. Joan Dunn; 26. AHM; 27. Katherine Ann Chisholm; 28. AHM; 29. AHM; 30. Bill Landry; 31. Mona MacDonald; 32. Roy Smith 33. Allan Armsworthy; 34. Waldren Collection, Dalhousie University Archives 35. Waldren Collection, Dalhousie University Archives; 36. Joan Phee; 37. Kenny Farrell; 38. Phil Arsenault; 39. St. Francis Xavier University Archives

Women's Work: 1. AHM; 2. Gilbert Landry; 3. Neil MacIsaac; 4. Gordon and Joan Randall; 5. Cape George Heritage School; 6. Gordon and Joan Randall; 7. AHM; 8. Joyce Pembroke; 9. Pomquet Historical Society; 10. Cape George Heritage School; 11. Peter and Angela DeGruchy; 12. Francis DeWolfe and Claire Dickson; 13. Alfred Landry; 14. AHM; 15. Marlene McLarty; 16. Gordon and Joan Randall; 17. Ronnie Gunn; 18. Joyce MacEachern; 19. Sara Carty; 20. Marleen Hubley

Religion: 1. Gilbert Landry; 2. AHM; 3. AHM; 4. Al and Margaret Jennings; 5. AHM; 6. Dolan Simpson Marsh; 7. Henry Van de Weil; 8. AHM; 9. AHM; 10. Joanne DeCoste; 11. Archie Mills; 12. Pat Skinner; 13. Gilbert Landry; 14. Francis Johnson; 15. Mae Bouchard; 16. Pomquet Historical Society; 17. Pomquet Historical Society; 18. Rick Grace; 19. Allan Armsworthy; 20. Joan Dunn

Education: 1. AHM 2. John Woodruff/National Archives of Canada/ PA-038044; 3. Ray A. MacLean; 4. AHM; 5. McNaughton Coll., AHM; 6. Roy Smith; 7. Edith Williams; 8. Gordon and

Joan Randall; 9. Sara Carty; 10. Edna Boudreau; 11. John P. MacEachern; 12. AHM; 13. AHM; 14. Hattie Farrell; 15. Dux MacKenzie's Scrapbook, St. Francis Xavier University Archives; 16. AHM; 17. Jean Graham; 18. Dux MacKenzie's Scrapbook, St. Francis Xavier University Archives

Transportation: 1. T.C. Weston/National Archives of Canada/PA-038945; 2. Gordon and Joan Randall; 3. AHM; 4. AHM; 5. AHM; 6. AHM; 7. Elizabeth May; 8. Gordon and Joan Randall; 9. Edna Boudreau; 10. Christina Connors; 11. Shirley McCormick; 12. Robert Williams; 13. Don Chapman; 14. Paul MacDonald; 15. Archie Mills; 16. Ronnie Gunn; 17. AHM; 18. AHM; 19. Hattie Farrell; 20. Isabel Whidden

Recreational Pastimes: 1. AHM; 2. AHM; 3. Catherine Steele; 4. The *Casket*, 1884; 5. Gordon and Joan Randall; 6. Ronnie Gunn; 7. AHM; 8. Joan Phee; 9. Hattie Farrell; 10. David Crerar; 11. AHM; 12. Cunningham Collection, AHM; 13. Dr. David McCurdy; 14. Cunningham Collection, AHM; 15. Francis DeWolfe and Claire Dickson; 16. Cunningham Collection, AHM; 17. Cunningham Collection, AHM; 18. Bethany Archives; 19. AHM; 20. AHM; 21. AHM; 22. AHM; 23. AHM; 24. Bill Hardie; 25. Francis DeWolfe and Claire Dickson; 26. Francis Johnson; 27. CJFX Album, AHM; 28. Eileen Adams; 29. Janice MacGillivray; 30. John Graham MacDonald; 31. Christina Connors

Sports: 1. Katherine Ann Chisholm; 2. AHM; 3. AHM; 4. Hattie Farrell; 5. Waldren Collection, Dalhousie University Archives; 6. Archibald Collection, AHM; 7. AHM; 8. AHM; 9. AHM; 10. Jean Graham; 11. AHM; 12. Roy Smith; 13. Jean Swansburg; 14. Gerard MacDonald; 15. Anita MacKay

Local Events 1. AHM; 2. AHM; 3. Jean Graham; 4. Joan MacIsaac; 5. Roy Smith; 6. Mary Barry; 7. Isabel Whidden; 8. Murph Chisholm; 9. AHM; 10. Allan Armsworthy; 11. Stephen Jewkes; 12. Jean Graham; 13. AHM; 14. C.J. MacGillivray, AHM; 15. St. Francis Xavier University Archives; 16. Royal Canadian Legion--Antigonish Arras Branch 59; 17. Berkley Cameron; 18. AHM

The Many Faces of Antigonish: 1. Clara Dennis Collection, Public Archives and Records Management; 2. Highland Society of Antigonish; 3. AHM; 4. Bill Landry; 5. AHM; 6. Margaret Enright; 7. Lawrence MacDonald; 8. Cella MacLellan; 9. Val Perry Chisholm; 10. Hattie Farrell; 11. Marian Kerr; 12. St. Francis Xavier University Archives; 13. Annie Prosper; 14. Pat Skinner; 15. Nancy MacLean; 16. Jean Graham; 17. Mary Brown; 18. AHM; 19. Dr. David McCurdy; 20. Jean Graham; 21. Jean Graham; 22. Dadie MacDonald; 23. Arthur C. Chisholm; 24. Kevin Fehr; 25. William Paulette; 26. Peter and Angela DeGruchy; 27. Yvonne Maas; 28. Clara Dennis Collection, Public Archives and Records Management; 29. Clara Dennis Collection, Public Archives and Records Management; 30. Clara Dennis Collection, Public Archives and Records Management; 31. Catherine MacKenzie; 32. Francis DeWolfe and Claire Dickson; 33. Margaret Bowie; 34. Rev. Greg MacKinnon and Pat MacNeil; 35. Mary Rose Wong; 36. Eileen Adams; 37. Christina Connors; 38. Owen McVicar; 39. Sisca Bekkers

The originals or copies of all the photographs in this volume have been kindly donated by the contributors to this project to the Antigonish Heritage Museum.